# CHRISTOPHER MORLEY'S
# PHILADELPHIA

# CHRISTOPHER
# MORLEY'S
# PHILADELPHIA

EDITED, AND WITH AN INTRODUCTION,

BY KEN KALFUS

ILLUSTRATED BY

WALTER JACK DUNCAN

AND

FRANK H. TAYLOR

## FORDHAM UNIVERSITY PRESS

NEW YORK

974.811
mor

First paperback printing 1992

**Morley, Christopher,** 1890–1957.
[Philadelphia]
Christopher Morley's Philadelphia / edited, and with an
introduction, by Ken Kalfus ; illustrated by Walter Jack Duncan and
Frank H. Taylor.—New York : Fordham University Press, c1990.
xvi, 329 p. : ill. ; 21 cm.
Essays and articles previously published in the author's Travels in
Philadelphia, 1920, and in various periodicals, 1918–1951.
ISBN 0-8232-1269-6 (cloth)    ISBN 0-8232-1270-X (paper)
1. Philadelphia (Pa.)—Description and travel.   2. Philadelphia
(Pa.)—Social life and customs.   I. Kalfus, Ken.   II. Title.
F158.5.M84   1990              974.8'11—dc20              90-80081
                                                    AACR 2   MARC

Printed in the United States of America

# CONTENTS

## NEIGHBORHOODS

## DAY TRIPS

## TOWARD MICKLE STREET

## EPILOGUE

# A NOTE ON SOURCES

Unless otherwise noted, the essays in this volume are taken from Christopher Morley's *Travels in Philadelphia* (David McKay, 1920).

"In Philadelphia" appeared in *Hide and Seek* (George H. Doran Company, 1920).

"The Urchin at the Zoo," "Making Marathon Safe for the Urchin," and "Walt Whitman Miniatures" appeared in *Mince Pie* (George H. Doran Company, 1920).

"Pershing in Philadelphia," "Pine Street," "An Early Train," "Ridge Avenue," "In West Philadelphia," "The University and the Urchin," and "A City Notebook" appeared in *Pipefuls* (Doubleday, Page & Co., 1921).

"Going to Philadelphia" appeared in *Plum Pudding* (Doubleday, Page & Co., 1921).

"In Honorem: Martha Washington" appeared in *The Powder of Sympathy* (Doubleday, Page & Co., 1923).

"Notes on Rosy" first appeared in the *Saturday Review*, December 24, 1927, and was published in book form in *Off the Deep End* (Doubleday, Doran & Co., 1928).

"Elegy in a Railroad Station" appeared in *Gentleman's Relish* (Norton, 1955).

"A Westminster Abbey in Philadelphia" appeared in the Philadelphia *Evening Public Ledger*, June 24, 1918. This is its first publication in book form.

The passage about Haverford opens Morley's autobiographical novel *John Mistletoe* (Doubleday, Doran & Company, 1931).

"Footnote on Philadelphia Cricket" appeared in *A Century of Philadelphia Cricket*, edited by John A. Lester (University of Pennsylvania Press, 1951).

"Gentles, Attend!" appeared in facsimile form in Alfred P. Lee's *A Bibliography of Christopher Morley* (Doubleday, Doran & Company, 1935). According to Lee, the text was published originally on newsprint paper. Shortly after Morley arrived in New York, he offered the piece, as a "passport," to a friend moving to Philadelphia.

A number of people and institutions have assisted the collection of these essays. I wish to thank Inga Saffron, Howard Mansfield, Steven Rothman, the Print and Pictures Department of the Free Library of Philadelphia, the Pennsylvania Historical Society, the Quaker Room at Haverford College's Magill Library, and the University of Pennsylvania's Van Pelt Library.

KK

# INTRODUCTION

PHILADELPHIA, the writer Christopher Morley declared early in this century, is "a surprisingly large town at the confluence of the Biddle and Drexel families. It is wholly surrounded by cricket teams, fox hunters, beagle packs, and the Pennsylvania Railroad."

The city has changed somewhat since Morley, the late novelist, essayist, playwright, poet, raconteur, columnist, and prodigious luncher, first wrote about it so engagingly and facetiously. The Biddles and the Drexels no longer dominate the city's imagination, and neither do cricket nor the hunt. Amtrak, of course, now sprints the track laid by the Pennsylvania Railroad. Philadelphia nevertheless remains a surprisingly large town, one with a character and physiognomy that Morley might still recognize, and a history and literature that has become, alas, neglected.

Morley, best known for his novels *Parnassus on Wheels* and *Kitty Foyle* and his Bowling Green column in *The Saturday Review of Literature,* died in 1957, after publishing some 50 books. Despite enjoying literary distinction in the 1920s and 1930s, Morley had faded into relative obscurity by the time of his death. The work he left behind, about itinerant booksellers and "White-Collar Working Girls" like Miss Foyle, about great American cities and the pleasures of the table, is largely unfamiliar to the current generation of readers, who, given the opportunity, are likely to relish his style, his wit, his exuberant championing of the written word, and his keen appreciation of the places in which he found himself.

Morley became the quintessential New York journalist-about-town, but he accomplished some of his best work before that as a young man in Philadelphia. For two years (1918–1920) he was a columnist for the Philadelphia *Eve-*

*ning Public Ledger,* publishing a series of casual essays in its editorial pages. The best of these pieces, now in your hands, comprise the most illuminating, lively, and endearing prose yet written in this century about this city.

At a time when America was still getting used to the idea of immigration from eastern and southern Europe, Morley ventured deep into Philadelphia's "Mediterranean colony," the famous Italian Market, whose shops, as the reader of this collection will discover, often embraced "a queer union of trades," such as the combined "funeral agent and detective bureau" and the "bookbinder and flower shop." From his Chestnut Street newspaper office he listened for "the light sliding swish of the trolley poles along the wire, accompanied by the deep rocking rumble of the car, and the crash as it pounds over the crosstracks." And throughout his columns, in the years during which the monumental amenities along the Benjamin Franklin Parkway were being raised, he voiced an abiding optimism in Philadelphia: "I walked down the Parkway yesterday morning visualizing that splendid emptiness of sunshine as it will appear five or ten years hence, lined with art galleries, museums and libraries, shaded with growing trees, leading from the majestic pinnacle of the City Hall to the finest public estate in America."

When he left for the *New York Evening Post* early in 1920, Morley collected his articles in a volume entitled *Travels in Philadelphia,* in which most of the following essays appeared. The book, published by the David McKay Company at 604–608 South Washington Square and reprinted for the last time in 1937, was introduced by A. Edward Newton, the Philadelphia bibliophile and writer whose home is described in Morley's "Darby Creek" essay. Newton confesses some astonishment that Philadelphia could be worth writing about. He asks, "Who, but [Morley], could find in the commonplace, sordid, and depressing streets of our city, subjects for a sheaf of dainty little essays, as delightful as they are unique? For say what you will, to most of us the streets of Philadelphia are dirty and depressing." Newton notes that it is "a thousand pities" that Morley was leaving for New York, but he doesn't blame him for the defection.

Indeed, Newton was grateful for the literary presence with which Morley invested Philadelphia. Elevating the city into a place fit for our imaginations to inhabit, Morley discovered protagonists and stories in its alleys and parks, among its new citizens and among the pedestrian elements of daily life (especially those elements having to do with eating). Years later Morley looked back and said it was in Philadelphia that he "first learned to some small extent, what I call a sense of human life and human significance, a sense of the significance of human life and human suffering, human aspiration and passion and despair, which is the vibration in which literature and art begin."

Philadelphia is too often obsessed by 1776; these essays, most of them fixed upon a single, previously unremarked moment in Philadelphia's history, reveal just one of the city's many other pasts. These essays shed light on our present, too, for much of the city that Morley explored remains intact for the "saunterer" with the eye and the patience to discover it.

CHRISTOPHER DARLINGTON MORLEY was born in the Philadelphia suburb of Haverford on May 5, 1890, to British parents. His father, a professor of mathematics at Haverford College, took a position at Johns Hopkins University when Chris was 10, moving the family to Baltimore. Chris, who would later write about his Haverford childhood with great warmth, returned to the college in 1906 as a freshman. His first book, a poetry collection entitled *The Eighth Sin*, was published in England in 1912, while he was studying at Oxford. The following year he went to work at Doubleday, Page and Company in Garden City, Long Island, as a reader and a book publicist. Publishing magnate Cyrus H. K. Curtis repatriated him to Philadelphia in 1917, first as an employee of the *Ladies' Home Journal,* and then of the *Evening Public Ledger.* Morley, his wife, Helen, and their infant son took up digs at 1722 Pine Street and in suburban Wyncote, upon which he bestowed the name Marathon. (In keeping with this Persian Wars theme, he would later call their Roslyn, Long Island, home Salamis Estates.)

Morley worked in a number of positions at the paper. Many of his contributions appearing on the paper's spirited editorial page were unbylined, or bore pseudonyms like "Dove Dulcet," "Socrates," or simply the tag line "CDM." Morley's favorite pseudonym was Andrew McGill; he and his best friend Page Allinson, whom he called Mifflin, shared the conceit that they were the McGill brothers. When he was promoted to columnist, Morley dashed off a characteristically playful note:

> Dear Mifflin, Better take to
> reading the Evg. Ledger, as
> they've bought A. McG. body,
> soul and bungstarter!
> —Andrew.

Morley's column first ran on March 11, 1918 and appeared at irregular intervals two or three times each week. The articles were usually found on the lower right-hand side of the page underneath the day's editorial cartoon, sometimes alongside his own verses. He also introduced a column, the Chaffing Dish, which was a grab bag of verse and sketches, including readers' submissions.

It was in Philadelphia that Morley established his literary character: good-natured, whimsical, and, being somewhat disengaged from the period's progressive literary movements, ultimately middle-browed. *Parnassus on Wheels* was published while he was in Philadelphia and he wrote its sequel, *The Haunted Bookshop*, here, as well as numerous essays and poems for national periodicals. By the time he left for New York, the 29-year-old author already owned a large reputation.

Morley's indefatigable and fluent writing made him a fixture on the New York literary and newspaper scene. At the *Evening Post* he started the Bowling Green column, which he later brought to the *Saturday Review*. He continued to write novels, short stories, and poetry, and to produce plays, and the later work in this collection shows that he maintained his affection for Philadelphia throughout his life. In New York he helped establish the famed organization of Sherlock Holmes enthusiasts, the Baker Street Irregulars, and he played key roles in the births of the *Saturday Review* and the Book-of-the-Month Club. *Kitty Foyle*, which was made into a 1940 movie starring Ginger Rogers, won him more fame and the kind of money one could not earn from books alone.

In the three years that the adult Morley lived in Philadelphia, the city rushed from wartime, with its accompanying shortages and labor unrest, through the influenza pandemic (which claimed more Philadelphians than the war did), and then into Normalcy. The appeal of Morley's articles lies in part in their contemporary flavor, heightened by references to the League of Nations, bolsheviks, Henry Ford, and General Pershing. These references are often parsed in the day's idiom, some of which may puzzle the reader and, with its condescensions and casual bigotries, may also offend him. Morley's essays, as you shall see, are evocative of their era's failings as well as its charms.

Perhaps Philadelphia, which Morley saw as profoundly conservative, never fully embraced the Jazz Age, nor the other Ages scheduled to follow, but time has worked itself on the city all the same. Gone are Dumont's Minstrels on Arch, the Indian Pole (blown down in a hurricane, say local residents), and Orange Street by Washington Square. The

Ronaldson Cemetery on Bainbridge Street is now the site of a playground and ballfield. Willow Grove is no longer known for its amusement park, though a massive mall there now accommodates today's preferred pastime, shopping. The celebrated Mercantile Library on South 10th Street has been replaced by a more ordinary facility on Chestnut. Morley's beloved Ludlow Street, then an alley of book-stores just south of Market, has been almost entirely sub-merged beneath block-sized buildings and parking lots.

Yet much of Morley's Philadelphia continues to show through the patina of postmodernity. The Italian Market still "breathes the Italian genius for good food." The Mint is still here; so is Penn Treaty Park, now virtually unknown to modern Philadelphians. The Poe House has been ele-vated, per Morley's request, into a national landmark. Philly and Camden still share claims to Walt Whitman, and Walt's ferries, recalled herein, will soon be running again between the two cities. The stone building engraved with the name of the Tripoli Barber Supply Company, on Ninth below South Street, no longer offers "the Vesuvius Quinine Tonic"; it's now an antique shop, but the building and the engraving remain, as if materialized directly from these pages.

The editor of this collection hopes the reader will use it as a guide book, a literary companion to a place whose literary qualities have been either denied or long forgotten. From a space of 70 years, Morley reveals to us the city we so carelessly inhabit, demonstrating that these "dirty and depressing" streets mark a landscape of human endeavor—a city worth reading about and a city worth tending.

KEN KALFUS

*Philadelphia*
*August 1989*

# CENTER CITY

# SAUNTERING

$S$OME FAMOUS lady—who was it?—used to say of anyone
she richly despised that he was "a saunterer." I
suppose she meant he was a mere trifler, a lounger, an idle
stroller of the streets. It is an ignominious confession, but I
am a confirmed saunterer. I love to be set down haphazard
among unknown byways; to saunter with open eyes, watching the moods and humors of men, the shapes of their
dwellings, the criss-cross of their streets. It is an implanted
passion that grows keener and keener. The everlasting lure
of round-the-corner, how fascinating it is!

I love city squares. The most interesting persons are
always those who have nothing special to do: children,
nurses, policemen, and actors at 11 o'clock in the morning.
These are always to be found in the park; by which I mean
not an enormous sector of denatured countryside with
bridle paths, fishponds and sea lions, but some broad patch
of turf in a shabby elbow of the city, striped with pavements, with plenty of sun-warmed benches and a cast-iron
zouave erected about 1873 to remind one of the horrors of
commemorative statuary. Children scuffle to and fro; dusty
men with spiculous chins loll on the seats; the uncouth and
pathetic vibrations of humankind are on every side.

It is entrancing to walk in such places and catalogue all
that may be seen. I jot down on scraps of paper a list of all
the shops on a side street; the names of tradesmen that
amuse me; the absurd repartees of gutter children. Why? It
amuses me and that is sufficient excuse. From now until
the end of time no one else will ever see life with my eyes,
and I mean to make the most of my chance. Just as Thoreau
compiled a Domesday Book and kind of classified directory
of the sights, sounds and scents of Walden (carefully record-
ing the manners of a sandbank and the prejudices of a

3

woodlouse or an apple tree) so I love to annotate the phenomena of the city. I can be as solitary in a city street as ever Thoreau was in Walden.

And no Walden sky was ever more blue than the roof of Washington square this morning. Sitting here reading Thoreau I am entranced by the mellow flavor of the young summer. The sun is just goodly enough to set the being in a gentle toasting muse. The trees confer together in a sleepy whisper. I have had buckwheat cakes and syrup for breakfast, and eggs fried both recto and verso; good foundation for speculation. I puff cigarettes and am at peace with myself. Many a worthy waif comes to lounge beside me; he glances at my scuffed boots, my baggy trousers; he knows me for one of the fraternity. By their boots ye shall know them. Many of those who have abandoned the race for this world's honors have a shrewdness all their own. What is it Thoreau says, with his penetrative truth?— "Sometimes we are inclined to class those who are once and a half witted with the half witted, because we appreciate only a third part of their wit." By the time a man is thirty he should be able to see what life has to offer, and take what dishes on the menu agree with him best. That is whole wit, indeed, or wit-and-a-half. And if he finds his pleasure on a park bench in ragged trousers let him lounge then, with good heart. I welcome him to the goodly fellowship of saunterers, an acolyte of the excellent church of the agorolaters!

These meditations are incurred in the ancient and noble city of Philadelphia, which is a surprisingly large town at the confluence of the Biddle and Drexel families. It is wholly surrounded by cricket teams, fox hunters, beagle packs, and the Pennsylvania Railroad. It has a very large zoölogical garden, containing carnivora, herbivora, scrapple-ivora, and a man from New York who was interned here at the time of the Centennial Exposition in 1876. The principal manufactures are carpets, life insurance premiums, and souvenirs of Independence Hall. Philadelphia was the first city to foresee the advantages of a Federal constitution and oatmeal as a breakfast food.

And as one walks and speculates among all this visible panorama, beating one's brains to catch some passing snapshots of it, watching, listening, imagining, the whole hullabaloo becomes extraordinarily precious. The great faulty hodge-podge of the city, its very pavements and house-corners, becomes vividly dear. One longs to clutch the whole meaning in some sudden embrace—to utter some testament of affection that will speak plain truth. "Friday I tasted life," said Emily Dickinson, the American Blake. "It was a vast morsel." Something of that baffled exultation seizes one in certain moments of strolling, when the afternoon sun streams down Chestnut street on the homeward pressing crowd, or in clear crisp mornings as one walks through Washington Square. Emily utters her prodigious parables in flashing rockets that stream for an instant in the dusk, then break and sink in colored balls. Most of us cannot ejaculate such dazzles of flame. We pick and poke and stumble our thoughts together, catching at a truth and losing it again.

Agreeable vistas reward the eye of the resolute stroller. For instance, that delightful cluster of back gardens, old brick angles, dormer windows and tall chimneys in the little block on Orange street west of Seventh. Orange street is the little alley just south of Washington Square. In the clean sunlight of a fresh May morning, with masses of green trees and creepers to set off the old ruddy brick, this quaint huddle of buildings composes into a delightful picture that has been perpetuated by the skilful pencil of Frank H. Taylor. A kindly observer in the Dreer seed warehouse, which backs upon Orange street, noticed me prowling about and offered to take me up in his elevator. From one of the Dreer windows I had a fascinating glimpse down upon these roofs and gardens. One of them is the rear yard of the Italian consulate at 717 Spruce street. Another is the broader garden of The Catholic Historical Society, in which I noticed with amusement Nicholas Biddle's big stone bathtub sunning itself. Then there is the garden of the adorable little house at 725 Spruce street, which is particularly interesting because, when seen from the street, it appears to have no front door. The attic window of that house is just our idea of what an attic window ought to be.

A kind of philosophy distills itself in the mind of the saunterer. Painfully tedious as people often are, they have the sublime quality of interesting one. Not merely by what they say, but often by what they don't say. Their eyes— how amazing is the thought of all those millions of little betraying windows! How bravely they struggle to express what is in them. A modern essayist has spoken of "the haggard necessities of parlor conversation." But the life of the streets has no such conventions. It is real: it comes hot from the pan. It is as informal, as direct and as unpretentious as the greetings of dogs. It is a never-failing remedy for the blues.

BACK GARDENS ON ORANGE STREET
by Frank H. Taylor. Courtesy Free Library of Philadelphia.

# MEETING THE GODS
# FOR A DIME

I F WE HAD TO choose just one street in Philadelphia to
the exclusion of all others, probably our greatest affection would be for Ludlow street. We have constituted
ourself the president, publicity committee and sole member of the Ludlow Street Business Men's Association and
Chamber of Commerce. We propose in this manifesto to
make known to the world just where Ludlow street is, and
why it is so fair.

Ludlow street is not in any sense a thoroughfare. It does
not fare through, for its course is estopped by several bulky
buildings. It reappears here and there in a whimsical,
tentative manner. We do not pretend to know all about
Ludlow street, nor have we charted its entire course. But
the pith and quintessence of this runnel of culture is trod
almost daily by our earnest feet.

Our doings with Ludlow street begin when we turn off
Eleventh street and caress the flank of the Mercantile
Library in an easterly gambit. Then, with our nose cocked
for any wandering savors from the steaming roast beeves of
a Tenth street ordinary well known to epicureans, we dart
along until our progress is barred by the Federal Building.
This necessitates a portage through the Federal Reserve
Bank on to the roaring coast of Chestnut street. We double
back on Ninth street and find Ludlow reappearing just
above Leary's Book Store.

Here it is that our dear Ludlow street finds its mission
and meaning in life. From the tall-browed façade of the
Mercantile Library it has caught a taste for literature and
against the north wall of Leary's it indulges itself to the
full. Perhaps you would think it a grimy little alley as it
twists blithely round Leary's, but to us it is a porchway of

Paradise. How many hours we have dallied under that little penthouse shelter mulling over the ten-cent shelves! All the rumors and echoes of letters find their way to Ludlow street sooner or later. We can lay our ear to those battered rows of books as to a whorled conch shell and hear the solemn murmur of the vast ocean of literature. There we may meet the proud argosies or the humble derelicts of that ocean for ten cents.

Yes, they all come to Ludlow street in the end. We have found Wentworth's Arithmetic there, old foe of our youth; and George Eliot, and Porter (Jane) and Porter (Gene Stratton). There used to be a complete set of Wilkie Collins, bound in blue buckram, at the genteel end of the street among the twenty-five centers. We were buying them, one by one (that was before the days of thrift stamps), when some plutocrat came along and kidnapped the whole bunch. He was an undiscerning plutocrat, because he took the second volume of "The Woman in White" while we were still reading the first. When we went gayly to buy Volume II, lo! it was gone.

Clark Russell is there, with his snowy canvassed yachts dipping and creaming through azure seas; and once in a while a tattered Frank Stockton or a "Female Poets of America" or "The Mysteries of Udolpho." We have learned more about books from Ludlow street than ever we did in any course at college. We remember how we used to hasten thither on Saturday afternoons during our college days and, fortified with an automatic sandwich and a cup of coffee, we would spend a delirious three hours plundering the jeweled caves of joy. Best of all are the wet days when the rain drums on the little shelter-roof and drips down the back of the fanatic. But what true fanatic heeds a chilled spine when his head is warmed by all the fires of Olympus?

Ludlow street has quiet sorrows of its own, however. At the end of the ten-cent shelves, redeemed and exalted, even intoxicated by these draughts of elixir, it staggers a

9

little in its gait. It takes a wild reeling twist round behind Leary's, clinging to that fortress of the Muses as long as it may. And then comes the thorn in its crown. Just as it has begun to fancy itself as a highbrow pathway to Helicon, it finds itself wearing against its sober brick wall one of the Street Cleaning Department's fantastic and long-neglected ash piles. This abashes the poor little street so that when it strikes Eighth street it becomes confused, totters feebly several perches to the north and commits suicide in a merry little cul-de-sac frequented by journeymen carpenters, who bury it in their sweet-smelling shavings.

O blessed little Ludlow street! You are to Philadelphia what the old book stalls on the Seine bank are to Paris, what Charing Cross Road is to London. You are the home and haunt of the shyest, sweetest Muses there are: the Muses of old books. The Ludlow Street Business Men's Association, in convention assembled, drinks a beaker of Tom and Jerry to your health and good fortune!

# CHESTNUT STREET
# FROM A FIRE ESCAPE

JUST OUTSIDE our office window is a fire-escape with a little iron balcony. On warm days, when the tall windows are wide open, that rather slender platform is our favorite vantage ground for watching Chestnut street. We have often thought how pleasant it would be to have a pallet spread out there, so that we could do our work in that reclining posture that is so inspiring.

But we can tell a good deal of what is going on along Chestnut street without leaving our desk. Chestnut street sings a music of its own. Its genial human symphony could never be mistaken for that of any other highway. The various strands of sound that compose its harmony gradually sink into our mind without our paying conscious heed to them. For instance, there is the light sliding swish of the trolley poles along the wire, accompanied by the deep rocking rumble of the car, and the crash as it pounds over the cross-tracks at Sixth street. There is the clear mellow clang of the trolley gongs, the musical trill of fast wagon wheels running along the trolley rails, and the rattle of hoofs on the cobbled strip between the metals. Particularly easy to identify is the sound every citizen knows, the rasping, sliding clatter of a wagon turning off the car track so that a trolley can pass it. The front wheels have left the track, but the back pair are scraping along against the setts before mounting over the rim.

Every street has its own distinctive noises and the attentive ear accustoms itself to them until they become almost a part of the day's enjoyment. The deep-toned bell of Independence Hall bronzing the hours is part of our harmony here, and no less familiar is the vigorous tap-tap of Blind Al's stick. Al is the well-known news-dealer at the

11

corner of Chestnut and Fifth. Several times a day he passes along under our windows, and the tinkle of his staff is a well-known and pleasant note in our ears. We like to imagine, too, that we can recognize the peculiarly soft and easy-going rumble of a wagon of watermelons.

But what we started to talk about was the balcony, from which we can get a long view of Chestnut street all the way from Broad street almost to the river. It is a pleasant prospect. There is something very individual about Chestnut street. It could not possibly be in New York. The solid, placid dignity of most of the buildings, the absence of skyscrapers, the plain stone fronts with the arched windows of the sixties, all these bespeak a city where it is still a little bit bad form for a building to be too garishly new. I may be wrong, but I do not remember in New York any such crisscross of wires above the streets. Along Chestnut street they run at will from roof to roof over the way.

Gazing from our little balcony the eye travels down along the uneven profile of the northern flank of Chestnut street. From the Wanamaker wireless past the pale, graceful minaret of the Federal Reserve Bank, the skyline drops down to the Federal Building which, standing back from the street, leaves a gap in the view. Then the slant of roofs draws the eye upward again, over the cluster of little conical spires on Green's Hotel (like a French château) to the sharp ridges and heavy pyramid roof of the Merchants' Union Trust Company. This, with its two attendant banks on either side, is undoubtedly the most extraordinary architectural curiosity Chestnut street can boast. The façade, with its appalling quirks and twists of stone and iron grillwork, its sculptured Huns and Medusa faces, is something to contemplate with alarm.

After reaching Seventh street, Chestnut becomes less adventurous. Perhaps awed by the simple and stately beauty of Independence Hall and its neighbors, it restrains itself from any further originality until Fourth street, where

12

the ornate Gothic of the Provident claims the eye. From our balcony we can see only a part of Independence Hall, but we look down on the faded elms along the pavement in front and the long line of iron posts beloved of small boys for leapfrog. Then the eye climbs to the tall and graceful staff above the Drexel Building, where the flag ripples cleanly against the blue. And our view is bounded, far away to the east, by the massive tower of the Victor factory in Camden.

It is great fun to watch Chestnut street from the little balcony. On hot days, when the white sunlight fills the street with a dazzle of brightness and bands of dark shadow, it is amusing to see how all pedestrians keep to the shady southern pavements. When a driving shower comes up and the slants and rods of rain lash against the dingy brownstone fronts, one may look out and see passers-by huddled under the awnings and the mounted policemen's horses sleek as satin in the wet. The pavement under our balcony is notable for its slipperiness: it has been chipped into ribs by stonemasons to make it less so. In the rain it shines like a mirror. And our corner has its excitements, too. Once every few months the gas mains take it into their pipes to explode and toss manholes and paving sixty feet in air.

The part of Chestnut street that is surveyed by our balcony is a delightful highway: friendly, pleasantly dignified, with just a touch of old-fashioned manners and homeliness. It is rather akin to a London street. And best of all, almost underneath our balcony is a little lunch room where you can get custard ice cream with honey poured over it, and we think it is the best thing in the world.

# PERSHING IN
# PHILADELPHIA

THE PAVEMENT in front of Independence Hall was a gorgeous jumble of colours. The great silken flags of the Allies, carried by vividly costumed ladies, burned and flapped in the wind. On a pedestal stood the Goddess of Liberty, in rich white draperies that seemed fortunately of sufficient texture to afford some warmth, for the air was cool. She graciously turned round for Walter Crail, the photographer of our contemporary, the *Evening Public Ledger*, to take a shot at her.

Down Chestnut Street came a rising tide of cheers. A squadron of mounted police galloped by. Then the First City Troop, with shining swords. Fred Eckersburg, the State House engineer, was fidgeting excitedly inside the hall, in a new uniform. This was Fred's greatest day, but we saw that he was worried about Martha Washington, the Independence Hall cat. He was apprehensive lest the excitement should give her a fit or a palsy. Independence Hall is no longer the quiet old place Martha used to enjoy before the war.

The Police Band struck up "Hail to the Chief." Yells and cheers burst upward from the ground like an explosion. Here he was, standing in the car. There was the famous chin, the Sam Browne belt, the high laced boots with spurs. Even the tan gloves carried in the left hand. There was the smile, without which no famous man is properly equipped for public life. There was Governor Sproul's placid smile, too, but the Mayor seemed too excited to smile. Rattle, rattle, rattle went the shutters of the photographers. Up the scarlet lane of carpet came the general. His manner has a charming, easy grace. He saluted each one of the fair ladies garbed in costumes of our Allies, but taking care not to linger too long in front of any one of them lest any embracing should get started. A pattering of tiger lilies or some such things came dropping down from above. He passed into the hall, which was cool and smelt like a wedding with a musk of flowers.

While the Big Chief was having a medal presented to him inside the hall we managed to scuttle round underneath the grand stand and take up a pencil of vantage just below the little pulpit where the general was to speak. Here the crowd groaned against a bulwark of stout policemen. Philadelphia cops, bless them, are the best tempered in the world. (How Boston must envy us.) Genially two gigantic bluecoats made room against the straining hawser for young John Fisher, aged eleven, of 332 Greenwich Street. John is a small, freckle-faced urchin. It was amusing to see him thrusting his eager little beezer between the vast, soft, plushy flanks of two patrolmen. He had been there over two hours waiting for just this adventure. Then, to assert the equality of the sexes, Mildred Dubivitch, aged eleven, and Eva Ciplet, aged nine, managed to insert themselves between the chinks in the line of cops. An old lady more than eighty years old was sitting placidly in a small chair just inside the ropes. She had been in the square more than five hours, and the police had found her a seat.

"Are you going to put Pershing's name in, too?" asked John as we noted his address.

Independence Square never knew a more thrilling fifteen minutes. The trees were tossing and bending in the thrilling blue air. There was a bronzy tint in their foliage, as though they were putting on olive drab in honour of the general. Great balloons of silver clouds scoured across the cobalt sky. At one minute to 11 Pershing appeared at the top of the stand. The whole square, massed with people, shook with cheers.

Had it been any other man we would have said the general was frightened. He came down the aisle of the stand with his delightful, easy, smiling swing; but he looked shrewdly about, with a narrow-eyed, puckered gaze. He was plainly a little flabbergasted. He seemed taken aback by the greatness of Philadelphia's voice. He said something to himself. On his lips it looked like "What the deuce," or something of similar purport. He sat down on a chair beside Governor Sproul. Not more than four feet away, amazed at our own audacity, we peered over the floor of the stand.

He was paler than we expected. He looked a bit tired. Speaking as a father, we were pleased to note the absence of Warren, who was (we hope) getting a good sleep somewhere. We had a good look at the renowned chin, which is well worth study. It must be a hard chin to shave. It juts upward, reaching a line exactly below the brim of his cap. Below his crescent moustache there is no lower lip visible: it is tucked and folded in by the rising thrust of the jaw. It is this which gives him the "grim" aspect which every reader of the papers hears about. He is grim, there's no doubt about it, with the grimness of a man going through a tough ordeal. "I can see him all right," squeaked little John Fisher, "but he doesn't see me." The first two rows of seats at the right of the aisle were crammed with generals, two-star and three-star. From our lowly station we could see a grand panorama of mahogany leather boots and the flaring curves of riding breeches. It was a great day for Sam Browne. The thought came to us that has reached us before. The higher you go in the A. E. F. the more the officers were tailored after the English manner. It is the finest proof of international cousinship. When England and America wear the same kind of clothes, alliance is knit solid.

Pershing sat with his palms on his knees. He looked worried. There was a wavering crease down his lean cheeks. The plumply genial countenance of Governor Sproul next to him was an odd contrast to that dry, hard face. The bell in the tower tolled eleven times. He stood up for the photographers. Walter Crail, appearing from somewhere, sprang up on the parapet facing the general. "Look this way!" he shouted as the general turned toward some movie men. That will be Walter's first cry when he gets to heaven, or wherever. Mayor Smith's face was pallid with excitement. His nicely draped trouserings, which were only six inches from our notebook, quivered slightly as he said fifteen words of introduction.

As Pershing stood up to speak the crowd surged forward. The general was worried. "Don't, don't! Somebody will get hurt!" he called sharply. Then Mayor Smith surged forward also and said something to the police about watching the crowd.

The general took off his cap. Holding it in his left hand (with the gloves) he patted his close-cropped hair nervously. He frowned. He began to speak.

The speech has already been covered by our hated rivals. We will not repeat it, save to say that it was as crisp, clean-cut, and pointed as his chin. He was nervous, as we could see by the clenching and unclenching of his hands. His voice is rather high. We liked him for not being a suave and polished speaker. He gestured briskly with a pointing forefinger, and pronounced the word *patriotic* with a short

17

A—"pattriotic." Later he stumbled over it again and got it out as *patterotism*. We liked him again for that. He doesn't have to pronounce it, anyway. We liked him best of all for the unconscious slip he made. "This reception," he said, "I understand is for the splendid soldiery of America that played such an important part in the war with our Allies." A respectful ripple of laughter passed over the stand at this, but he did not notice it. He was fighting too hard to think what to say next. We liked him, too, for saying "such an important part." A man who had been further away from the fighting would have said that it was America, alone and unaided, that won the war. He is just as we have hoped he would be: a plain, blunt man. We have heard that he is going to enter the banking business. We'd like to have an account at that bank.

# THE PARKWAY, HENRY FORD, AND BILLY THE BEAN MAN

I WALKED down the Parkway yesterday morning visualizing that splendid emptiness of sunshine as it will appear five or ten years hence, lined with art galleries, museums and libraries, shaded with growing trees, leading from the majestic pinnacle of the City Hall to the finest public estate in America. It is a long way from those open fields of splintered brick and gravel pits, where workmen are now warming their hands over bonfires, to the Peace Conference in Paris. But the hope occurred to me that the League of Nations will not tie itself down too closely to the spot where its archives are kept. It will be a fine thing if the annual meetings of the League can be held in different cities all over the world, visiting the nations in turn. This process would do much to educate public sentiment to the reality and importance of our new international commission. And in the course of time it is to be supposed that the league might meet in Philadelphia, where, in a sense, it was founded. The world is rich in lovely cities—Rio, Athens, Edinburgh, Rome, Tokio and the rest. But the Philadelphia of the future, as some citizens have dreamed it, will be able to hold up its head with the greatest. I like to think of a Philadelphia in which the lower Schuylkill would be something more than a canal of oily ooze; in which the wonderful Dutch meadows of the Neck would be reclaimed into one of the world's loveliest riverside parks, and in which the Parkway will stretch its airy vista from the heart of the city, between stately buildings of public profit, out to the sparkling waters of Fairmount.

The city shows a curiously assorted silhouette as one walks down the Parkway from Twenty-fifth street. There is

19

the plain dark dome of the Cathedral, with its golden cross flashing in the sun and the tall cocoa-colored pillars. No one would guess from the drab exterior the splendor of color and fragrance within. There is, of course, the outline of William Penn on his windy vantage, the long, dingy line of Broad Street Station's trainshed and the tall but unpretentious building of the Bell Telephone Company, where the flag swims against the sky on its slender staff. As one walks on, past the Medico-Chirurgical Hospital, with its memorable inscription (*Think not the beautiful doings of thy soul shall perish unremembered; they abide with thee forever*), the thin white spire of the Arch Street Methodist Episcopal Church and the monstrous oddity of the Masonic Temple spring into view. In an optimistic mood, under a riot of sunlight and a radiant sky, one is tempted to claim a certain beauty for this incongruous panorama. Yet if there is beauty no one can claim a premeditated scheme for it. Granite, marble, brick and chocolate stone jostle one another. Let us hope that the excellent ruthlessness with which the paths of the Parkway have been made straight will be equaled by diligent harmony in the new structures to come.

The great churches of the Roman communion are always an inspiration to visit. At almost all hours of the day or night you will find worshipers slipping quietly in and out, generally of the humblest classes. I slipped into the Cathedral for a few minutes and sat there watching the shimmer of color and blended shadows as the vivid sunlight streamed through the semicircular windows above the nave. The body of the church is steeped in that soft dusk described once for all as "a dim religious light," but the great cream-colored pillars with their heavy gold ornaments lift the eyes upward to the arched ceiling with its small tablets of blue and shining knots of gold. In the dome hung a faint lilac haze of intermingled gentle hues, sifting through the ring of stained windows. The eastern window over the high altar shows one brilliant note of rich blue in the folds of the

Madonna's gown. Over the gleaming terrace of white marble steps hangs a great golden lamp with a small ruby spark glowing through the twilight. Below these steps a plainly dressed little man knelt in prayer all the time I was in the church. The air was faintly fragrant with incense, having almost the aroma of burning cedar wood. A constant patter of hushed footfalls on the marble floor was due to the entrance and exit of stealthy worshipers coming in for a few minutes of silence in the noon recess.

Just around the corner from the Cathedral one looks across the broad playground of the Friends' Select School on to the bright, cheerful face of Race street. In that 1600 block Race is a typical Philadelphia street of the old sort—plain brick houses with slanted roofs and dormer windows, white and green shutters and scoured marble steps. I was surprised to notice the number of signs displayed calling attention to "Apartments," "Vacancies" and "Furnished Rooms." Certainly I can imagine no pleasanter place to lodge, with the sunny windows looking over the school ground to the soaring figure of Penn and the high cliffs behind him. Romance seems to linger along that sun-warmed brick pavement, and I peered curiously at the windows so discreetly curtained with lace and muslin, wondering what quaint tales the landladies of Race street might have to impart if one could muster up courage enough to question them. In the news-stand and cigar store at the corner of Sixteenth I made a notable discovery—a copy of Henry Ford's new Sunday school paper, the Dearborn Independent—the Ford International Weekly, he proudly subtitles it. I bought a copy and took it to lunch with me. I cannot say it left me much richer; nor, I fear, will it leave Henry that way. Much can be forgiven Henry for the honest simplicity of his soul, but the lad who's palming off those editorial page mottoes on him, in black-face type, ought to face a firing squad. This is the way they run:

21

*"Where buy we sleep?" inquired the royal shirk;*
*The sweetest rest on earth is bought with work.*

And this:

*The truth of equal opportunity is this:*
*Life, death; love, hope and strife, no man may miss.*

Or again:

*When profit is won at the cost of a principle,*
*The winner has lost—this law is invincible.*

Henry, Henry—didn't that cruise on the Oskar teach you *anything?* It seems too bad that Henry should go to the expense of founding a new humorous journal when *Life* is doing so well.

Coming back along Arch street I fell in with Billy the Bean Man. You may have seen Billy selling necklaces of white and scarlet beans on Broad street, clad in his well-known sombrero, magenta shirt and canvas trousers. Billy is a first-class medicine man, and he hits this town about once a year. He wore the cleanest shave I ever saw, but his dark William J. Bryan eyes were mournful. He tried to lure me into buying a necklace by showing me how you can walk on the beans without breaking them. "Picked and strung by the aboriginal Indians of the Staked Plain," he assured me; "and brought by me to this home of eastern culture. A sovereign remedy for seasickness and gout."

"Billy," I said, "you amaze me. Last year those same necklaces were curing mumps and metaphysical error."

He looked at me keenly. "Oh, it's you, is it? Say, this is a bum town. Business is rotten. I'm going on to Washington tomorrow."

"Sell one to Senator Sherman," I said; and passing by the allurements of Dumont's matinee—"The Devil in Jersey: He Terrified Woodbury, but He Couldn't Scare Us"—I gained the safety of the office.

# MAROONED IN
# PHILADELPHIA

IF A PHILADELPHIAN of a hundred years ago could walk
along our streets at night, undoubtedly the first thing
that would startle him would be the amazing dazzle of light
that floods from all the shop windows. Particularly during
the few weeks directly preceding Christmas city streets at
night present a panorama that would cure the worst fit of
the blues. What a glowing pageant they are, blazing with
radiance and color! Here and there you will find a display
ornamented with Christmas trees and small red, blue and
green electric bulbs. Perhaps there will be a toy electric
train running merrily all night long on a figure-eight-shaped
track, passing through imitation tunnels and ravines with
green artificial moss cunningly glued to them; over ravish-
ing switches and grade crossings, past imposing stations
and little signal towers. Perhaps you may be lured by the
shimmer of a jeweler's window, set with rows and rows of
gold watches on a slanting plush or satin background.
There, if you are a patient observer, you will usually find
one of the ultra-magnificent time-pieces that have an old-
fashioned railroad train engraved on the case. We have
always admired these hugely, but never felt any overwhelm-
ing desire to own one. They are sold for $14.95, being
worth $150.

Sometimes even the most domestic man is marooned in
town for the evening. It is always, after the first pang of
homesickness is over, an enlarging experience. Instead of
the usual rush for train or trolley he loiters after leaving the
office, strolling leisurely along the pavements and enjoying
the clear blue chill of the dusk. Perhaps the pallid radiance
of a barber's shop, with its white bowls of light, lures him
in for a shave, and he meditates on the impossibility of

avoiding the talcum powder that barbers conceal in the folds of a towel and suddenly clap on his razed face before they let him go. It avails not to tell a barber "No powder!" They put it on automatically. We know one man who thinks that heaven will be a place where one may lie back in a barber's chair and have endless hot towels applied to a fresh-shaved face. It is an attractive thought.

But the most delightful haunt of man, about 7 o'clock of a winter evening, is the popular lunch room. This admirable institution has been hymned often and eloquently, but it can never be sufficiently praised. To sit at one of those white-topped tables looking over the evening paper (and now that the big silver-plated sugar bowls have come back again there is once more something large enough on the table to prop the newspaper against) and consume sausages and griddle cakes and hot mince pie and revel in the warm human glitter round about, is as near a modest 100 per cent of interesting satisfaction as anything we know. Joyce Kilmer, a very human poet and a very stout eater, used to believe that abundant meals were a satisfactory substitute for sleep. For our own part, we are always ready to postpone bed if there is any prospect of something to eat. But we do not like to elaborate this subject any further, for it makes us hungry to do so, and we dare not leave the typewriter just yet.

Our marooned business man, after a stroll along the streets and a meal at the lunch room, may very likely drop in at the movies. Most of us nowadays worship now and then at this shrine of Professor Muybridge. The public is long suffering, and seems fairly well pleased at almost anything that appears on the screen. But the extraordinary thing at a movie is hardly ever what is on the screen, but rather the audience itself. Observe the mute, expectant, almost reverent attention. The darkened house crowded with people prayerfully and humbly anxious to be amused or thrilled! One wonders what their evenings must have been like when there were no movies if their present reaction is so passionately devout. A movie audience is a more moving spectacle than any of the flashing shadows that beam before it. If all this marvelous attention-energy, gathered every evening in every city in the land, could be focussed for a few moments on some of the urgent matters that concern the world now—say the League of Nations— it would be a wonderful aid to good citizenship. The movies are blindly groping their way, by means of current-event films, war films and the like, toward an era in which they will play a leading and indispensable part in education and civic life.

It should be a function of every large city government to provide "municipal movies," by which we mean not free motion-picture shows, but reels of film distributed free among all the motion-picture theatres in the city, exhibiting various phases of municipal activity and illustrating by suggestion how citizens may co-operate to increase the welfare of the community. We hear a good deal about street-cleaning evils, about rapid-transit problems, about traffic congestion, about the evils of public spitting, the danger of one-way streets and a score of other matters. All these could be interestingly illuminated on the screen, with serious intent, and yet with the racy human touch that always enlivens the common affairs of men. And when some discussion arises that concerns us all, such as the character of the proposed war memorial, various types of memorials could be illustrated in films to stimulate public suggestion as to what is most fitting for our environment. None of us know our own city as well as we would like to. Let the city government, through some film bureau, show us our own citizens at work and play and so quicken our curiosity and civic pride or shame, as the case may be.

Another public clubhouse which the marooned business man finds delightful and always full of good company is the railroad terminal. A big railroad station is an unfailing source of amusement and interest. From news-stand to lunch counter, from baggage room to train gate, it is rich in character study and the humors of humanity in flux. People are rarely at their best when hurried or worried, and many of those one meets at the terminal are in those moods. But, for any rational student of human affairs, it is as well to ponder our vices as well as our virtues, and the statistician might tabulate valuable data as to the number of tempers lost on the railway station stairs daily or the number of cross words uttered where commuters stand in line to buy their monthly tickets. The influence of the weather, the time of year and the time of day would bring interesting factors to bear upon these figures.

There is just one more pastime that the castaway of our imagination finds amusing, and that is acting as door-opener for innumerable cats that sit unhappily at the front doors of little shops on cold evenings. They have been shut out by chance and sit waiting in patient sadness on the cold sill until the door may chance to open. To open the door for them and watch them run inside, with tail erect and delighted gesture, is a real pleasure. With a somewhat similar pleasure does the marooned wanderer ultimately reach his own front door and rededicate himself to the delights of home.

# SOUTH BROAD STREET

ONE OF THE singularly futile and freakish little "literary" magazines that flourish among desiccated women and men whose minds are not old enough for the draft proudly raises the slogan that it "Makes no compromise with the public taste."

What I like about South Broad street is that it does make compromise with the public taste, every possible compromise. In the course of a three-mile stroll from the City Hall down to the South Broad street plaza one may see almost every variety of human interest. It is as though South Broad street had made up its mind to see all phases of life before leaping into the arms of Uncle Sam at League Island. It is like the young man's last night with the boys before enlisting.

"Broad and Chestnut" is a Philadelphia phrase of great sanctity. It is uttered with even greater awe than the New Yorker's "Broadway and Forty-second," as though the words summed up the very vibration and pulse of the town's most sacred life. And yet why is it that Broad street seems to me more at ease, more itself, when it gets away from the tremendous cliffs of vast hotels and office mountains? Our Philadelphia streets do not care to be mere tunnels, like the canyon flumes of Manhattan. We have a lust for sun and air.

So when Broad street escapes from the shadow of its own magnificence it runs just a little wild. In its sun-swept airy stretches perhaps it abuses its freedom a little. It kicks up its heels and gets into its old clothes. Certainly as soon as one gets south of Lombard street one sees the sudden change. Even the vast and dignified gray façade of the Ridgway Library does not abash our highway for more than a moment. It dashes on between a vast clothing factory and the old "Southern and Western Railroad Station." It indulges itself in small clothing stores, lemonade stands and all manner of tumble-down monkey business. It seems to say, "I can look just like Spring Garden street, if I want to."

Perhaps it is because William Penn on the City Hall is looking the other way that South Broad street feels it can cut up without reserve.

The Ridgway Library ought to be able to daunt this frisking humor, for a more solemn and repressive erection was never planned. But what a fascinating place it is, though I fear not much of South Broad street ever takes the trouble to open those iron gates marked "Pull." Perhaps if they had been marked *"Push"* the public would have responded more eagerly. But who are we to discuss the subtleties of advertising psychology? As I pass the long, heavily-pillared frontage of the library I seem to hear the quiet, deliberate ticking of the clock in the cool, gloomy reading room and smell the faint, delicious, musty fragrance of the old volumes. It is no small thrill to step inside and revel in the dim scholarly twilight of this palace of silence, to pore over the rare books in the glass showcases and explore the alcoves where the marvelous collection of chess books is kept. Those alcoves look out over a little playground at the back, where the shady benches would be an ideal place for a solemn pipe; but alas! no men are admitted. The playground is reserved for women and children.

Very different is the old railroad station across the way, now used as a freight depot. Built in 1852, it was Philadelphia's crack terminus fifty years ago, and as one studies the crumbled brownstone front one thinks of all the eager and excited feet that must have passed into the great arched hall. Now it is boarded up in front, but inside it is crammed with box cars and vast cases stenciled *"Rush—Military Supplies—U. S. Army."* Sixty freight cars can be loaded there at one time. One thinks what emotions that glass-roofed shed must have seen in Civil War times. I suppose many a train of men in blue said good-by to mothers and sweethearts along those platforms. That thought was with me as I stood inside the old station, which in spite of its bustle of freight is filled with the haunting sadness of all places that are old and decayed and echoing with the whispers of long ago. Does it seem absurd to sentimentalize over a railway station less than seventy years old? Well, I think a railway station is one of the most romantic places in the world. I like to imagine the old locomotives with their flaring stacks. And as I crossed Washington avenue (which runs just south of the station) I remembered a hot day in June twenty years ago when I tugged a roll of steamer rugs down that street from the trolley to the American Line pier. We were going on board the old *Belgenland*, bound for Liverpool. Somewhere along the hot, grimy pavement a barrel of molasses had broken open; I recall the strong, sweet smell. Childhood does not forget such adventures.

Below the quartermaster depot of the marine corps and the Third Regiment Armory, Broad street recalls its more sober responsibilities. Suddenly it realizes the fleeting uncertainty of life; perhaps because half the houses hereabouts are the offices of doctors and undertakers. It falls into a quiet residential humor about Wharton street and lines itself with trees and shady awnings. It seemed to me I could discern a breath of Italy in the air. At an Italian undertaker's a large and sumptuous coffin was lying on the pavement without any embarrassment, nameplate and all; presumably waiting for its silent passenger. Among the womenfolk white stockings and sparkling black eyes betrayed the Latin blood. And I saw that a church lettered its notice board both in Italian and English. "Ingresso Libero," it said, which I take to mean "Everybody welcome!" The same sort of hospitality is evinced by the doctors and

29

dentists. They all have little notices on their doors: "Walk in without knocking."

In a quaint effort to retrieve its brief escapade into shabby Bohemianism, Broad street now goes in for an exaggerated magnificence. It has a taste for ornate metal doorknobs and brass handles. (I cannot resist the thought that these mannerisms were caught from the undertakers.) Moving-picture theatres are done in a kind of Spanish stucco. Basement gratings are gilded; parlor windows are banded with strips of colored glass. The brownstone fronts are gabled and carved; cornices are fret worked. There are plaster statues in the little side gardens. It is the opposite swing of the architect's pendulum from the plain and beautiful old houses of Pine and Spruce streets, where Philadelphia expresses herself in the lovely simplicity of rich old brick and white shutters.

Apparently Broad street lost hope of gaining salvation by ornamenting its house fronts, for about Morris and Mifflin streets it turns to education and philanthropy. It puts up large hospitals, and the vast gray building of the South Philadelphia High School, where, reading backward through the stained glass transom I discerned the grave and very Bostonian motto: "Work—Self-reliance—Culture—Life." But more exhilarating to me was the Southern Home for Friendless Children at Morris street. Its large playground is surrounded by a high stone wall. I could easily have scaled it and would have loved to smoke a pipe sitting up there to watch the children playing inside. (I could hear their laughter, and caught a glimpse of a small boy as he flew up in the air on a swing.) But I feared penalties and embarrassments. It does not do to love anything too well; people naturally are suspicious of you. And though my heart was warm toward the Southern Home, I didn't quite like to do what I yearned for. That would have been to ring the door-bell and ask to go in and play in the garden with the others. Instead I snooped round the wall until I found a corner with a glimpse into the shady ground where the urchins were busy. One small boy was working in his garden, others were burning up rubbish and hammering at something along the wall. I stood there a long time, listening to the warm, drowsy hum of the afternoon, and almost wished I were a friendless child.

After this excursion into culture and charity, Broad street feels the need of one more whistle-wetting before it wanders off onto the vast expanse of sunny, pollen-scented meadows that stretch toward the dry zones of League Island. For this purpose exists the cool haven of McBride, on the corner of Moyamensing avenue. There I encountered one of the best beakers of shandygaff in my experience. And—wonder of wonders—it can still be bought for a nickel.

# THE RECLUSE OF
# FRANKLIN SQUARE

WHO CAN DESCRIBE the endless fascination, allurement and magic of the city? It is like a great forest, full of enchantment for the eye and ear. What groves and aisles and vistas there are for wandering, what thickets and underbrush to explore! And how curious it is that most of us who frequent the city follow only little beaten paths of our own, rarely looking round the corner or investigating (in the literal sense) unfamiliar byways. We tread our own routine, from terminal or trolley to office, to the customary lunching place, back to the office, and home. Year after year we do this, until the city is for us nothing but a few tedious streets we know by heart.

But how dull it is to be confined to one life, one habit, one groove of conduct. Do you ever pine to shed the garment of well-worn behavior, to wander off into the side-paths of the city, to lose yourself in its great teeming life? The thought is fascinating to me. I like to imagine myself disappearing one day from my accustomed haunts, slipping away into some other quarter of the town, taking up entirely new habits and environment. Ah, that would be an adventure!

I think I would emigrate to Franklin Square which, after all, is only a few blocks north of the territory where I oscillate every day; but it seems almost like a different continent. I would go up to Franklin Square, take a room at one of those theatrical lodging houses on the western side of the square, grow a beard, wear a wide sombrero hat, and keep my pockets full of sweetmeats for the children of the square. In the course of a few months quite a legend would accumulate about me. I would be pointed out as one of the characters of the neighborhood. Newspaper reporters

32

would be sent to interview me. Then I would shave and move on to some other home.

Franklin Square is a jolly place on a warm day. There are red and pink geraniums round the pool in the middle. There is the drowsy whirr and hum of lawn mowers. There is a sweet, dull air moving gently across the wide grass plots; the flag waves heavily on the tall staff. There is a whole posse of baby carriages gathered together in a shady patch of pavement, with usually one small girl left to "mind" them while the other little guardians are sprinkling themselves with water at the stand-pipe, or playing hop-scotch in the sun. You mind my baby and I'll mind yours, is the tacit understanding of these ragged little damsels. But, really it is surprising how little minding the Franklin Square babies seem to need. They lie in their carriages furling and unfurling their toes with a kind of spartan restraint. They refuse to bawl or to hurl themselves upon the paving below, because they know that their young nurses are having a good time.

Franklin Square policemen are stout and very jovial. An Italian woman was sitting on a bench opposite mine; she had a baby on her lap, one leaning against her knee, three sitting on the bench with her, and two in the carriage. Seven in all and I gathered from her remarks that six of them were boys. "Quite an army!" said the stout police-man, passing by. Her face gleamed with the quick pleasure of the Latin race. "Ah, yes," she said, "Italians good for boys!"

On the west side of the square are the theatrical boarding houses, where ladies with very short skirts and silk stock-ings air little fuzzy white dogs that just match the soiled marble steps. Midway in the row is a bulky chocolate-colored church, Deutsche Evang. Lutherische, according to its signboard. Gottesdienst, Morgens 10:45, Abends 7:30. It is well for us to remember that God is worshiped in all languages. And up at the little news-stall at the corner of

Vine street, the literary and dramatic leanings of Franklin Square seem to be reflected in the assortment of paper-backed volumes on display. "The Confessions of an Actress," "The Stranglers of Paris," and "Chicago by Night" are among the books there, also some exceedingly dingy editions of Boccaccio and Napoleon's Dream Book. I could learn a good deal, I am sure, by studying those volumes.

Franklin Square is full of color. The green spaces are islanded in a frame of warm, red brick. The fountain bubbles whitely, the flag is an eager spot of brightness on the tall white mast. Shop windows seem to display a broader, more lilting kind of poster than they do on Market street. There is one on a by-street representing a young man blowing heart-shaped smoke rings and a glorious young woman is piercing them with a knitting needle or some other sharp instrument.

I don't know just what I would do for a living on Franklin Square. The only thought that has occurred to me is this: some one must have to look after those little white dogs while their debonair mistresses are at the theatre. Why couldn't I do that, for a modest fee? I would take them all out at night and tow them through the fountain pool. It would serve to bleach them.

Another thing I could do, which I have always wanted to do, would be to decipher the last line of the small tombstone that stands over the pathetic grave of Benjamin Franklin's little son. That is not far from the square. The stone reads, as far as I can make it out, *Francis F., Son of Benjamin and Deborah Franklin, Deceased Nov. 21, 1736. Aged 4 years.* The number of months and days I can't make out, nor the last line of the epitaph, which begins with the sadly expressive word *Delight*. It is much effaced, and without squatting on Ben Franklin's tomb I can't read it. And as there are usually some young ladies sitting knitting on the bench by the grave I am too bashful to do that. But if I lived in Franklin Square I would find a way somehow.

But much as I love it, I doubt if I could live in Franklin Square long. There is an air of unrest about it, of vagabond whimsy. The short-skirted ladies would come and go, and sooner or later the bearded recluse, with his pocket full of candy, and his sombrero hat, would disappear and only the children would lament his going. For I know that if I were a wandering blade I could never resist a summons like this, which I found posted up just off the square. Here speak Romance and Adventure, with golden lute:

MEN WANTED TO TRAVEL
WITH R——'S CIRCUS
A CHANCE TO SEE THE COUNTRY
EXCELLENT BOARD AND COMFORTABLE
SLEEPING CARS PROVIDED BY THE MANAGEMENT

GRAVE OF BENJAMIN AND DEBORAH FRANKLIN
by Frank H. Taylor. Courtesy Free Library of Philadelphia.

# A SLICE OF SUNLIGHT

ABOUT A QUARTER to 9 in the morning, at this time of year, a slice of our pale primrose-colored March sunlight cuts the bleak air across the junction of Broad and Chestnut streets and falls like a shining knife blade upon the low dome of the Girard Trust Building. Among those towering cliffs of masonry it is hard to see just where this shaving of brightness slips through, burning in the gray-lilac shadows of that stone valley. But there it is, and it always sets me thinking.

Man has traveled far in his strange pilgrimage and solaced himself with many lean and brittle husks. It is curious to think how many of his ingenious inventions are merely makeshifts to render tolerable the hardships and limitations he has imposed upon himself in the name of "civilization." How often his greatest cunning is expended in devising some pathetic substitute for the joy that once was his by birthright! He shuts himself up in beetling gibraltars of concrete, and thinks with pride of the wires, fans and pipes that bring him light, air and warmth. And yet sunshine and sky and the glow of blazing faggots were once common to all! He talks to his friends by telephone, telegraph or machine-written letters instead of in the heart-easing face-to-face of more leisured times. He invents printing presses to do his thinking for him, reels of translucent celluloid to thrill him with vicarious romance. Not until the desire of killing other men came upon him did he perfect the loveliest of his toys—the airplane. How far, in his perverse flight from the natural sources of joy, has his love of trouble brought him!

So it is that one poor, thin, thwarted filament of sunlight, falling for a few precious minutes across a chasmed city street, seems so dazzling a boon and surprise that he passes enchanted on his darkened pavement. Man, how easily you are pleased!

Is there any one, in our alternate moods of bafflement and exultation, who has not brooded on this queer divergence of Life and Happiness? Sometimes we feel that we have been trapped: that Life, which once opened a vista so broad and golden, has somehow jostled and hurried us into a corner, into a narrow treadmill of meaningless gestures that exhaust our spirit and our mirth. In recent years all humanity has been herded in one vast cage of confusion and dread from which there seemed no egress. Now we are slowly, bitterly, perplexedly groping our way out of it. And perhaps in the difficult years of rebuilding each man will make some effort to architect his existence anew, creeping humbly and hopefully a little closer to the fountains of beauty and strength that lie all about us. When did we learn to cut ourselves apart from earth's miracles of refreshment? To wall ourselves in from the sun's great laughter, to forget the flamboyant pageantry of the world? Earth has wisdom for all our follies, healing for all our wounds, dusk and music for all our peevishness. Who taught us that we could do without her? Can you hear the skylark through a telephone or catch that husky whisper of the pines in a dictograph? Can you keep your heart young in a row of pigeonholes? Will you forego the surf of ocean rollers to be serf to a rolltop desk?

Little by little, and in haphazard ways, wisdom comes to a man. No matter how resolutely he shuts his ears, Truth keeps pricking within him. What a futility, what a meanness and paltriness of living this is that would send us hence with all Life's great secrets unlearned, her ineffable beauties unguessed, her great folio only hastily glimpsed. Here is this spinning ball for us to marvel at, turning in an ever-changing bath of color and shadow, blazed with sunshine, drenched with silver rain, leaning through green and orange veils of dusk, and we creep with blinkered eyes along

37

narrow alleys of unseeing habit. What will it profit us to keep a balance at the bank if we can't keep a balance of youth and sanity in our souls? Of what avail to ship carloads of goods north, east, south and west, if we cannot spare time to know our own dreams, to exchange our doubts and yearnings with our friends and neighbors?

In every man's heart there is a secret nerve that answers to the vibration of beauty. I can imagine no more fascinating privilege than to be allowed to ransack the desks of a thousand American business men, men supposed to be hard-headed, absorbed in brisk commerce. Somewhere in each desk one would find some hidden betrayal of that man's private worship. It might be some old newspaper clipping, perhaps a poem that had once touched him, for even the humblest poets are stout partisans of reality. It might be a photograph of children playing in the surf, or a little box of fish-hooks, or a soiled old timetable of some queer backwoods railroad or primitive steamer service that had once carried him into his land of heart's desire.

I remember a friend of mine, a man much perplexed by the cares of earth, but slow to give utterance to his inner and tenderer impulses, telling me how he first grasped the meaning and value of these inscrutable powers of virtue that hurl the whole universe daily around our heads in an unerring orbit. For some reason or other—he was writing a book, I think, and sought a place of quiet—he had drifted for some winter weeks to the shore of a southern bay, down in Florida. When he came back he told me about it. It was several years ago, but I remember the odd look in his eyes as he tried to describe his experience. "I never knew until now," he said, "what sunshine and sky meant. I had always taken them for granted before." He told me of the strange sensation of lightness and quiet smiling that had flooded through him in that land where Nature writes her benignant lessons so plainly that all must draw their own conclusions. He told me of sunset flushes over long, purple waters, and of lying on sand beaches wrapped in sunshine, all the problems of human intercourse soothed away in a naked and unquestioning content. What he said was very little, but watching in his eyes I could guess what had happened. He had found more than sunshine and color and an arc of violet sea. He had found a new philosophy, a new strength and realization of the worthiness of life. He had traveled far to find it: it might just as well be learned in Independence Square any sunny day when the golden light falls upon springing grass.

It is strange that men should have to be reminded of these things! How patiently, how persistently, with what dogged and misdirected pluck, they have taught themselves to ignore the elemental blessings of mankind, subsisting instead on pale and wizened and ingenious substitutes. It is like a man who should shoulder for a place at a quick lunch counter when a broad and leisurely banquet table was spread free just around the corner. The days tick by, as busy, as fleeting, as full of empty gestures as a moving picture film. We crowd old age upon ourselves and run out to embrace it, for age is not measured by number of days but by the exhaustion of each day. Twenty days lived at slow pulse, in harmony with earth's loveliness, are longer than two hundred crowded with feverish appointments and disappointments. Many a man has lived fifty or sixty hectic years and never yet learned the unreckonable endlessness of one day's loitering, measured only by the gracious turning of earth and sun. Some one often asks me, "Why don't you wind the clocks?" But in those rare moments when I am sane clocks do not interest me.

Something of these thoughts flashes into my mind as I see that beam of pale and narrow sunlight fallen upon the roof of that bank building. How strange it is, when life is bursting with light and strength, renewing itself every day in color and freshness, that we should sunder ourselves from these great sources of power. With all the treasures of earth at hand, we coop ourselves in narrow causeways where even a sudden knife-edge of brightness is a matter for joyful surprise. As Stevenson once said, it is all very well to believe in immortality, but one must first believe in life. Why do we grudge ourselves the embraces of "Our brother and good friend the Sun"?

# DARKNESS VISIBLE

O F ALL GIFTS to earth, the first and greatest was darkness. Darkness preceded light, you will remember, in Genesis. Perhaps that is why darkness seems to man natural and universal. It requires no explanation and no cause. We postulate it. Whereas light, being to our minds merely the cleansing vibration that dispels the black, requires some origin, some lamp whence to shine. From the appalling torch of the sun down to the pale belly of the glowworm we deem light a derivative miracle, proceeding from some conceivable source. We can conceive darkness without thought of light; but we cannot conceive light without darkness. Day is but an interval between two nights. In other words, darkness is a matter which includes light just as the conception of a joke includes that of humor. One can think (alas!) of jokes without humor; but no one can conceive of humor without jokes.

This philosophy, probably scoffable for the trained thinker, is a clumsy preface to the thought that city streets at night are the most fascinating work of man. Like all other handouts of nature, man has taken darkness and made it agreeable, trimmed and refined and made it acceptable for the very nicest people. And the suburbanite who finds himself living in town for a week or so is likely to spend his whole evenings in wandering espial, poring over the glowing caves of shop windows and rejoicing in the rich patterns of light wherewith man has made night lovely. Night by herself, naked and primitive and embracing, is embarrassing; she crowds one so; there is so much of her. So we push her up the side streets and into the movie halls and out to the suburbs, and taking her a little at a time we really learn to enjoy her company.

There is a restaurant on Arch street near Ninth where

one may dine on excellent jam omelet and coffee, after which it is good to stroll along Ninth street (which with its tributary Ludlow I esteem the best street we have) to admire the different tints of light that man has set out in order to get a look at the darkness. There is the wan white glow of the alabaster inverted bowls that are favored in barbers' shops. There is the lucent gold of jewelers' windows where naked electric bulbs of great candlepower are masked in silvered reflectors along the top and bottom of the pane. There is the bleak moonshine of tiled and enameled restaurants, where they lose much lightness by having everything too white. If (for instance) the waitresses would only wear scarlet or black dresses, how much more brilliant the scene would be. There is the pale lilac and lavender of the arcs, and the vicious green glare of mercury vapor tubes in the ten minute photograph studios that are always full of sailors. Over all soars the orange disc of the City Hall clock, which has been hailed by so many romantic wastrels as the rising or setting moon. And the fierce light that is said to beat upon a throne is twilight compared to that which shimmers round our jewelled soda fountains.

The long, musty corridor of the postoffice on Ninth street is an interesting place about 8 o'clock in the evening. Particularly in these last weeks, when movies, saloons and theatres have been closed on account of the influenza epidemic, the postoffice has become a trysting place for men in uniform and young ladies. The gloomy halls at each end of the corridor are good ground for giggling colloquy; light love (curiously) approves the dusk. Through the little windows one catches glimpses of tiers of pigeonholes packed with letters, and wonders what secrets of the variable human heart are there confided to the indulgent secrecy of Uncle Sam. If a novelist of imaginative sympathy might spend a week in reading through those pigeonholes, what a book he could make of them! Or could we only peer over the shoulders of those who stand writing at the blackened, ink-stained desks, what meshes of joy and pain we might see raveled in the lives of plain men and women! The great tapestry of human life lies all round us, and we have to pluck clumsily at its patterns thread by thread.

One who is interested in bookish matters ought to make a point of going upstairs to the registered mail room on the second floor. In a corner of that room, sitting in a well-worn chair under a drop light, you may be fortunate enough to find one of the postoffice guards, an elderly philosopher who beguiles the evening vigil with a pipe and a book. He is a genial sage and a keen devourer of print. He eats books alive. Marie Corelli and Marion Crawford are among his favorites for lighter ministration, but in the past few weeks his mind has been on graver matter. He has just finished a life of Napoleon and a biography of Joan of Arc. Tonight when I went in to register a letter his chair was empty (he was having his supper of sandwiches and a little bucket of coffee at a table in the dim hallway outside), but on the shelf lay his book, pipe and tobacco pouch. I could not resist peeking to see what the volume was. Little's *Life of Saint Francis of Assisi*. Verily, if our government officials are taking to reading of Saint Francis, the world looks forward to happier days.

The Secretary of the Treasury says in a notice "Loitering about this building is prohibited," but I fear I have committed what Don Marquis used to call lèse-McAdoo in often halting to scrutinize the bulletin board in the north hall of the postoffice. Here are posted statements of stores and materials needed by the Federal departments. One finds such notices as this: *Sealed proposals will be received by the undersigned until 2 o'clock p. m., October 30, for supplying this building with three dozen scrubbing brushes.* And the Navy Yard's bulletin board, near by, always has interesting requirements: *Wanted, for United States naval training camp, seventy-five bubbling heads sanitary drinking fountains.* (Imagine how amazed seamen of the tarry pigtail era would be at the idea of drinking from a sanitary drinking fountain!) The Inspector of Engineering Material, U. S. N., Cleveland, O., announces that he desires space for storing one five-passenger Ford touring car and washing it at least once each week for the period ending June 30, 1919. It would be a bit inconvenient, we think, to store the flivver here in Philadelphia. The Navy Yard desires bids for supplying submarines with copper-jacketed gaskets, which has a business-like sound. The Public Works Department admits that one dozen mouse traps, revolving, are needed, to be delivered and inspected at Building No. 4, Navy Yard. *Wanted for overseas vessels* (here our heart leaps up at the prospect of something exciting) *eleven revolving office chairs, oak finish, and eleven dozen pencils.* The Naval Hospital at League Island asks bids on 100 poinsettias, 50 cyclamens, 100 primroses, 100 carnations, 12 hydrangeas, all in pots. And there are requisitions posted for wires and shackles, for anchors and propellers, for chemicals and talcum powder and vast radio towers to be erected at a naval base in France. War, you see, is not all a matter of powder and shot. If you are ever tempted to wonder what the Government does with the Liberty Loans, go up to the Federal Building and look over a few of those invitations for bids posted on the bulletin boards.

Ninth street, as I said, often seems to me the most alluring street in town. Perhaps it is because of certain bookshops; perhaps it is because at a table d'hôte restaurant above Market street I first learned the pleasant combustion of cheap claret and cigarettes ignited by the spark of youthful converse. To these discoveries of a dozen years ago I am happy to add others; for example, that the best spaghetti I have ever eaten is served on Ninth street; and that there is a second-hand bookstore which is open at night. Nor am I likely to forget a set-to with sausages and corncakes and sirup that I enjoyed on Ninth street the other evening with the Soothsayer. We had been motoring in the suburbs, a crisp and bravely tinted October afternoon, and getting back to town after 8 o'clock as hungry as bolshevik commissars, we entered into the joy of the flesh in a Ninth street hash cathedral. Here and now let me pay tribute to those blissful lunch rooms that stay open late at night to sustain and replenish the toiler whose business it is to pass along the lonely pavements of midnight. Waiters and waitresses of the all-night shift, we who are about to eat salute you! Let it be a double portion of corned-beef hash and "coffee with plenty." And many a midnight luncher has blessed you for your unfailing good humor. Is it not true, admit it, that most of the happy recollections of mankind deal with food we have enjoyed?

You will find it well worth while to take a stroll up Ninth street some evening. You will usually find a roasted chestnut cart at the southeast corner of Market street. The noble savor of cooking chestnuts is alone worth the effort of the walk. Then you can pass on northward, by the animal shop, where the dogs sleep uneasily in the window, agitated by the panorama outside; past the cuckoo clock shop and the old Dime Museum. As the street leads on to less exalted faubourgs you will notice that it grows more luxurious. Windows glow with gold watches, diamond studs, cut glass carafes. Haberdashers set out $8 silk shirts, striped with the rainbow, infinitely more glorious than anything to be found on Chestnut street. And then, at Race street, you can turn off into the queer sights of Chinatown.

# PINE STREET

OUR NEIGHBOURHOOD is very genteel. I doubt if any one who has not lived in Philadelphia can imagine how genteel it is. Visitors from out of town are wont to sigh with rapture when they see our trim blocks of tall brick dwellings—that even cornice running in a smooth line for several hundred yards really is quite a sight—and exclaim, "Oh, I wish we had something like this in New York!" But our gentility is a little self-conscious, for we live on the very frontier of a region, darker in complexion, which is far from scrupulous in deportment. Uproarious and naïve are the humours of South Street, lying just behind us. Stanleys have gone exploring thither and come back with merry tales. South Street on a bright evening, its myriad barber shops gleaming with lathered dusky cheeks, wafting the essence of innumerable pomades and lotions, that were a Travel indeed. On South Street the veins of life run close to the surface.

We are no less human on our street, but it takes a bit more study to get at the secret. There is a certain reticence about us. It would take an earthquake to cause much fraternization along Pine Street. Perhaps it is because three houses out of every four bear the tablets of doctors. The average layman fears to stop and speak to his neighbour for fear it will develop into a professional matter. We board up our front windows at night with heavy wooden shutters. We have no druggists, only "apothecaries." These apothecaries are closed on Sundays. They sell stamps in little isinglass capsules, to be quite sanitary, two twos in a capsule for five cents. In their shops you can still get soda water with "plain cream" and shaved ice, such as was customary twenty-five years ago. When our doctors go away for the summer, someone comes twice a week from June to October to polish up the little silver name plate. It is the custom in our neighbourhood (so one observes through drawing room windows) to have reading lamps with rosy pink shades and at least two beautiful daughters of débutante age. I hope I am not unjust, but our street looks to me like the kind of place where people take warm baths, in a roomy old china tub, on Sunday afternoons. After that, they go downstairs and play a hymn on the piano, at twilight.

There are a number of very odd features about our neighbourhood. There is a large schoolhouse at the next corner, but as far as I can see, it is not used as a school, not for children, at any rate. Sometimes, about 8 o'clock in the evening, I see the building gloriously illuminated, and a lonely lady stooped and assiduous at a table. She seems quite solitary. Perhaps her researches are so poignant that the school board has prescribed entire silence. But midway down the block is a very jolly little private school, to which very genteel children may be seen approaching early in the morning. The little girls come with a bustle of starch, on foot, accompanied by governesses; the small boys arrive in

limousines. They are small boys dressed very much in the English manner, with heavy woollen stockings ending just below the knee. They probably do not realize that their tailor has carefully planned them to look like dear little English boys. Then there is a very mysterious small theatre near by. If it were a movie theatre, what a boon it would be! But no, it is devoted to a strange cult called the Religion of Business, which meets there on Sundays. Before that, there was a Korean congress there. There is a lovely green room in this theatre, but not much long green in the box office. Philadelphia prefers Al Jolson to Hank Ibsen.

We have our tincture of vie de Bohème, though, in our little French table d'hôte, a thoroughly atmospheric place. Delightful Madame B., with her racy philosophy of life, what delicious soups and salads she serves! Happy indeed are those who have learned the way to her little tables, and heard her cheerful cry "À la cuisine!" when one of her small dogs prowls into the dining room. Equally unique is the old curiosity shop near by, one of the few genuine "notion" shops left in the city (though there is a delightful one on Market Street near Seventeenth, to enter which is to step into a country village). This is just the kind of shop bought by the old gentleman in one of Frank Stockton's agreeable tales, "Mr. Tolman," in the volume called *The Magic Egg*. The proprietress, charming and conversable lady, will sell you anything in the "notions" line, from a paper of pins to garter elastic. Then there is the laundry, whose patrons carry on a jovial game known as "Looking for Your Own." Every week, by some cheery habit of confusion, the lists are lost, and one hunts through shelves of neatly piled and crisply laundered garments to pick out one's own collars, pyjamas, or whatever it may be. The amusing humours of this pastime must be experienced to be understood.

The little cigar and magazine shop on the corner is the political and social focus of the neighbourhood. I shall never forget the pallid and ghastly countenance of the newsdealer when the rumour first went the rounds that "Hampy" was elected. Every evening a little gathering of local sages meets in the shop; on tilted chairs, in a haze of tobacco, they while the hours away. In tobacco the host adheres to the standard blends, but in literature he is enterprising. Until recently this was the only place I know in Philadelphia where one could get the *Illustrated London News* every week.

There are twinges of modernity going on along our street. Some of the old houses have been remodeled into apartments. There is an "electric shoe repairer" just round the corner. But the antique dealers and plumbers for which the street is famous still hold sway; the fine old brick pavement still collects rain water in its numerous dimpled hollows, and the yellowish marble horse-blocks adorn the curb. The nice shabby stables in the little side streets have not yet been turned into studios by artists, and the neighbourhood's youngest urchins set sail for Rittenhouse Square every morning on their fleet of "kiddie-cars." Their small stout legs, twinkling along the pavements in white gaiters on a wintry day, are a pleasant sight. Even our urchins are notably genteel. Surrounded on all sides by the medical profession, they are reared on registered milk and educator crackers. If Philadelphia ever betrays its soul, it does so on this delightful, bland, and genteel highway.

# MARKET STREET

## I. Edgar Allan Poe

During the whole of a dull and oppressive afternoon, when the very buildings that loomed about
me seemed to lean forward threateningly as if to crush me
with their stony mass, I had been traveling in fitful jerks in
a Market street trolley; and at length found myself, as the
sullen shade of evening drew on, within view of the melancholy tower of the City Hall. I know not how it was—
but, with the first glimpse of the building a sense of
insufferable gloom pervaded my spirit. I say insufferable,
for the feeling was unrelieved by any of that half-pleasura-
ble sentiment with which the mind usually receives even
the sternest images of the desolate or terrible. I looked
upon the simple visages of the policemen on guard in the
courtyard—upon the throng of suburban humanity pressing
in mournful agitation toward their solemn hour of trial—
upon a deserted litter of planks left by the heedless hand
of the subway contractor—and an icy anguish seized upon
my spirit. What was it—I paused to think—what was it that
so unnerved me in the contemplation of the City Hall? Was
it the knowledge that any one of these bluecoats could,
with a mere motion of his hand, consign me to some terrible
dungeon within those iron walls—or the thought that in
this vast and pitiless pile sat men who held the destiny of
my fellow citizens in their hands—or the knowledge that
time was flying and I was in imminent peril of missing my
train? It was a mystery all insoluble, and I mused in
shadowy fancy, caught in a web of ghastly surmise.

At last I raised my head, breaking away from these unanalyzed forebodings. I gazed upward where the last fire of the setting sun tinged the summit with a gruesome glow—O horror more than mortal!—O fearful sight that drove the blood in torrents on my heart—*God shield and guard me from the arch-fiend,* I shrieked—had William Penn gone Bolshevist? For they had painted the base of his statue—*a glaring, bloodlike red!*

## II. HENRY JAMES

THORNCLIFF WAS thinking, as he crossed the, to him, intolerably interwoven confusion of Market street, that he had never—unless it was once in a dream which he strangely associated in memory with an overplus of antipasto—never consciously, that is, threaded his way through so baffling a predicament of traffic, and it was not until halted, somewhat summarily, though yet kindly, by a blue arm which he after some scrutiny assessed as belonging to a traffic patrolman, that he bethought himself sufficiently to inquire, in a manner a little breathless still, though understood at once by the kindly envoy of order as the natural mood of one inextricably tangled in mind and not yet wholly untangled in body, but still intact when the propulsive energy of the motortruck had been, by a rapid shift of gears and actuating machinery, transformed to a rearward movement, where he might be and how.

"This is Market street," said the officer.

"Market street? Ah, thank you."

Market street! Could it be, indeed? His last conscious impression had been of some shop—a milliner's, perhaps?—on, probably, Walnut street where he had been gazing with mild reproach at the price tickets upon the hats displayed, or, if not displayed, a term implying a rather crude concession to commercialism, at least exhibited, and considering whether or not it would be advisable, on so hot a day or a day that had every promise of becoming hot unless those purple clouds that hung over the ferries should liquidate into something not unlike a thunder shower, to carry with him a small hat as an act of propitiation and reconcilement with Mrs. Thorncliff. So this was Market street. He gazed with friendly interest into the face of the policeman, a gaze in which there was not the slightest sign of any animating rebuke at the interruption in his meditation, a meditation which, after all, had been unconscious rather than actively cerebrated and with some vague intention of inquiring ultimately whether it were safe, now and here, to cross the highway or whether it would be better to wait until the semaphore (which, as he had just noticed, was turned to STOP) gave him undoubted privilege to pass unhindered, remarked again, but without malicious motive, which indeed would have been foreign to his mood and purpose: "Market street? How interesting."

## III. WALT WHITMAN

I SEE the long defile of Market street,
And the young libertad offering to shine my shoes
(I do not have my shoes shined, for am I not as worthy
    without them shined? I put it to you, Camerado.)
And I see the maidens and young men flocking into the
    movies.
And I promulge this doctrine, that the government might
    have imposed twice as heavy a tax on amusements, and
    still young men and maidens would throng to the
    movies,
(O endless timidity of statesmen)
And I wonder whether I, too, will go in and give the
    eidolons the once over,
But putting my hand in my pocket I see that I have only
    thirteen cents
And it will cost me three cents to get back to Camden.
In a window I see a white-coated savan cooking griddle
    cakes,

And I think to myself, I am no better than he is,
And he is no better than I am,
And no one is any better than any one else
(O the dignity of labor,
Particularly the labor that is done by other people;
Let other people do the work, is my manifesto,
Leave me to muse about it)
Work is a wonderful thing, and a steady job is a wonderful
    thing,
And the pay envelope is a wonderful institution,
And I love to meditate on all the work that there is to be
    done,
And how other people are doing it.
Reader, whether in Kanada or Konshohocken,
I strike up for you.
This is my song for you, and a good song, I'll say so.

## IV. KARL BAEDEKER

\*   \*   \*   MARKET STREET (Marktstrasse). Issuing from
the majestic terminus of the Camden ferries the traveler
will behold the long prospect of Market street, ending with
the imposing tower (548 feet) which was until the recent
rise in prices the highest thing in Philadelphia. On the
summit of the tower will be observed the colossal statue of
William Penn, said to be of German extraction (1644–1718).
The Market street is the business center of Philadelphia. A
curious phenomenon, exhibiting the perspicacious shrewdness of the natives of this great city, may be observed on
any warm day about noon: the natives keep to the shady
side of the street. As the thoroughfare runs due east and
west, a brief astronomical calculation will show this to be
the southern side of the way. Between October and April,
however, it is quite safe to walk at a leisurely pace on the
sunny side. By all means observe the great number of
places where soft drinks may be obtained, characteristic of
the American sweet tooth, but expensive (war tax, one cent

per ten cents or fraction thereof). The dignified edifice at the corner of Ninth street is the federal building, often carelessly spoken of as the postoffice. An entertaining experiment, often tried by visitors, is that of mailing a letter here. (See note on Albert Sidney Burleson, elsewhere in this edition.) The visitor who wishes to make a thorough tour of Market street may cover the ground between the river (Delaware, a large sluggish stream, inferior to the Rhine) and the City Hall in an hour, unless he takes the subway. (Allow 1½ hrs.)

# BENJAMIN FRANKLIN
## Jan. 17, 1919

BENJAMIN FRANKLIN, sagacious and witty,
The greatest of all who have lived in this city,
Earnest and frugal and very discerning,
Always industrious, bent upon learning,
Athlete, ambassador, editor, printer,
Merchant and scientist, writer, inventor,
None was more canny or shrewder of brain,
None was more practical or more humane,
> None was e'er wiser
>> With common sense ripe,
> Great advertiser
>> And founder of type.

Troubles he suffered, but he didn't dodge any:
Born the fifteenth of a numerous progeny
> (Seventeen children Josiah had sired,
>> A whole little font of good lower-case types;
> A fact that the census man must have admired—
>> I think old Josiah might well have worn stripes,
But that was in Boston where folks are prolific)
He passed through a boyhood by no means pacific.
Through most of his teens, young Benjamin lent his
Best efforts to being his brother's apprentice,
But Jimmy was crusty—they didn't get on,
And one autumn morning young Benny was gone.
He vowed he would make his sour kinsman look silly,
And so he took ship and descended on Philly.
The very first thought that came into his nob
(After buying some buns) was to look for a job.
> So up from the ferry
>> Our Benjamin stalked,
> And hungrily, very,
>> Ate buns as he walked.
> A certain blithe flapper,

A whimsical lass,
Observed the young strapper
And thought he lacked class,
And so, in the manner of feminine strafing,
The superior damsel just couldn't help laughing;
But Ben, unabashed by this good-natured chaffing,
Although young Deborah
Was certainly rude,
He thought he'd ignore her
And cheerfully chewed.
With the best kind of repartee later he parried her,
For seven years afterward he went and married her.


Well, you all know of his varied successes,
Electrical hobbies and his printing presses.
See how his mind, with original oddity
Touched and found interest in every commodity:
Busy with schemes to domesticate lightning,
Inventing a stove for home warming and brightening,
Scribbling a proverb, a joke or a sermon,
Publishing too (what I am loth to mention
For fear of its bringing up any dissension)
Printing, I say, a newspaper in German—
Also, for which he's remembered by most,
He founded the *Saturday Evening Post*,
For which Irvin Cobb has consistently praised him—
And its circulation would have much amazed him!
Busy with matters too many for telling—
Saving of daylight and simplified spelling—
Still his chief happiness, as one may think,
Came when he found himself dabbling in ink,
And all his writings, though slight he did think 'em,
Brought him a very respectable income.
His was a mind that was chiefly empirical,
Not at all given to theory or miracle—
Nothing chimerical,
Nothing hysterical,—
Though he wrote verses, they weren't very lyrical,
And he was touched with a taste for satirical.

## PHILADELPHIA

Though his more weighty affairs were so numerous
Yet he was quaintly and constantly humorous,
Loved Philadelphians, but when he was one of them
Nothing he liked quite so well as make fun of them.

Scarce an invention since his time has burst
But Benjamin Franklin had thought of it first;
Indeed it would cause me no ejaculations
To hear he suggested the new League of Nations.
He truly succeeded in most that he tried, he
Confounded his enemies, and when he died he
Was guiltless of sin except being untidy.
He died of old age, not of illness or tumor,
And wrote his own epitaph, full of good humor.
Every tradition and custom he broke,
This first Philadelphian who dared make a joke!

# CLAUD JOSEPH WARLOW

Some DAYS AGO we were passing the new office of the Philadelphia Electric Company at Tenth and Chestnut streets, when our eye was caught, through the broad plate-glass windows, by a shimmer of blue at the back of the store. Being of a curious disposition, we pushed through the revolving doors to investigate.

On the rear wall of the office we found a beautiful painting representing Philadelphia seen from above in the twilight of a snowy winter evening. It is a large canvas, about twenty-five feet long by ten high. Now we are totally unfamiliar with the technical jargon adopted by those who talk about art; we could not even obey the advice given to us by an artist friend, always to turn a picture upside down and look at it that way before passing judgment; but this painting seemed to us a mighty fine piece of work.

As we said, it shows the city as seen from some imaginary bird's-eye vantage, perhaps somewhere above the Girard Avenue Bridge. The bending course of the Schuylkill is shown in a ribbon of deep blue; the broader and paler stretch of the Delaware closes the canvas to the east; the whole city from Cramps' shipyard down to Hog Island lies under the gaze, with the brilliance of the evening lights shining up through the soft blue dusk. The prevailing tone of the painting is blue; but examined closely the white of snow-covered roofs and the golden glow of street lights sparkling upward from the channels of the city, together with the varied tints of the masonry, lend a delightful exuberance of color, though always kept within the restrained and shadowy soberness of a winter twilight.

This painting seemed to us so remarkable an achievement that we were immediately interested and made some inquiries to find out who had done it. The story is interesting, as any story of achievement is, and it also has a touch of poignant tragedy.

In the bitter snowy days of the winter of 1917–18—and there is no Philadelphian who does not remember what that winter was like—a young artist of this city spent the daylight of almost every snowy day out on the streets with his paint box. He climbed to the top of high buildings, he haunted the Schuylkill bridges with his sketchbook, and with numbed fingers he sat on ice-crusted cornices or leaned from giddy office window-sills noting down colors, contours and the aspect of the city from various viewpoints. Time and again watchmen and policemen took him to the station house as a suspected spy until his errand was explained to the city authorities and he was given an authoritative passport. But his passion for painting snow scenes and his desire to crown handicapped years of study by a really first-rate canvas spurred him on. He had spent the previous summer in getting the topography of the city by heart, mapping the course of various streets until he knew them house by house. Then, when the bitterest winter in our history came along, the snow that bothered most of us was just what he had yearned for. He revelled in the serene sparkling colors of the winter twilight, when blazing windows cast their radiance across the milky whiteness and the sky shimmers a clear gem-like emerald and blue and mother-of-pearl.

Even those who know the city through a long lifetime of street wandering will admit the difficulty of representing the vast area as it would be seen from an imaginary gazing-point high in air. Infinite problems of perspective, infinite details of accuracy and patient verification must enter into such a work. But the artist never wavered through his long task. The sketches he had made through that long blizzard winter were gradually put on his big canvas through the hot days of last summer. Undoubtedly it was a happy task, working on that broad snowscape in the hot drowsy weather, with the growing certainty that he was doing something that measured up to his dream of portraying the city he loved, picturing it with the accurate fidelity of a map and yet with the loving eye of an artist who lingers over the beauty that most of us only intuitively suspect. The painting was finished early in the autumn and the ambitious young artist looked forward eagerly to the triumphant day when it would be hung in the new office of the Electric Company, which had encouraged the work and made it possible.

Then came the influenza epidemic, and the artist was among the first to be carried off by that tragic pestilence. He died without seeing his painting put up in the place of honor it now occupies. In his modesty he did not even put his name on the canvas—or at least if he did it is written so minutely that one hunts for it in vain.

It is good to know that the Philadelphia Electric Company is going to erect a bronze tablet in his memory beside the splendid painting on which he worked for a year and a half.

The name of the artist was Claud Joseph Warlow, well remembered at the Academy of the Fine Arts as one of its most promising pupils in recent years. He was born in Williamstown, Pa., March 31, 1888, and died in this city October 6, 1918. His skill as an artist was apparent even as a boy; chalk drawings that he made on the blackboard at school were so good that they were allowed to remain on the board for months after he had done them as an incentive to other children. After leaving school he started a sign-painting business, sketching in oils in his spare time. Owing to his father's death, about 1906, he had to postpone for some years his ambition to enter the Academy classes, finally attaining that desire in 1911. At the Academy he was awarded several prizes, notably the Cresson traveling fellowship, which he was not able to enjoy on account of the war.

We hope that all lovers of Philadelphia will take occasion to step into the office of the Electric Company to see this beautiful painting. There are no words competent to express the tragedy of those who have worked patiently for an ideal and yet die too soon to see their dreams come to full fruit. Yet it is good to remember that those pinched and bitter days of last winter, when we were all bemoaning Black Mondays and ways clogged with snow, gave Claud Warlow his opportunity to put on canvas the beauty that haunted him and which made his life a triumph. And a civilization that is wise enough to beautify an electrical office with so fine a mural canvas, that builds railroad stations like Greek temples, puts one of the world's finest organs in a department store and a painting of mosaic glass in a publishing plant, is a civilization that brings endless hope to birth.

# AT THE MINT

I DON'T KNOW just why it was, but all the time I was in
the Mint yesterday I kept on thinking about Lenine
and Trotzky and how much they would have liked to be
there.

I found my friend, the assistant assayer, in his laboratory
making mysterious chalk marks on a long blackboard and
gazing with keen gray eyes at a circle of little bottles
containing pale bluish fluids. At the bottom of each vessel
was a white sediment that looked like a mixture of cream
cheese and headache powder. "Silver," said the assistant
assayer, in an offhand way, and I was duly impressed.

You may expect to be impressed when you visit the Mint
on Spring Garden street. Most of us know, in a vague way,
that two-thirds of our coinage comes from that dignified
building, which is probably the finest mint building in the
world. Fewer of us know that most of South America's coins
come from there too, and when the citizens of Lima or
Buenos Aires pay out their bright centavos for a movie show
or a black cigar their pockets jingle with small change
stamped in Philadelphia. And none of us can realize,
without a trip to that marvelous home of wonders, the spirit
of devoted and delicate science that moves among the men
who have spent self-effacing lives in testing precious metals
and molding them into the most beautiful coinage known
on earth.

The assistant assayer, after a last lingering look at his
little blue flasks—he was testing the amount of silver in
deposits of ore brought in to the Mint from all over the
country—if you find any in your back yard the Mint will
pay you a dollar an ounce for it—was gracious enough to
give me some fleeting glances at the fascinating work going
on in the building. The first thing one realizes is the

presence of the benign and silent goddess of Science. Those upper floors, where the assayers work in large, quiet chambers, are like the workrooms of some great university, some university happily exempt from the turbulent and irritating presence of students, where the professors are able to lose themselves in the worship of their own researches. Great delicate scales—only you mustn't call them "scales," but "balances"—that tremble like a lover's heart if you lay a hair on one platform, shelter their gossamer workings behind glass cases. My guide showed me one, a fantastic delicacy so sensitive that one feels as clumsy as Gibraltar when one looks at it. Each division on its ivory register indicates one-tenth of a milligram, which, I should say, is about as heavy as the eyelash of a flea. With a pair of calipers he dropped a tiny morsel of paper on one balance and the needle swung over to the extreme end of the scale. With his eyes shining with enthusiasm he showed how, by means of a counterpoise made of a platinum wire as slender as a mosquito's leg, he could swing the needle back toward the middle of the scale and get the exact reading.

At another balance a scientist was snipping shreds from a long ribbon of gold. I was allowed to hold it in my hand, and though its curator explained deprecatingly that it was only 999.5 thousandths pure, it seemed pure enough for all my purposes. It is wonderful stuff, soft enough to tie in knots and yet so tough that it is very difficult to cut with heavy shears. That strip of about sixty ounces was worth well over $1200—and they didn't even search me when I left the building. "Proof gold," it seems, which is 1000 pure, is worth $40 an ounce, and all the proof gold used for scientific purposes in this country is refined in the Philadelphia Mint. The assistant assayer showed me lots of nice little nuggets of it in a drawer. Almost every drawer he opened contained enough roots of evil to make a newspaperman happy for a year.

In a neat little row of furnaces set into a tiled wall I was shown some queer little cups heating to 1700 degrees in a rosy swirl of fire. These little "cupels," as they call them, are made of compressed bone-ash and are used to absorb the baser metals in an alloy. Their peculiar merit is that at the required temperature they absorb all the copper, lead or whatever other base metal there may be and leave in the cup only the gold and silver. Then the gold and silver mixture is placed in boiling nitric acid, which takes out all the silver and leaves only the globule of pure gold. The matter that puzzles the lay observer is, how do you find these things out in the first place? But I would believe anything after one marvel my friend showed me. He picked up a glass that looked like an innocent tumbler of spring water. "This," he said, "is nitrate of silver; in other words, dissolved silver. Don't spill it on your clothes or it will eat them right off your back." I kept off, aghast. Into the tumbler he dropped a little muriatic acid. The mixture boiled and fumed and long streamers of soft, cheesy substance began to hasten toward the bottom of the glass, waving like trees in a gale. "That's the silver," he said, and while I was still tremulous showed me wafers of gold dissolving in aqua regia. When completely dissolved the liquid looks like a thin but very sweet molasses. He then performed similar magic upon some silver solution by unloading a pipette of salt water on it and shaking it in a little machine called an "agitator." After which he felt I was sufficiently humble to show me the furnace room.

If you have an affection for the nice old silver cartwheel dollars, keep away from the furnace room of the Mint, for one of the first things you will see is whole truckloads of them moving silently to their doom. I was told that there is a shortage of silver in Europe these days, particularly since troubles in Mexico have reduced that country's output of ore, and in order to accommodate foreign friends Uncle Sam has recently melted 200,000,000 of our old friends into bars and 50,000,000 more of them are on the way to the furnace. None have been coined since 1904, as apparently they are not popular.

The pride of the Mint centers just now upon the two new electric furnaces, the larger of which has only been installed a few weeks (a Swedish invention, by the way), but the old gas ovens are more spectacular to the visitor because the flames are more visible. When the heavy door is slid aside you can see the crucible (made of graphite from Ceylon) with its mass of silver dollars, standing patiently in the furious glow. Then, if you are lucky, you will see them ladling out the liquid silver into the molds. One of the workmen held a slip of paper to the boiling metal: it burst into flame and he calmly lit his pipe with it. In other furnaces sheets of nickel from which Argentine coins had been punched were being melted, surrounded by a marvelous radiance of green and golden fire. All about you are great ingots of copper, silver, nickel and boxes of queer little nickel nuggets, formed by dropping the hot liquid into ice water. It is a place in which one would willingly spend a whole day watching the wonders which those accustomed to them take so calmly. In the vault just outside the furnace room I was shown between eighteen and nineteen million dollars' worth of gold bars stacked up on shelves. Again—I don't know just why—I thought of Lenine and Trotzky.

There were also more truckloads of the old silver dollars on their way to the fire. Some of them, though dated back in the seventies, seemed as good as new; others were badly worn. They were piled up in lots of 40,000, which when new, would weigh 34,375 ounces; one lot, I was told, had lost 208 ounces through abrasion.

In the big coining room the presses were busily at work stamping out new coins, and women operators were carefully examining the "blanks" for imperfections before they go under the dies. To one who expected to see vast quantities of shining new American coinage it was odd to learn that almost all the machines were busy turning out small change for Peru and Argentina. Next week, the foreman said, they start on a big order of the queer coins of Siam, which have a hole in the middle, like the Chinese money. But I saw one machine busy turning out Lincoln pennies at the rate of 100 a minute. The one-cent piece requires a pressure of forty tons to stamp the design on the metal; the larger coins, of course, need a heavier pressure, up to 120 tons.

The Mint's wonderful collection of coins and medals of all lands would deserve an article of its own. One of the rarities of which the curator is most proud is a terra-cotta medallion of Franklin, made by Nini at Chaumont in 1777. It is in perfect condition and was bought by the Mint from a New York newspaperman. A brand-new acquisition, only set up within the last few weeks, is a case of French military decorations presented by the French Government—the five grades of the Legion of Honor, the four grades of the Croix de Guerre and the Médaille Militaire. Near these are the United States military and naval medals, a sad and ugly contrast to the delicate art of the French trophies.

I was unfortunate in not being lucky enough to meet Superintendent Joyce, under whose administration the Philadelphia Mint has become the most remarkable place of coinage in the world; or Mr. Eckfeldt, the assayer in chief, who has served the Mint for fifty-four years and is the son of the former assayer and grandson of the Mint's first "coiner," Adam Eckfeldt. These three generations of Eckfeldts have served the Mint for 123 years. But my friend, Mr. Homer L. Pound,* the assistant assayer, who modestly speaks of his own thirty years of service as a mere trifle, had by this time shown me so much that my brain reeled. He permitted me to change my pocket money into brand new coinage of 1919 as a souvenir, and then I left. And as for Lenine and Trotzky, the experience would have killed them!

*Homer L. Pound was the father of the poet Ezra Pound [ed. note].

# THE MERCANTILE
# LIBRARY

THERE IS A legend of an old booklover who was pasturing among his folios one evening by candle light. Perhaps he sat (as Charles Lamb used to) with a tumbler of mild grog at his elbow. Perhaps he was in that curious hypnotic trance induced by utter silence, long reading and insufficient air. In the musty fragrance of his library the tapers cast their mellow gush of gold about him, burning up the oxygen from under his very nose. At any rate, in a shadowy alcove something stirred. A bookworm peeped out from a tall vellum binding. It flapped its wings and crew with a clear lively note. Startled, the aged bibliophile looked up and just glimpsed the vanishing flutter of its wings. It was only a glimpse, but it was enough. He ran to his shelves, his ancient heart pounding like an anvil chorus. The old promise had come true. For if any man shall live to see a bookworm, all the volumes on his shelves immediately turn to first editions, signed by the author. But the joyous spasm was too much for the poor scholar. The next morning he was found lying palsied at the foot of his bookcase. The fact that at least two fingers of grog remained in his glass, undrunk, led his fellow booklovers to suspect that something strange had happened. As he lay dying he told the story of his vision. He was the only man who ever saw a bookworm.

But if a bookworm should ever flap its wings and crow in Philadelphia, certainly the place where it would do so would be the Mercantile Library. I imagine that when Mr. Hedley, the delightful librarian, shuts up at night, turns off the green-shaded lamps and rings the bell to thrust out the last lingering reader from the long dark tables, he treads hopefully through those enchanted alcoves. The thick sweet savor of old calf and the dainty bouquet of honest rag paper, the subtle exhalation of rows and rows of books (sweeter to the nostril of the bibliosoph than any mountain air that ever rustled in green treetops), is just the medium in which the fabled bookworm would crow like chanticleer. It is fifty years this month since the Mercantile Library moved into the old market building on Tenth street, and while fifty years is a mere wink of the eyelash to any bookworm, still it is long enough for a few eggs to hatch. For that matter, some of the library's books have been in its possession nigh a hundred years, for it will celebrate its centennial in 1922.

The Mercantile is everything that a library ought to be. It has the still and reverent solemnity that a true home of learning ought to have, combined with an undercurrent of genial fellowship. It is not only a library but a club. Through the glass panels at the back one may see the chess players at their meditative rites, and the last inner fane where smoking is permitted and the votaries puff well-blackened briars and brood round the boards of combat in immortal silence. The quaint old stained windows at the western end of the long hall look down on the magazine tables where one may be reading the *Cosmopolitan* and the next the *Hibbert Journal*. From these colored panes Franklin, Milton, Beethoven and Clovio gaze approvingly. They are surmounted by four symbolic figures, representing (I suppose) their respective arts of Science, Poetry, Music and Art. Of Clovio the miniaturist one does not often hear, and I may as well be honest and admit I had to look him up in the encyclopedia.

To the heart of the booklover the Mercantile speaks with a magical appeal. One wishes there were a little cloister attached to it where the true saints of the bookworld might be buried. It seems hard that those who have so long trodden the alcoves of peace should be interred elsewhere. To many devout souls libraries are the greatest churches of humanity. Even the casual dropper-in realizes that the Mercantile is more than a mere gathering of books. It is a guild, a sort of monastery. The members have secret raptures and side-long glances whereby they recognize one another. As they walk down the long entrance passage they are purged of the world and the world's passions. As they pass through the little swinging gates that shut out the mere visitor, as they bury themselves in shadowy corners and aisles pungent with book-perfume, they have the grateful bearing of those secure in a strong fortress where the devil cannot penetrate. For my own part, I have only one test of a good library, which I always employ when I get anywhere near a card catalogue. There is a certain work, in three volumes, famous chiefly because Robert Louis Stevenson took the second volume with him on his immortal *Travels With a Donkey*. It is called *Pastors of the Desert*, by Peyrat, a history of the Huguenots. If you will turn again to R. L. S.'s chapter called "A Camp in the Dark" you will see that he says:

> I had felt no other inconvenience, except when my feet encountered the lantern or the second volume of Peyrat's Pastors of the Desert among the mixed contents of my sleeping bag.

I am happy to assert that the Mercantile has a set of these volumes, and therefore one may pronounce it an A-1 library.

Of course the Mercantile has many more orthodox treasures than Peyrat, though its function is not to collect incunabula or rare editions, but to keep its members supplied with the standard things, and the important books and periodicals of the day. Mr. Hedley was gracious enough to take me into the locked section of the gallery, where there are alcoves teeming with old volumes and rich in the dust that is so delightful to the lover of these things. He showed me, for instance, a first edition of the Authorized or King James Bible, imprinted at London by Robert Barker in 1611. Inside the front cover some one has written in pencil "Charge 5£." I am no expert on these matters, but I wonder if many a collector would not pay a hundred times as much for it nowadays? On another shelf I saw a beautiful edition of Eusebius's Chronicles, printed at Venice in 1483, the paper as fresh and the rubrication as bright as when it was new. Opening it at random, I found the following note, which seemed quaintly topical:

Anno salutis 811, Anno mundi 6010, Locustes gregatim ex Affrica volantes Italiam infestant.

(Year of grace 811, Year of the earth 6010. The locusts flying in swarms from Africa, infest Italy.)

In this book some former owner has written, with the honorable candor of the true booklover:

De isto pretioso volumino animadvertere libet, quod non est "edition premiere" sicut opus Deburii falso ostendit.
W. H. Black, 4 Feb., 1831.

(Concerning this precious volume it is permitted to remark that it is not the first edition, as the work of Deburius falsely maintains.)

Ignoble Deburius, shame upon him!

Mr. Hedley also showed me the famous Atlas Major of John Blaeu, the Dutch publisher, issued (in Spanish) in Amsterdam in 1662, eleven huge tomes in white vellum, stamped in gold. These marvelous large-scale maps, magnificently colored by hand, with every town marked by a tiny dot of gleaming gold, set the lover of fine work in a tingle of amazement. Lucky indeed the bibliophile who finds his way to that sacred corner. One would not blame any bookworm for crowing with a shrill cry of exultation if he were hatched in that treasury. There was not time to find out whether John Blaeu's atlas contained plates of American geography, but I hope to go again and study these fascinating volumes more at leisure, by Mr. Hedley's kindness.

Perhaps the most curious feature of the Mercantile is the huge vaulted cellar which underlies the length of the whole building. Constructed originally for storage of market produce, before the days of modern refrigeration, it is now a dark and mysterious crypt extending under the adjoining streets, where the rumble of wheels sound overhead. The library's stamping press, used to incise the covers of books, gives one of the chambers a medieval monkish air, and the equally medieval spelling of the janitor in some memoranda of his own posted upon a door do not detract from the fascinating spell. With a flashlight Mr. Hedley showed me the great extent of these underground corridors, and I imagined that if so friendly a librarian should ever hold a grudge against an author it would be an admirable place to lure him and leave him lost in the dark. He would never find his way out and his copyrights would expire long before his bones would be found. Joan Gutenberg, the library cat, dwells in that solemn maze of heavy brick arches, and she finds it depressing that the only literature stored down there is the overplus of old government documents.

# WILD WORDS WE HAVE KNOWN

About noon on Saturday the city heaves a sigh of
relief. Indeed, it begins a little earlier than that.
About eleven-forty even the most faithful stenographer
begins to woolgather. Letters dictated in that last half hour
are likely to be addressed "Mrs. Henrietta Jenkins, Esq.,"
or "Miss John Jones." The patient paying teller has to
count over his notes three times to be sure of not giving a
five instead of a one. The glorious demoralization spreads
from desk to desk. No matter who we are or how hard we
have worked, it is Saturday noon, and for a few hours we
are going to forget the war and spend our pocketful of
carefree fresh-minted minutes. As Tom Daly, the poet
laureate of Philadelphia, puts it—

"Whenever it's a Saturday and all my work is through,
I take a walk on Chestnut street to see what news is new."

Every Jack and Jill has his or her own ideas of a Saturday
afternoon adventure. Our stenographer hastens off with a
laughing group to the Automat and the movies. Our friend
with the shell-rimmed spectacles, tethered by a broad silk
ribbon, is bound to the Academy of the Fine Arts to censure
the way Mr. Sargent has creased John D. Rockefeller's
trousers, and will come back bursting with indignation to
denounce the portrait "a mere chromo." We ourself hasten
to the Reading Terminal to meet a certain pair of brown
eyes that are sparkling in from Marathon for lunch and a
mobilization of spring millinery. And others are off to breast
the roaring gusts of March on the golf meads or trundle
baby carriages on the sunny side of suburban streets.

But there is another diversion for Saturday afternoon that

is very dear to us, and sometimes we are able to coax B—
W— to agree. That is to spend two or three glorious hours
in the library mulling over the dictionaries. Talk about
chasing a golfball over the links or following Theda Bara
serpentining through a mile of celluloid, or stalking Tom
and Jerry, mystic affinities, from bar to bar along Chestnut
street—what can these excitements offer compared to a
breathless word-hunt in the dictionaries! Words—the noblest quarry of the sportsman! To follow their spoor through
the jungles and champaigns of the English language; to
flush them from their hiding places in dense thickets of
Chaucer or Spenser, track them through the noble aisles of
Shakespeare forest and find them at last perching gayly on
the branches of O. Henry or George Ade! The New Oxford
Dictionary, that most splendid monument of human schol-
arship, gives moving pictures of words from their first
hatching down to the time when they soar like eagles in
the open air of today.

We know no greater joy than an afternoon spent with
dear old Dr. Johnson's Dictionary of the English Language,
published after seven years' patient labor in 1755. Probably
somewhere in Philadelphia there is a copy of the first
edition; but the one we know (at the Mercantile Library) is
the revised fourth edition which the doctor put out in 1775.
One can hardly read without a lump in the throat that noble
preface in which Doctor Johnson rehearses the greatness
and discouragement of his task. And who can read too often
his rebuff to the Earl of Chesterfield, who, having studi-
ously neglected to aid the lexicographer during the long
years of his compilation, sought by belated flattery to
associate himself with the vast achievement? "Is not a
Patron, my Lord, one who looks with unconcern on a man
struggling for life in the water, and, when he has reached
ground, encumbers him with help?" And who does not
chuckle over the caustic humor of the doctor's definitions
of words that touched his own rugged career? "Lexicogra-

pher: a harmless drudge"; "book-learned: versed in books or literature; a term implying some slight contempt"; "Grub street: a street in London much inhabited by writers of small histories, dictionaries and temporary poems."

O. Henry was a great devotee of word-beagling in dictionaries, and his whimsical "review" of Webster deserves to be better known:

"We find on our table quite an exhaustive treatise on various subjects written in Mr. Webster's well-known, lucid and piquant style. There is not a dull line between the covers of the book. The range of subjects is wide, and the treatment light and easy without being flippant. A valuable feature of the work is the arranging of the articles in alphabetical order, thus facilitating the finding of any particular word desired. Mr. Webster's vocabulary is large, and he always uses the right word in the right place. Mr. Webster's work is thorough, and we predict that he will be heard from again."

What exhilaration can Theda Bara or the nineteenth putting green offer compared to the bliss of pursuing through a thousand dictionary pages some Wild Word We Have Known, and occasionally discovering an unfamiliar creature of strange and dazzling plumage?

# NOTES ON ROSY

Dr. ROSENBACH is one of the world's greatest hunters—and finders—of manuscript; yet there will be no manuscript (in any exact sense) of his own very interesting *Books and Bidders*. It was dictated, and a remarkable job of dictation it was. Avery Strakosch, who was at the notebook end of the collaboration, must possess in high degree the great gift of translucency, for the Doctor's own easy colloquy and lively humour come through with every symptom of identity. It is a book packed full of Dr. Rosenbach's learning, but also rich in merry anecdote. One remembers the great day when an editor of the *World*, wishing to pay high tribute to Miss Amy Lowell's Life of Keats, avouched in print that he "had read nothing so nugatory in a long time." It was his idea, evidently, that "nugatory" meant "full of nuggets." And if that were the meaning, *Books and Bidders* would also be nugatory, delightfully so.

The gift of jocundity seems to be a characteristic of the great bibliophiles. Here again, popular tradition is wrong as usual. The general notion of book collectors as prosy ancients, shiny at elbows, soupy on the vest, shrivelled and stooped by years among fungus-smelling pages, is certainly false in my observation. So far as I have seen them they are pink and plump, connoisseurs of vivacity, tellers of phosphorescent adventure, frolic amateurs of all life's more generous pastime. They seem to get more fun out of this planet than any other class of human beings. They extra-illuminate the book of life with fore-edge painting.

Book Collecting, like horse racing, has always been the supreme sport of the Rich and Powerful. But it now stands on a peculiar apex of joy in America, for it has seriously entered the ranks of Big Business. Dr. Rosenbach often shows the specially amused and quiet smile of the scholar who has outwitted so many great merchants at their own game—as indeed the scholar so often can, if he cares to. Not without humour he tells of the hard-headed investors who tuck away Conrad MSS. and Whitman items in safe deposit boxes as negotiables more stable in time of crisis than many an engraved certificate. Dealers themselves confess their amazement at the soar of prices. The old bookseller, once the symbol of musty eccentricity, is now often a power in finance. Ernest Dressel North, in the preface to his 25th anniversary catalogue, points out that the price of a single book offered in that catalogue (a 1667 *Paradise Lost,* priced at $5500) exceeds the total of the prices of the 401 items listed in his first catalogue in 1902. And he adds, remarking on the prices lately paid for Shakespeare folios and Gutenberg Bibles, that perhaps in another twenty-five years only Henry Ford and John D. Rockefeller, Jr., will be able to afford such books. Dr. Rosenbach himself, who is slow to make predictions, suggests that $250,000 will be a modest price for a Gutenberg Bible ten years hence. None of us have forgotten how Mitchell Kennerley, two or three years ago, brought home the Melk copy of the Gutenberg from England in two suitcases—one volume in each case—and kept them in his cabin under his berth. It was the wisest thing to do. He would not even entrust them to the purser's safe, for he wanted to be able to grab them instantly in case of any sudden taking to the boats. So also did Colonel Isham, generously carrying some of the incredible richness of his Boswell MSS. to show to a sanhedrim of the Three Hours for Lunch Club, entrust them to a gruesome old wicker valise that looked only likely to contain a week-end wash. No one, in any horrid emergency, would have suspected such luggage of secreting anything notorious. It was that copy of the Gutenberg Bible, incidentally, that Dr. Rosenbach bought for $106,000, and which is now at Yale University.

There will always be many to deplore so much discussion of these great memorabilia of human life in terms of price and trading; yet that sentimentality may easily become only an empty snobbery. Money after all is the only esperanto we have, the sole universal measure of our possessive passion for things that (for reasons of our own) are precious. And in the case of the perfect amorist, the paramour of print, he only thinks of the thing in terms of price before he has got it. Once acquired, the money phase is oddly irrelevant. It was only a few years ago that Dr. Rosenbach with characteristic humour gave tranquil Walnut Street in Philadelphia a considerable shock. He put a collection of Shakespeare folios and quartos in his show window with a small card stating that the price of the lot was $985,000. I cannot resist the feeling that (except for the amusement it would have caused him) he would have been very unhappy if anyone had walked in, paid the price, and taken away the books. It would have been a sound investment, too, for anyone who could afford to tie up a million cash for a few years.

Perhaps it was because Dr. Rosenbach was born in Philadelphia in its great romantic year, the year of its famous Centennial in '76, that he was endowed with his miracle of book instinct. For, though the metaphor is not appropriate to his solid form, he is a willow-wand for the hidden springs of book lore. He is the Pied Piper of rare editions. He blows an airy wheedling note, and the old vellums and calfskins come trotting after him. They disappear into his twin Venusbergs—on Walnut Street or on Madison Avenue—and if he happens to take a fancy to keep them himself they are never heard of again. There is no one in the world rich enough to buy from Rosy anything that he thinks belongs on his own private shelves. There is no man more generous with his treasures, and no man who gets a finer sentimental pleasure out of the things he values for associations of their own. When he was only eighteen, still an undergraduate at the University of Pennsylvania, he spotted the fact that a group of old pamphlets bound up together included the long-lost first edition of Dr. Johnson's famous Drury Lane Prologue. These, with beating heart, he bought for $3.60 in Stan Henkels' old auction-room in Philadelphia. And I think the most significant comment on Rosy's career is that a few years later, when he needed money very badly, he refused an offer of $5000 for his treasure. The panting customer toiled after him in vain. He still has it.

There's a little scrap of paper in Rosy's private collection that brings you very close to some great and vanished things—into the very "shadow of a magnitude." It is a bill from the Mermaid Tavern. It was preserved in the family of the Goodyeares—Andrew Goodyeare was the host of the Mermaid in Shakespeare's time—and it gives you a pretty good notion of the sort of dinner you'd have had if you had dropped in to eat with Shakespeare and Drayton or Ben Jonson. When they spoke of "meat and drink" in those days, that's exactly what they meant. Vegetables, you'll observe, weren't on the menu at all.

The document—I believe it's never been published before, and so we are specially in Dr. Rosenbach's debt—goes like this:

*Visitation Dinner*

1588
September
14
Superfine bread xi d.
Beer & ale xiiii d.
Wine ii s. xi d.
Sugar x d.
Boiled beef x d.
Roast beef v s.
Boiled mutton iii s. iii d.
Capon v s.

Fire iiii d.
SUMMA XX s. iiii d.

ANDREW GOODYEARE.

Some of the items are not easy to decipher. I was a bit uncertain whether that "capon" might not have been "capers," for the proximity to Boiled Mutton certainly suggests caper sauce. The gorgeous thing about the whole menu is its extreme Britishness. Only add a cabbage or a brussels sprout and it might well be to-night's dinner at any Fleet Street ordinary.

There was a tradition (wasn't there?) that it was at a drinking bout with Drayton, Shakespeare contracted his fatal fever? But the Elizabethans died young not from too much drinking but from too much meat. Strange that such heavy diet bred—as Beaumont said of the "nobly wild" Mermaid evenings:

> "words that have been
> So nimble and so full of subtle flame
> As if that every one from whence they came
> Had meant to put his whole wit in a jest
> And had resolved to live a fool the rest
> Of his dull life."

As one might expect from one who has risen so high in his own line, Dr. Rosenbach's book is full of good wisdom for the beginning collector, pointing out the very necessary fact that one does not have to begin with high-priced books. He is shrewd enough to know, though too modest to point out, that the great prizes in the collecting game will always go to those who have that queer specific instinct for which there is no counterfeit and no substitute. But the real fun, if you are a beginner in the collecting field, is to stake your own judgment. To choose something in which you yourself believe—perhaps the work of some still unknown author.

The "wild vicissitudes of taste" in this matter are part of the sport. I see, for instance, in a current catalogue, that H. M. Tomlinson's *The Sea and the Jungle*, which I bought for $1 in 1920, is now listed at $90. I haven't the faintest intention of selling my copy; but it is a pleasant confirmation of one's own judgment. Can any zigzagging of the stock market give one better fun than that? The kind of collecting that appeals to me is not chasing after things that everyone knows are great, but trying to hunt out the things that are going to be great ten or twenty years later. And this means, as Dr. Rosenbach points out, a lot of brooding over catalogues. He himself has a special marsupial overcoat, with a large pouch built in, to carry his brood of catalogues which he studies diligently as he rides to and fro between Philadelphia and New York.

*Books and Bidders* is so full of nourishing anecdote that I have made no attempt to cull any of its plums. Those who are interested in the comfortable folly of book-collecting will find them for themselves. But one thing should be said: that Dr. Rosenbach has an unerring instinct for knowing how a story should be told. He always begins with a vivid little "lead," as reporters say, that lures you into the narrative unawares. Like this—

"The *First Folio* had lain idly at anchor for two long, sultry days . . ."

"The gas lamps in Stan Henkels' auction-rooms were being extinguished . . ."

"It was a cold winter in my uncle Moses Polock's shop in Philadelphia . . ."

I'm sorry there's no manuscript of this book. If there were, I think I should go after it for my own collection.

# A WESTMINSTER
ABBEY IN
PHILADELPHIA

WALKING DOWN Tenth Street just below Market we noticed the other day that workmen are again busy in St. Stephen's Church. The interior of the church is being redecorated in harmony with the uniquely beautiful chancel (the gift of Miss Anna Magee, in memory of her sister Fannie Magee). This interesting edifice, one of the plainest of the city's churches in exterior, is inwardly a marvel of beauty. The exquisite eastern windows, which gleam with brilliant blue and opal tints through a delicate lacework of white marble (almost unbelievably frail and graceful), are a vision of quiet loveliness. On Saturday morning the doors of the church were open while the workmen were busy within, and many passers-by who had not seen the windows before were lured by this gleam of deep and sparkling blue to step inside the church and admire.

During the energetic rectorship of Dr. Carl Grammer, who has occupied St. Stephen's pulpit since 1905, the treasures of the church have been notably increased. The generosity of St. Stephen's friends has been unfailing, and considering the number of remarkable memorials and beauties his church houses, Doctor Grammer's own name for the shrine seems not inappropriate. He speaks of it as "Philadelphia's Westminster Abbey."

St. Stephen's is notable as an example of the many services that may be performed by an active church in the heart of the business district. Many men who do not attend any religious services regularly are grateful to St. Stephen's for the noon services held there daily during Lent. These services, which have been held for many years, are remarkably popular, the annual attendance having exceeded 25,000, with a daily average of more than 600. In June, 1917, the church opened clubrooms for men in the service, and more than 50,000 soldiers and sailors have registered there in the last year. The church's service flag shows fifty stars.

The severely plain and fortresslike edifice of St. Stephen's, so familiar to all who pass along Tenth Street, was originally a Methodist church, taken over and remodeled for the new congregation in 1823. That period was one of great expansion in the Episcopal Church, which had by that time outlived the prejudice against it (inherited from Revolutionary times) as the Church of England. From the beginning St. Stephen's seems to have had a friendly relation with the South and became a favorite place of worship for Southerners in Philadelphia. One of the earliest monuments erected in the church stands in the vestry, a tablet to the memory of three young Southerners, medical students at the University of Pennsylvania, who died in the course of their studies. This was in 1825.

Dr. Henry W. Ducachet, a man of very great charm and social attractiveness, was rector 1834–1865, and under his care St. Stephen's became one of the leading social churches of the city. Many old Philadelphia families of wealth and refinement worshiped here, but the church has never forgotten that the duties of a sacred edifice extend to every caste. Under Doctor Ducachet's rectorship St. Stephen's became an illustrious example of the Episcopalian tendency to ally the church with the arts. Colonel Edward Shippen Burd, who died in 1848, left instructions in his will for a memorial to be erected to the memory of his three deceased children. The Burd memorial, executed in Italian marble by the famous German sculptor Steinhauser, is one of the most beautiful pieces of its kind in the country. A replica of it was erected in Bremen, the sculptor's native city. It is known as "The Angel of the Resurrection."

The recumbent effigy of Colonel Burd and the magnificent marble font (also by Steinhauser) were the gift of Colonel Burd's widow in 1849 and 1859. The font is very interesting: three cherubs support the bowl on their wings. Each cherub holds one of the instruments of the Savior's torture—the nail, the thorn and the spear. The cherub with the nail is shown testing the sharpness of the point on his chubby hand. Inside the bowl are carved several fish, representing, of course, the secret symbol of early Christian faith.

In 1889 the Venetian mosaic of the Last Supper, which contains more than 180,000 tesserae, was erected by the generosity of the Magee family. This was executed partly by Italian workmen and partly by the artist, Henry Holiday, of London, the versatile craftsman who is also well known for a very different type of work in his illustrations for Lewis Carroll's "Hunting of the Snark." The new organ was also given by the Magee family, and "voiced" in the church under the supervision of Dr. David Wood, the famous blind musician, who was organist of St. Stephen's for forty-six years.

It is impossible in the compass of a few paragraphs to mention all the beauties of St. Stephen's, but no account, however brief, can omit the touching memorial to Maria Gouverneur Mitchell, the daughter of Dr. S. Weir Mitchell. This monument was done by Saint Gaudens, and the figure, of exceptional grace and simplicity, represents "The Angel of Purity."

St. Stephen's is a church of very great interest to all Philadelphians. No one can read the names engraved on the old-fashioned silver pew-plates without realizing how many old Philadelphia families have loved this church and worshiped there. The walls are lined with tablets and lit with richly tinted windows, each one of which is a story in itself. It is a curious coincidence that Doctor Grammer, the present rector, was called to St. Stephen's from Christ

Church, Norfolk, the same church from which Doctor Ducachet came. Doctor Grammer is noteworthy in cherishing the traditions of his predecessors, and there is no church that better repays a visit from art lovers than old St. Stephen's.

# MEDITATIONS ON OYSTERS

Sansom Street, below Ninth, runs a modest course through the middle of the afternoon, scooped between high and rather grimy walls so that a coolness and a shadow are upon it. It is a homely little channel, frequented by laundry wagons taking away great piles of soiled linen from the rear of the Continental Hotel, and little barefoot urchins pushing carts full of kindling wood picked up from the litter of splintered packing cases. On one side of the street is a big power-house where the drone and murmur of vast dynamos croon a soft undertone to the distant clang and zooming of the trolleys. Beyond that is the stage door of a burlesque theatre, and a faint sweetness of greasepaint drifts to the nose down a dark, mysterious passageway.

We walked down this little street, noticing the For Rent sign on a saloon at the corner and the pyramided boxes of green and yellow apples on a fruit stand, and it seemed to us that there was an unmistakable breath of autumn in the air. Out beyond, where the street widens and floods itself again with sun, there were heat and shimmer and the glittering plate-glass windows of jewelry dealers, but in the narrower strip of alley we felt a premonitory tang of future frost. At the end of August the sunlight gets yellower, more oblique; it loses the pale and deadly glare of earlier days. It is shallower, more colorful, but weaker of impact. Shall we say it has lost its punch?

And then we saw a little oyster café, well known to many lovers of good cheer, that has been furbishing itself for the jolly days to come. No one knows yet whether the U-boats have frightened the oysters, whether the fat bivalves will be leaner and scarcer than in the good old days; no one knows whether there will even be enough of them to last out until next Easter; but in the meantime we all live in hope. And one thing is certain—the oyster season begins on Monday. The little café has repainted its white front so that it shines hospitably; and the sill and the cellar trapdoor where the barrels go in, and the shutters and the awning poles in front, are all a sticky, glistening green. The white marble step, hollowed by thousands of eager feet in a million lunch-time forays, has been scrubbed and sand-soaped. And next Monday morning, bright and early, out goes the traditional red and green sign of the R.

The "poor patient oyster," as Keats calls him (or her, for there are lady oysters, too, did you know?), is not only a sessile bivalve mollusk, but a traditional symbol of autumn and winter cheer. Even if Mr. Hoover counts out the little round crackers in twos and threes, we hope there will be enough of the thoughtful and innocent shellfish to go around. When the cold winds begin to harp and whinny at street corners and wives go seeking among camphor balls for our last year's overcoats, you will be glad to resume your acquaintance with a bowl of steaming bivalves, swimming in milk, with little clots of yellow butter twirling on the surface of the broth. An oyster stew, a glass of light beer and a corncob pipe will keep your blue eyes blue to any weather, as a young poet of our acquaintance puts it.

# OUR OLD DESK

WE SEE THAT there has been a fire at a second-hand furniture warehouse on Arch street. We think we can offer an explanation for the blaze. Our old desk was there.

That desk was always a hoodoo. Last autumn, when we gave up commuting and moved into town, we had to get rid of some of our goods in order to squeeze ourselves into an apartment. The very first thing we parted with was our old desk. We did not tell genial Mr. P., the dealer in second-hand furniture, that the piece was a Jonah, for we were afraid it would knock fifty cents or so off his offer, but now we feel rather shamefaced for not having warned him.

We bought the desk before we were married, at a department store in New York. It was almost the last article that store, a famous one in its day, got paid for. Soon after selling it the house failed.

We moved the desk out to a cottage in the country. We sat down in front of it. We didn't know it then, but we are convinced now there was some evil genius in it. It must have been built of slippery elm, full of knots, cut in the dark of the moon while a brindle cat was mewing. The drawers stuck once a week and had to be pared down with a jack-knife. We sat at that desk night after night, with burning visions of literary immortality. We wrote poems that no one would buy. We wrote stories that gradually became soiled and wrinkled around the folds of the manuscript. We wrote pamphlets eulogizing hotels and tried to palm them off on the managers as advertising booklets. The hotels accepted the booklets and went out of business before paying for them. Sitting at that desk we composed sparkling essays for a newspaper in Toledo, and after the paper had printed a bunch of them we wrote to the editor and asked him how about a check. He replied that he did not understand we were writing that stuff for actual money. He was quite grieved to have misunderstood us so. He thought we were merely writing them for the pleasure of uplifting the hearts of Toledo.

There was another odd thing about that desk. There was some drowsy sirup in its veins. Perhaps the wood hadn't been properly seasoned. Anyway, we couldn't keep awake while sitting at it. Night after night, assiduously, while the jolly old Long Island mosquitoes hummed in through the open windows like Liberty motors, we would begin to scribe. After an hour or so we would always fall asleep over the tawny keys of our ancient typewriter. It may be that the trouble lay partly in the typing bus, for we were so inexpert that we couldn't pound rapidly enough to keep ourself awake. We remember memorizing the letters on the first row of keys in a vain hope that if we could say *qwertyuiop* off by heart it would help us to move along faster, but it did no good. We started a novel, but after six months of wrestling we decided that as long as we worked at that desk we would never get it done. We tried writing on the kitchen table, in front of the stove—it was winter by that time— and we got the novel done in no time.

When we moved to Marathon, the van containing that desk broke down near a novelty factory in Trenton. Probably that novelty factory was its home and the old flat-top had nostalgia. In order to get the desk into the Marathon house its top had to be unscrewed and the screws were lost. After that, whenever we were trying to write a poem in the small hours of the night, when we got aroused in the heat of composition and shifted round on our chair, the whole top of the desk would slide off and the inkwell would cascade on to the floor.

There was one drawer in that desk that we look back on with particular affection. We had been asked by a publisher in Chicago to contribute the section on Etiquette for a Household Encyclopedia that was to be issued. That was about 1914, if we remember rightly. We knew nothing whatever about Etiquette. The article was to deal with the origin and history of social usages, coming down to the very latest thing in table manners, accepting and declining invitations, specimen letters dealing with every social emergency, such as being invited to go to a clambake, a wedding or the dedication of a sanitary dog-pound. We had an uproarious time compiling the essay. It was to contain at least fifteen thousand words and we were to get fifty dollars for it. In the chapter on specimen letters we let ourself go without restraint. In these specimen letters we amused ourself by using the names of all our friends. We chuckled to think of their amazement on finding themselves enshrined in this Household Encyclopedia, writing demure and stilted little regrets or acceptances for imaginary functions.

The manuscript of this article had to be mailed to Chicago on a certain date or the fifty dollars would be forfeit. Late the night before we toiled at our desk putting the final touches on The Etiquette of Courtship and Etiquette for Young Girls at Boarding School. Never having been a young girl at boarding school, our ideas were largely theoretical, but still we thought they were based on sound sense and a winsome instinct as to comely demeanor. We threw our heart into the task and felt that Louisa Alcott herself could not have counseled more becoming decorum. It was long after midnight when we finished the last reply of a young girl to the young man who had called her by her first name three months before we felt he had any right to do so. We put these last two sections of the manuscript into a drawer of the desk, to give them a final reading the next morning.

Late that night there came a damp fog, one of those pearly Long Island fogs. The desk drawer swelled up and retired from active life. Containing its precious freight, it was immovable. We stood the desk upside down, we tugged frantically at it, we hammered and chiseled and strove but in vain. The hour for mailing the copy approached. At last baffled, we had to speed to a mail-box and post the treatise on Etiquette without those two chapters. The publisher, we knew, would not miss them, though to us they contained the cream of our whole philosophy of politeness, containing our prized aphorisms on Consideration for Others The Basis of Good Manners.

We were never able to get that drawer open again. When we sold the desk to Mr. P. it was still tightly stuck. Some months ago we were passing along Arch street, just under the Reading Railway viaduct, and we saw a familiar sight on the pavement. It was our old desk, covered with dust and displayed for sale, but unmistakable to our recognitory eye. Furtively we approached it and gave the well-known bottom drawer a yank. It was still jammed, and presumably the manuscript was still within. We thought for a moment of buying the old thing again, splitting it open with an ax and getting out our literary offspring. But we didn't. And now this fire has come along and undoubtedly the desk perished in the flames. If only that chapter on Young Girls at Boarding School could have been rescued . . . . We have a daughter of our own now, and it might have given us some hints on how to bring her up.

# GENTLES, ATTEND!

March 30, 1920, 11 P.M.

THIS BEING A PASSPORT AND HANDY COMPANION UNTO
THE GRACIOUS CITY OF PHILADELPHIA ISSUED UNTO
SIDNEY WILLIAMS, GENT.

HAVING JUST dispatched a grog, consisting of the juice
of one orange, two fingers of "old vatted Scotch"
from the cellars of the Hotel Traymore (*ex domo* M. Hawley
McLanahan), a lump of ice and two teaspoons of sugar, I
apply myself, lighting a new pipe of French briar root
(unpainted) to the task of writing out for one SIDNEY
WILLIAMS, ESQ., gentleman and man of letters, a passport to the noble city of Philadelphia, with a feeling of
sadness that I cannot, *propria persona,* go with him among
the manifold amenities of that delicious and tranquilizing
town.

Among the citizens of that brotherly city, I mention first
three gentlemen to whom said WILLIAMS will present
these credentials, applying to them, in the name of Allah
the beneficent, for genial courtesies and fulness of grace.
These are known among the elect as the Three Great
Caliphs. *Quorum primus inter pares* I will name The Caliph
of Precious Ink, A. EDWARD NEWTON, who may be
reached at N.E. corner 19th and Hamilton by a 2-cent
stamp. This is not that Great Caliph of whom it is said,
Allah in his goodness set out to make one perfect man, but
the mould was broken ere the casting was complete. In his
frantic zeal he made haste to repeat the exploit, and came
near success. His second effort was this Great Caliph, on
whose face there shines the lustre of unutterable seemli-
ness. This is the Great Caliph known to all the world,

91

whose shrine at Daylesford, above the headwater of Darby Creek (O fairest of stripling streamlets!) is a wall of first editions undefiled.

Second of the Caliphs I will mention the Lord M. HAWLEY McLANAHAN, known among the discreet (and such as can keep privy counsel) as The Giver of Good Gifts. Of this great Khan I will restrain myself to observe that he is a kitchen friar, a lord of rich tabling and august cheer, magnificent of aspect toward the lowly and meek, a builder of palaces by the sea, one whose voice over the telephone is full of seduction and mystery. This noble prince may be found in the Bell Telephone Company, their book.

Third, now, in this roster of golden names, but no whit lagging in grandeur of spirit, is The Caliph of Sweet Madrigals, the Great Rhetorician and Consumer of the Friday Fish, THOMAS AUGUSTINE DALY, who may be found in the office of *The Philadelphia Record,* an admirable journal staunch in the tenets of the Democratic Party in a city where the Democratic Party was said to be a myth and a vapour of old time. This great Lord of Language—beloved trencherman, the Robert Burns of American soil, the Titus Oates of the Quaker Oats city, the Prince of Papists, the merry madrigal of the Elizabethan tradition, this benignant and antic sweetmeat, hath the key and inner password to the messroom of the HOUSE of DOONER, and when called upon the telephone will explain satisfying reasons for his apparently incredible existence. This DALY, best loved motley of the eastern seaboard, is a man complete, a man (as Belloc saith) "a man absolute." Scrapple him in thy heart with hoops of steel.

Speak we of lesser fry:

Now first of bookstores. Let there be no undo favoritism, but these great beacons of the noblest trade must be first sued, then placated with gentle speech and fair, then trampled into decent submission. Those be harsh men and proud, lifting a scornish eyebrow towards such as have not the good fortune to be booksellers. Attend:—PHILIP WARNER, of Leary's, 9 South 9th Street, a man of strict serenity, righteous heart and fluent mind, a man of logic, a man of pity and easy bowels. A man of whom it is said: "He is always out at lunch,["] and therefore a man placable by oyster stew or a dozen of doughnuts such as may be found at Johnson's Doughnut Shop, Chestnut Street, north side between 9th and 10th. This is the optimus maximus of booksellers. He will do as I bid him: I hold him to the hollow of my palm. An he do not comport himself with charity, I will make him the villain of a bookshop melo-drama.

Other bookstores to be studied with care: JERRY CUL-LEN'S—He, the Jerry, reddish complect and hairless on the crown—of whom it is said, "Many are bald but few are Cullen.["] He, eke, abideth on 9th Street, and hath a great heart, merry and full of ycast and orris-root.

Highland's and McVey's, on Arch Street.

Wrigby's—Campion's—Sessler's—Fisher's—Jacobs'—aye, and John Wanamaker his book department; and in Ellis Gimbel his book department you will find one Isidor Kricheff, a youth of brains and understanding.

On the Great Lord Charles Sessler, in his shop on Walnut Street, you will call, crying fondly the name of CHARLES DICKENS, and the Great Lord will advance and give countersigns. In the beautiful new store of the Great Lord Campion, across the way, you will find hospitality and gentle treatment. Of the Great Lord ROSENBACH, peerless among booksellers, I speak not. All the world knows him. Ask CALIPH NEWTON.

Now of LESSER FRY again. There be the merry wags of The Franklin Inn, of whom to name all would tax patience, and to name but some were to omit others of equal lustre—yet meseems, I will call to paper the prodigious charms of such a puissant vizier as PROFESSOR

JOHN BACH McMASTER, president of the Club, a noble
lord indeed, whose heart abideth not on [hi]s sleeve but
who hath ever been of comfort and grace to us little ones.
There be such strange wags as Edward Mumford, Sam
Scoville, Jr., George Gibbs, Ellis Oberholtzer, Yarnall Ab-
bott, Lawrence Dudley, Tait McKenzie, Hill Loyd, Rupert
and Leicester Holland, aye and many more, roaring blades,
rollicking tosspots in days gone by, saturnine dogs, bloody
buccaneers when faint hearted publishers are toward—but
gentle in heart and of a mild benignant humor. To these,
salutation and greeting. They be of one blood, the[y] and
thou: the blood of rash publishers is upon their feet.

And one CRAVEN: H. T. CRAVEN, the man that barks
like a seal—the QUIZ EDITOR of the *Evening Public
Ledger*, a man of notable waggishness, a man of huge zest
at the dinner table, now shortly bound for France but soon
also to return, a man of bookishness and worth of thy
homage: clasp him with firmness, bespeak him sternly of
ungovernable oddity, a man wholy unique, a man of plump-
ness, both body and soul. This CRAVEN, and eke his
colleague, BART HALEY of the *Evening Ledger*, both old
*North American* servants, these be men for attention and
reverence. Of this HALEY, lo I could indite a volume and
not be done. This is He the latchet of whose shoes I am
not worthy to unloose: this is He, the preposterous Celt,
whose magnificent bean is a whimsical vision all compact,
this is he who will (being a bachelor and always unoccupied)
brother and shepherd thee through strange bypaths,
through side doors where the word is easily spoken and the
wood alcohol foams brightly in the beaker—this is he of an
infinite charity and comprehension who will go with thee
unto the doorsills of strange enchantment, yet would not
write thee a letter (be thou once severed from him) to spare
thee hell-pang itself. Get this HALEY to take thee voyag-
ing in his car, the Gladys of renown, and show thee the
wonders of Wissahickon.

Ah, sir, my hand grows numb to think of the pleasures that await thee in that heavenly city of the quiet ways! Oh to be in Philly, now that April is here. Sir, there be cities and cities, but few cities of the open heart such as she is. She has her own ways, and her citizens have fallen into an odd manner of deprecation (or else into an even odder manner of superb insolence, but of such we have no concern)—but I lay hand on heart and say unto you that nowhere, not even in the town whereof the hymn saith *Nearer My God to Thee*, may a man wander with such satisfaction to the flesh and the spirit. Touching lodgings, there is a gentle-hearted woman, one Mrs. Miller, a good friend of mine, who usually hath rooms to let at 285 South Sixth Street (on Washington Square) where you can find temporary shelter most strangely reasonable until such time as you find lasting quarters. For myself, I would seek rooms in Washington Square, or up some such street as Locust or Spruce—there are lovely old homes on South Washington Square. I would counsel that advice in this matter be taken of the Lords of the Franklin Inn, or of my sweet chuck, ROY HELTON, 2213 PINE STREET, a poet of rare gusto, a lovable errant. Or of said BART HALEY who hath knowledge of a rooming house at 1716 Chestnut Street or some such number, where he abideth in great contentment.

Of Clubs: The Franklin Inn cometh foremost, first your obvious cranny. Of other clubs I know only by guest entry: there be University Club, whereof men say it sleepeth; and the Art Club, whereof men say, what has it to do with Art; but either of these clubs will give thee jocund harbourage.

Ah, sir, and indeed, sir, the pen would be dipping in the pot all night were I to set out to open unto thee the mysteries, the jolly moods and manners of this town of Penn. It was ill chosen service to tell thee too much, so great is the pleasure of learning for one's self. There is the Mercantile Library—more than Library, a kind of club, where Master REDLEY the Librarian will greet thee kindly. There be Jack Hart's ordinary on 10th Street, beloved of MASTER HALEY, where English bloaters are to be had. There is Bellini's, on South 9th, hard by the ancient WALNUT THEATRE, home of glorious traditions where spaghetti is at its rarest. There is the secret table d'hôte of Madame BEURTHENOT, in the 1600 block on PINE STREET, next door to the two iron dogs that besprawl the pavement (I forget the number) where delicate French cooking is to be had. Open the door and walk in—there is no sign, but Madame welcomes the true believer. But most of all, for sage advice and genial counsel, I recommend that you promptly telephone two good friends of mine, Master HALEY, at the *Ledger* office, Master SWIFT NEWTON at the office of the CUTTER MFG. COMPANY (this latter being the son of the Great Caliph NEWTON aforesaid, and a man of infinite leisure and vivacity), for what these two do not know about the city of the Gentle Bosom, is indeed not knowable to the prophane.

AND SO, Master WILLIAMS, go in peace, and may the blessing of all such as love Philadelphia be upon thee and remain with thee as long as cider and scrapple and milk fed chickens retain their virtue.

AND to all before whom these presents may pass, We invoke hospitality and gentle service to our trusty and high-spirited friend, the bearer.

Sic subscribit,

CHRISTOPHER MORLEY

# CALLING ON
# WILLIAM PENN

I T WOULD BE a seemly thing, perhaps, if candidates for
political office were to take a private trip up the tower
of the City Hall and spend an hour or so in solitary musing.
Looking out over the great expanse of men and buildings
they might get a vision of Philadelphia that would be more
valuable to them than the brisk bickering business of
"showing each other up."

Under the kindly guidance of Mr. Kellett, the superintendent of elevators in the City Hall, I was permitted to go
up to the little gallery at the base of the statue. A special
elevator runs up inside the tower, starting from the seventh
floor. Through great echoing spaces, crossed with girders
and littered with iron work which the steeplejacks have
taken down from the summit for painting and repairs, the
small car rises slowly into the top of the dome, over 500
feet above the street. Then you step out onto the platform.
Along the railings are the big arc lights that illuminate the
pinnacle at night. Over your head is the projecting square
toe of William Penn, his sturdy stockinged legs, his coat-
tails and outstretched right hand as he stands looking
toward the treaty ground. He loved the "fruits of solitude,"
and he has them here. He is not often disturbed, save by
the nimble acrobats who swing in a bosun's chair at their
unenvied tasks. A bosun's chair, let one add, is only a
plank, not much bigger than a shingle, noosed in midair in
the loop of a rope.

The street-dweller knows curiously little of the atmospheric conditions. The groundling would have said that
yesterday was a day of crystal clearness. Yet from the top of
the tower, even in the frank morning sunlight, the view was
strangely restricted. The distances were veiled in summer

97

haze. Camden, beyond the shoreline, was a bluish blur; even League Island was not visible. On the west the view faded away into the greenery of Overbrook, and northward the eye did not reach to the suburbs at all. Enclosed by this softened dimness, the city seemed even vaster than it is.

At that height the clamor of the city is dulled to a gentle mumble, pierced by the groan of trolleys and the sharp yelps of motorcars trundling round the Hall. On the glittering pathway of the river ferries and tugs were sliding, kicking up a riffle of white foam behind them. One curious and applaudable feature is the absence of smoke. All over the roofs of the city float little plumes and wisps of steam, detaching and drifting away in the warm blue shimmer like dissolving feathers. A cool breeze was moving in from over the Park, where the tall columns of the Smith Memorial were rising over a sea of green. The Parkway seen from above stands out as the most notable feature of Philadelphia topography. From there, too, one sees how the northeastern corner of Broad Street Station cuts into the line of the Parkway, and wonders just how this will be rectified.

It is fascinating to lean over that sunny parapet and watch the city at its work. Down at the corner of Broad and Chestnut I could see a truck loaded with rolls of paper, drawn by three horses, turning into Chestnut street. On the roof of the Wanamaker store was a party of sightseers, mostly ladies, going round with a guide. Mr. Kellett and I got out our kerchiefs and gave them a wave. In a moment they saw us, and all fluttered enthusiastic response. We were amused to notice one lady who detached herself from the party and went darting about the roof in a most original and random fashion. From our eyrie it looked rather as though she was going to take a canter round the running track on the top of the store, and we waited patiently to see what she was up to. Then she disappeared. As one looks over the flat bare roofs of skyscrapers it seems curious that so few of them are put to any use. Only on one of the cliffs of offices could I see any attempt at beauty. This was on the roof of the Finance Building, where there are three tiny grass plots and a little white bench.

It is possible to climb up through William Penn's left leg by a narrow ladder, dodging among beams and girders and through a trap-door, and so up to the brim of his beaver. I was keen to essay it, but Mr. Kellett discouraged me by saying a suit of overalls was necessary. I am no respecter of garments, but I did not press the point, as I feared that my friendly guide might still think I had a grenade about my person, and was yearning for immortality by blowing William's head off. So we compromised by going down to see the inside of the huge clock dials, and the ingenious compressed air devices by which the hands are moved every thirty seconds. A minute space on each clock face is an arc of about fourteen inches, so the minute hand jumps about seven inches every half minute. In a quiet room at the base of the tower are the two master clocks that control the whole mechanism. They are very beautiful to watch, and it is interesting to see that they were made in Germany, by Strasser and Rohde, Glashütte, Saxony. Exact noon is telegraphed from Washington every day so that these clocks can be kept strictly on the tick.

If we were a city of mystics, instead of a city of hustling and perturbed business men, we would elect a soothsayer to dwell on the little gallery below William Penn. The pleasantest job in the world has always been that of an oracle. This soothsayer would be wholly aloof from the passion of the streets. (Passion, said William Penn, is a sort of fever in the mind, which always leaves us weaker than it found us.) He would spend his time reading the "Fruits of Solitude" and would occasionally scribble messages on slips of paper, which he would weight with marbles and throw overboard. Those who found these precious sayings would read them reverently, and go on about their folly undismayed. Baskets of victuals and raiment would occasionally be conveyed to this lofty dreamer by humble admirers. On his windy perch he would brood lovingly upon the great city of his choice. When election time came round he would throw down slips telling people whom to vote for. If he thought (not mincing words) that none of the proposed candidates was worth a damn, he would frown down forbiddingly, and the balloting would have to be postponed until candidates satisfactory to his vision had been put forward. When they told him that John Jones had hosts of friends, scraps of paper would be found in the City Hall courtyard saying "It is the friends of mayors who make all the trouble." And the people would marvel greatly. He would be the only completely blissful prophet in the world, as the only way for an oracle to be happy is to put him so far away from the marketplace that he can't see that the people pay no attention to his utterances. What William Penn used to call his "natural candle," that is, the light of his spirit, would burn with a cheerful and unguttered radiance. Just inside the door that leads to the tower gallery there is a comfortable meditative armchair of the kind usually found in police stations. So perhaps they are planning to have just such an oracle.

I wandered for some time in the broad corridors of the City Hall, which smell faintly of musky disinfectant. I peered into the district attorney's indictment department, where a number of people were gathered. Occasionally a clerk would call out names, and some would disappear into inner rooms. Whether they were plaintiffs or defendants I could not conjecture. In the calf-lined alcoves of the law library, learned men were reading under green lamps. I looked uncomprehendingly at the signs on the doors— *Court of Common Pleas, Court of Oyer and Terminer, Orphans' Court, Delinquent Tax Bureau, Inspector of Nuisances*. All this complex machinery that keeps the city in order makes the layman marvel at its efficiency and its apparent kindliness. He wants to do something horrible in order to see how the wheels go round. He feels a little guilty not to have committed some crime.

# ON THE
# SIGHTSEEING BUS

A FEELING OF sour depression, consequent upon mailing the third installment to Ephraim Lederer, led us to seek uplift and blithe cheer. The sightseeing bus was filled except one seat by the driver, and we hopped aboard. The car was generously freighted with Sir Knights and their ladies, here for a convention of Templars. There was also one baffled gentleman from South America, who strove desperately to understand what was happening to him. From some broken remarks he let fall we think he had boarded the vehicle under the impression that he was taking a taxi to a railway terminal, where he wanted to catch a train for New York. At any rate, when we approached Independence Hall he was heard to ask plaintively if this was Broad Street Station. He kept uttering this inquiry with increasing despondency throughout the voyage.

It was a merry and humorous occasion. The gentleman who sits on a little camp stool in the prow of the bus and emits history and statistics through a megaphone is a genuine wag. His information is copious and uttered with amazing fluency. But we were particularly interested in the Sir Knight who slept peacefully through most of the ride, which was a long one, as we were held up by the big industrial parade on Broad street and had to take a long detour up Thirteenth street and Ridge avenue. During a spirited wrangle between our guide and the conductor of a trolley car, who asserted that we were nesting on his rails and would not let him pass, the drowsy Knight awoke and took a keen interest in the proceedings. Otherwise he will look back on the tour in a pleasantly muddled haze of memory.

The pathetic zeal and eagerness with which the passengers hang upon the guide's words is worthy of high praise. It is an index of our national passion for self-improvement. But after two hours of continuous exhortation we began to wonder how much of it would stick in their minds. The following, we imagine, is not an unfair representation of the jumbled way in which they will remember it:

*Guide*: Observation car now leaving Keith's million-dollar theatre for a systematic tour of the City of Brotherly Love. As soon as William Penn had taken possession of the land he laid plans for a large city at the junction of the Drexel and Biddle families. On your left you see the site where Benjamin Franklin, the first postmaster general, discovered the great truth that a special delivery letter does not arrive any faster than the ordinary kind. Also on your left is Black's Hotel, where Benedict Arnold was married. On your right is Independence Hall, the office of the only Democratic newspaper published in the city. Further down this street is the Delaware river, which separates the city from Camden, the home of the largest talking soup factory in the world.

We are now turning north on Fifth street, approaching Market street, the city's fashionable residential thorough-fare. Directly underneath your comfortable seats in this luxurious car pass the swift conveyances of the subway, forming the cheapest entrance into the great department stores. By means of this superb subterranean passageway ocean steamers arrive and depart daily from all ports of the globe. On your right observe old Christ Church burial ground, all the occupants of which were imported from England. Under the large flat slab lies Benjamin Franklin, the first postmaster general, and his wife, the beautiful Rebecca Gratz, the heroine of Walter Scott's novel, "Hugh Wynne." Now touring past the Friends and Quakers' meeting house, the birthplace of Old Glory. On your left the Betsy Ross house, occupied by 1600 poor orphan boys. Not far from here is the Black Horse Tavern, the favorite worshiping place of General George Washington.

Touring west on Market street. Directly in front is the tower of the City Hall, 36 feet in height, surmounted by the statue of Russell H. Conwell. The building with the dome is Mr. Cattell, the city statistician, the author of the famous baseball poem, "Acres of Diamonds." The vast edifice on your left is Temple University, founded by Stephen Girard, the originator of the price "$1.98, marked down from $2." Here we make an interesting detour to avoid the congestion on Broad street. On your right the residence of the late Doctor Munyon, the famous hair restorer, the man who said that every self-respecting man should have a roof garden of his own. This is the city of homes: there are 375,000 single homes in the city, each one equipped with the little instrument you will notice attached to the second-story windows. This is called a Busybody, and is a reflecting mirror used to tell when the rent collector is at the front door. On your right is the North Penn Bank, where Benjamin Franklin flew his famous kited check, extracting electricity from the bank examiners.

We are now approaching Fairmount Park, the largest public playground in the world. On your left is the aquarium, the local headquarters of the Anti-Saloon League. It is open to the public six days a week and to the fish at all times. In this aquarium is held the annual regatta of the Schuylkill Navy. The building in the distance with the dome is Horticultural Hall, filled with all manner of weird tropical visitors. This commodious tunnel was carved out of the solid rock of the Vare organization by J. Hampton Moore, the well-known sculptor of public opinion. Across the river is the Zoological Garden, the summer residence of Robert Morris, the well-known cigarette maker. On your right, carved out of sandstone, are the lifelike figures of Tom Robins and the other three members of the committee of 1000, immortalized in Edgar Allan Poe's poem, "Tam o'

Shanter.'' Returning down the Parkway we pass the magnificent grand stands erected at the time of the Centennial
Exposition and maintained ever since for the resuscitation
of those unable to get seats on the Market street trolleys. I
thank you for your kind attention and have here some nice
postal cards—

# IN HONOREM: MARTHA WASHINGTON

AN AMERICAN figure of national consequence has passed away from the scene of her many glories. We refer to Martha Washington, the Independence Hall cat.

When we worked in the old Philadelphia *Ledger* office, and paragraphs were scarce, we had an unfailing recourse. We would go over to the State House (as they call it in its home town), descend to the cool delightful old cellar underneath the hall, and call on Fred Eckersberg, the engineer. We would see Martha sleeking herself on the flagstones by the cellar steps (she was the blackest cat we ever knew, giving off an almost purple lustre in hot sun-

light) or perhaps we would have to search her out among
the coal bins where she was fixing a layette for the next
batch of kittens. In any case, Martha having been duly
admired, Fred Eckersberg would gladly talk about her and
tell us what were the latest adventures of her historic life.
Which was always good copy, for Fred, having been on
friendly terms with Philadelphia reporters for many years,
knew the kind of anecdotes that would please them. One
of Fred's unconscious triumphs was the time he told us of
his perplexity about ringing in the New Year in the Independence Hall belfry. It was about Christmas time, 1919.
"Last January," he said, "I rang One-Nine-One-Nine to
welcome in the New Year. But what am I going to do this
time? How can I ring One-Nine-Two-Nought?" We told him
we saw no way out of it but to start early in the afternoon of
New Year's Eve and ring the whole One Thousand Nine
Hundred and Twenty tolls.

We could say a good deal about Martha Washington: her
kittens were surely the most noble in the land, charter
members of the Colonial Felines of America, all born in the
Hall, directly underneath the lobby where the Bell stands.
When the most famous brood of all were swaddled, four
fine jetty daughters born in November, 1918, Fred chris-
tened them Victory, Freedom, Liberty, and Independence.
He paid us the greatest compliment of our life by offering
us Victory, but at that time we were living in a small
apartment in the city and we didn't think it would be a
sufficiently dignified home for such a kitten, who deserved
nothing less than a residence on the Main Line (Oh,
Philadelphia!), with scrapple made on the premises.

But it is time to get down to the point of our story.
Martha has left the Hall. Poor Fred, in his bereavement,
has taken pen in hand. We can see him, sitting at his desk
down there in the ancient cellar, with all his emblems,
souvenirs, and clippings posted up above him and an oblong
of gold-and-green brightness shining down through the

doorway from the leafy sunshine of the Square. We can see him talking it over with his comrades "the boys"—the State House carpenter and the gardeners, as they sit at their lunch in the cellar. There is the empty saucer, dry and dusty now; in the good old days Fred always brought in a little bottle of milk every morning for Martha. And this is what Fred writes us, word for word:

PHILA Aug 3, 21.

DEAR FRIEND: I thought I would write you a few lines to let you know that I am still at the Hall but the Black cat is gone—without a press agent Martha just became a cat the boys miss her as we had a bag of grass seed the mice got in and they have to hang their lunch on a string but we have a pair of Robbins that sing in the square they would not be long there if Martha was strolling around. We kept one of her kittens when I was on my vacation it was sent to the Morris Refuge with one of the men, on a Friday the next day he got a yellow slip (good bye). Lot of people ask me about her and a Friend of yours left this card: *Dear friend It looks as if Martha is going to have a family—Will you save me two kittens if they are black like their ma!* But she did not have a black kitten so he did not get one.

She left them for a few days came back when they were sent away this was what got her in wrong, but when a fight between two Thomas cats on the lawn was pulled off Martha's doom was sealed. She had the same sleek black coat the same bright eyes but she was in wrong with our Superintendent so I called up and had a boy from the cat home call for her they said it would cost 50 cents so I left the cents and the job of putting her in the basket to one of the men, but her picture is still on the wall.

We are making changes and repairs about the buildings if the tower would interest you would be pleased to take you up when over in Phila had a party from New York up and they said they knew you.

The old janitor lived in the tower because he had to ring the bell for fires funerals and most everything that went on they tell me one son was born there he had three children, the rafter alongside the open fireplace is burned and we found some old shoes worn by children under the floor, and some bones we thought ment a Crime but upon investigation turned out to be soup bones from Sheep Legs. This is about all. Your Friend

FRED ECKERSBERG
Engineer, Independence Hall.

# SEPTEMBER
# AFTERNOON

WHAT AN afternoon it was! Sunshine and blue sky, blended warmth and crispness, the wedding of summer and autumn. Sunshine as tender as Cardinal Mercier's smile, northern breeze sober as the much-harassed lineaments of the Tomsmith. Citizens went about their business "daintily enfolded in the bright, bright air," as a poet has put it. Over the dome of the postoffice, where the little cups of Mr. Bliss's wind gauge were spinning merrily, pigeons' wings gleamed white in the serene emptiness. The sunlight twinkled on lacquered limousines in dazzles of brightness, almost as vivid as the "genuine diamonds" in Market street show windows. Phil Warner, the always lunching bookseller, was out snapping up an oyster stew. Men of girth and large equator were watching doughnuts being fried in the baker's windows on Chestnut street with painful agitation. The onward march of the doughnut is a matter for serious concern in certain circles, particularly the circle of the waist line.

Strolling up Ninth street one was privileged to observe a sign of the times. A lunch room was being picketed by labor agitators, who looked comparatively unblemished by toil. They bore large signs saying:

THE C——— RESTAURANT
IS UNFAIR TO
ORGANIZED LABOR.

Side by side with these gentry marched two blonde waitresses from the lunch room, wearing an air of much bitterness and oilcloth aprons emblazoned

OUR EMPLOYES ARE NOT ON STRIKE
ALL OUR HELP GET GOOD WAGES
SOME OF THE WAITERS WANT OUR WOMEN
TO QUIT SO THEY MAY TAKE THEIR PLACES.

"We're doing this of our own free will," said one of these
damsels to me. "These guys never worked here. Our boss
gives us good money and we're not going to walk out on
him." She leaned a blazing lamp toward one of the prowling
picketers, an Oriental of dubious valor. I would be sorry for
the envoy if the lady spreads her lunch-hooks across the
area by which his friends recognize him. Almost next door
to this campaigning ground is the famous postal-card shop
in which one may always read the secret palpitations of the
public mind. The first card I noticed there said:

MANY HAPPY RETURNS OF THE DAY
WHAT DAY? PAY DAY.

Arch street seemed to be taking a momentary halt for
lunch. On the sunny paths of old Christ Church burying
ground a few meditators strolled to and fro, and one young
couple were advancing toward the wooing stage on a shady
bench. The lady was knitting a sweater, the swain arguing
with persuasion. The Betsy Ross House, still trailing its
faded bunting and disheveled wreaths, looked more like an
old curio shop than ever. One wishes the D. A. R. would
give it a coat of paint and remove the somewhat confused
sign *POUR PATRIA*. A little further on one finds a sign

SELECT EVENING TRIP
DOWN THE DELAWARE
ON PALACE STEAMER THOMAS CLYDE
THEATRICAL MOONLIGHT

This reference to nautical pleasures brought it to my
mind that I had never enjoyed a voyage on the palace ferries

111

of the Vine street crossing, and I moved in that direction. On Front above Arch one meets the terminus of the Frankford L, a tangle of salmon-colored girders. Something perilous, I could not see just what, was evidently going on, for a workman in air shouted, "Watch yourself!" This terse phrase is one of the triumphs of the American language, as is also the remark I heard the other evening. It referred to a certain publican who conducts a speak-easy at an address I shall not name. This publican had apparently got into an argument solvable only by the laying on of hands, and had emerged bearing an eye severely pulped. "Some one's been workin' on him," was the comment of one of his customers.

Watching myself with caution, I dodged down the steep stairs by which Cherry street descends from Front to Delaware avenue. In the vista of this narrow passage appeared the sharp gray bow of the United States transport *Santa Teresa*. The wide space along the docks was a rumble of traffic, as usual: wagons of golden bananas, sacks of peanuts on the pavement. But along the waterside bulwark were the customary groups of colored citizens shooting dice. Crap, I surmise, is a truly reverent form of worship: nowhere else does one hear the presiding deities of the congregation addressed with such completely fervent petition. A lusty snapping of fingers and an occasional cry of "Who thinks he feels some?" rose from one group of happy competitors. Here again the student of manners may notice a familiar phenomenon, the outward thrust of the negro toe. It seems that the first thing our brother does on buying a new pair of shoes is cut out a section of leather so that his outmost phalange may sprout through.

The tranquil upper deck of the Race street recreation pier is a goodly place to sit and survey the shining sweep of the river. The police boat *Ashbridge* lies there, and one may look down on her burnished brasses, watch the tugs puffing up and down, and the panorama of shipping from Kaighn's Point to a big five-masted schooner drawn up at Cramps'.

112

Approaching the Vine street ferry a mood of reckless vagabondage is likely to seize the wayfarer. Posters inform that the Parisian Flitters with "40 French Babies 40" are in town, and one feels convinced that life still teems with irresponsible gaiety. A savor of roasting peanuts spreads upon the air. Buying a bag, one darts aboard the antique ship *Columbia*, built in 1877, and still making the perilous voyage to Cooper's Point.

There is an air of charming leisure about the Vine street ferry. Two mules, attached to a wagon, waved their tall ears in a friendly manner as we waited for the sailing date to arrive, and I tried to feed them some peanuts. All the mules I have ever been intimate with were connoisseurs of goobers, but somewhat to my chagrin these animals seemed suspicious of the offer. After several unavailing efforts to engage their appetites their amused charioteer informed me that he didn't think they hardly knew what peanuts were. These delightful mules watched me with an air of embarrassing intensity throughout the crossing. They had quite the air of ladies riding in a Pullman car whose gaze one has inadvertently interrupted and who have misconstrued the accident.

These mules were so entertaining that I almost forgot to study the river. On the Camden side I was somewhat tempted to go exploring, but a friendly seaman assured me the *Columbia* would shortly return to her home port and entreated me not to allow myself to be stranded abroad. So all I have to report of Cooper's Point is a life-size wooden figure of a horse near the ferry slip. Then we made the return trip over the sparkling beer-colored water, speaking a sister vessel of the Shackamaxon route.

There is much to catch the eye on a ramble up Vine street from the river, but probably most interesting is a very unexpected stable about number 120. Passing under an archway, one finds a kind of rural barnyard scene; great wooden sheds on each side of an elbow alley, with lines of

113

DOCK STREET

by Frank H. Taylor. Courtesy Free Library of Philadelphia.

wagons laid away. There is an old drinking trough of clear water, horses stand munching in the sunshine, and a queer tangle of ragged roofs and small windows overhangs this old-fashioned scene. A few doors further on is an equally unexpected sign in a barber shop window: Cups and Leeches Applied. One also finds a horseshoeing forge in full blast, with patient animals leaning their heads against the wall and rosy irons glowing in the darkness. With similar brightness shone a jug of beer that I saw a man carrying across the street at the corner of Fifth. The sunlight sparkled upon the bright brown brew, and as peanuts are thirsty fodder I pushed through the swinging doors.

# AN EARLY TRAIN

THE COURSE of events has compelled me for several months to catch an early train at Broad Street three times a week. I call it an "early" train, but, of course, these matters are merely relative; 7:45 are the figures illuminated over the gateway—not so very precocious, perhaps; but quite rathe enough for one of Haroun-al-Raschid temper, who seldom seeks the "oblivion of repose" (Boswell's phrase) before 1 A.M.

Nothing is more pathetic in human nature than its faculty of self-deception. Winding up the alarm clock (the night before) I meditate as to the exact time to elect for its disturbing buzz. If I set it at 6:30 that will give me plenty of time to shave and reach the station with leisure for a pleasurable cup of coffee. But (so frail is the human will) when I wake at 6:30 I will think to myself, "There is plenty of time," and probably turn over for "another five minutes." This will mean a hideous spasm of awakening conscience about 7:10—an unbathed and unshaven tumult of

116

preparation, malisons on the shoe manufacturers who invented boots with eyelets all the way up, a frantic sprint to Sixteenth Street and one of those horrid intervals that shake the very citadel of human reason when I ponder whether it is safer to wait for a possible car or must start hotfoot for the station at once. All this is generally decided by setting the clock for 6:50. Then, if I am spry, I can be under way by 7:20 and have a little time to be philosophical at the corner of Sixteenth and Pine. Of the vile seizures of passion that shake the bosom when a car comes along, seems about to halt, and then passes without stopping—of the spiritual scars these crises leave on the soul of the victim, I cannot trust myself to speak. It does not always happen, thank goodness. One does not always have to throb madly up Sixteenth, with head retorted over one's shoulder to see if a car may still be coming, while the legs make what speed they may on sliddery paving. Sometimes the car does actually appear and one buffets aboard and is buried in a brawny human mass. There is a stop, and one wonders fiercely whether a horse is down ahead, and one had better get out at once and run for it. Tightly wedged in the heart of the car, nothing can be seen. It is all very nerve-racking, and I study, for quietness of mind, the familiar advertising card of the white-bearded old man announcing "It is really very remarkable that a cigar of this quality can be had for seven cents."

Suppose, however, that fortune is with me. I descend at Market Street, and the City Hall dial, shining softly in the fast paling blue of morning, marks 7:30. Now I begin to enjoy myself. I reflect on the curious way in which time seems to stand still during the last minutes before the departure of a train. The half-hour between 7 and 7:30 has vanished in a gruesome flash. Now follow fifteen minutes of exquisite dalliance. Every few moments I look suddenly and savagely at the clock to see if it can be playing some saturnine trick. No, even now it is only 7:32. In the lively alertness of the morning mind a whole wealth of thought and accurate observation can be crammed into a few seconds. I halt for a moment at the window of that little lunchroom on Market Street (between Sixteenth and Fifteenth) where the food comes swiftly speeding from the kitchen on a moving belt. I wonder whether to have breakfast there. It is such fun to see a platter of pale yellow scrambled eggs sliding demurely beside the porcelain counter and whipped dextrously off in front of you by the presiding waiter. But the superlative coffee of the Broad Street Station lunch counter generally lures me on.

What mundane joy can surpass the pleasure of approaching the station lunch counter, with full ten minutes to satisfy a morning appetite! "Morning, colonel," says the waiter, recognizing a steady customer. "Wheatcakes and coffee," you cry. With one deft gesture, it seems, he has handed you a glass brimming with ice water and spread out a snowy napkin. In another moment here is the coffee, with the generous jug of cream. You splash in a large lump of ice to make it cool enough to drink. Perhaps the seat next to you is empty, and you put your books and papers on it, thus not having to balance them gingerly on your knees. All round you is a lusty savour of satisfaction, the tinkle of cash registers, napkins fluttering and flashing across the counters, coloured waiters darting to and fro, great clouds of steam rising where the big dish covers are raised on the cooking tables. You see the dark-brown coffee gently quivering in the glass gauge of the nickel boiler. Then here come the wheatcakes. Nowhere else on earth, I firmly believe, are they cooked to just that correct delicacy of golden brown colour; nowhere else are they so soft and light of texture, so hot, so beautifully overlaid with a smooth, almost intangible suggestion of crispness. Two golden butter pats salute the eye, and a jug of syrup. It is now 7:38.

As everyone knows, the correct thing is to start immediately on the first cake, using only syrup. The method of dealing with the other two is classic. One lifts the upper one and places a whole pat of butter on the lower cake. Then one replaces the upper cake upon the lower, leaving the butter to its fate. In that hot and enviable embrace the butter liquefies and spreads itself, gently anointing the field of coming action. Upon the upper shield one smilingly distributes the second butter pat, knifed off into small slices for greater speed of melting. By the time the first cake has been eaten, with the syrup, the other two will be ready for manifest destiny. The butter will be docile and submissive. Now, after again making sure of the time (7:40) the syrup is brought into play and the palate has the congenial task of determining whether the added delight of melting butter outweighs the greater hotness and primal thrill of the first cake which was glossed with the syrup only. You drain your coffee to the dregs; gaze pityingly on those rushing in to snap up a breakfast before the 8 o'clock leaves for New York, pay your check, and saunter out to the train. It is 7:43.

This, to be sure, is only the curtain-raiser to the pleasures to follow. This has been a physical and carnal pleasure. Now follow delights of the mind. In the great gloomy shed wafts and twists of thick steam are jetting upward, heavily coiled in the cold air. In the train you smoke two pipes and read the morning paper. Then you are set down at Haverford. It is like a fairyland of unbelief. Trees and shrubbery are crusted and sheathed in crystal, lucid like chandeliers in the flat, thin light. Along the fence, as you go up the hill, you marvel at the scarlet berries in the hedge, gleaming through the glassy ribs of the bushes. The old willow tree by the Conklin gate is etched against the sky like a Japanese drawing—it has a curious greenish colour beneath that gray sky. There is some mystery in all this. It seems more beautiful than a merely mortal earth vexed by sinful men has any right to be. There is some ice palace in Hans

119

Andersen which is something like it. In a little grove, the boughs, bent down with their shining glaziery, creak softly as they sway in the moving air. The evergreens are clotted with lumps and bags of transparent icing, their fronds sag to the ground. A pale twinkling blueness sifts over distant vistas. The sky whitens in the south and points of light leap up to the eye as the wind turns a loaded branch.

A certain seriousness of demeanour is noticeable on the generally unfurrowed brows of student friends. Midyears are on and one sees them walking, freighted with precious and perishable erudition, toward the halls of trial. They seem a little oppressed with care, too preoccupied to relish the entrancing pallor of this crystallized Eden. One carries, gravely, a cushion and an alarm clock. Not such a bad theory of life, perhaps—to carry in the crises of existence a cushion of philosophy and an alarum of resolution.

# IN PHILADELPHIA

## I

I HAVE SEEN sunsets gild the pillared steam
  Where Broad Street Station hoops with arches dark
  The western fire; and seen the looming, stark
Crags of the Hall grow soft in morning gleam.
  One drowsy eye I wandered far to mark
The Neck, a land of opal color-scheme;
And know no fairer place to watch and dream
  Than on a bench in old Penn Treaty Park.

And there are corners, glimpses, houses, streets,
  With curious satisfaction in the view,
And unconfessed sweet moments when one meets
  The destiny of human life anew.
A city rarely beautiful I know . . . .
It is not men alone who make it so.

## II

I have seen streets where strange enchantment broods:
Old ruddy houses where the morning shone
In seemly quiet on their tranquil moods,
Across the sills white curtains outward blown.
Their marble steps were scoured as white as bone
Where scrubbing housemaids toiled on wounded knee—
And yet, among all streets that I have known
These placid byways give least peace to me.

In such a house, where green light shining through
(From some back garden) framed her silhouette
I saw a girl, heard music blithely sung.
She stood there laughing in a dress of blue,
And as I went on, slowly, there I met
An old, old woman, who had once been young.

121

# GOING TO
# PHILADELPHIA

## I

EVERY INTELLIGENT New Yorker should be compelled, once in so often, to run over to Philadelphia and spend a few days quietly and observantly prowling.

Any lover of America is poor indeed unless he has savoured and meditated the delicious contrast of these two cities, separated by so few miles and yet by a whole world of philosophy and metaphysics. But he is a mere tyro of the two who has only made the voyage by the P. R. R. The correct way to go is by the Reading, which makes none of those annoying intermediate stops at Newark, Trenton, and so on, none of that long detour through West Philadelphia, starts you off with a ferry ride and a background of imperial campaniles and lilac-hazed cliffs and summits in the superb morning light. And the Reading route, also, takes you through a green Shakespearean land of beauty, oddly different from the flat scrubby plains traversed by the Pennsy. Consider, if you will, the hills of the idyllic Huntington Valley as you near Philadelphia; or the little white town of Hopewell, N. J., with its pointing church spire. We have often been struck by the fact that the foreign traveller between New York and Washington on the P. R. R. must think America the most flat, dreary, and uninteresting countryside in the world. Whereas if he would go from Jersey City by the joint Reading—Central New Jersey—B. & O. route, how different he would find it. No, we are not a Reading stockholder.

We went over to Philly, after having been unfaithful to her for too many months. Now we have had from time to time, most menacing letters from indignant clients, protesting that we have been unfaithful to all the tenets and duties of a Manhattan journalist because we have with indecent candour confessed an affection for both Brooklyn and Philadelphia. We lay our cards on the table. We can't help it. Philadelphia was the first large city we ever knew, and how she speaks to us! And there's a queer thing about Philadelphia, hardly believable to the New Yorker who has never conned her with an understanding eye. You emerge from the Reading Terminal (or, if you will, from Broad Street Station) with just a little superbness of mood, just a tinge of worldly disdain, as feeling yourself fresh from the grandeur of Manhattan and showing perhaps (you fondly dream) some pride of metropolitan bearing. Very well. Within half an hour you will be apologizing for New York. In their quiet, serene, contented way those happy Philadelphians will be making you a little shame-faced of the bustling madness of our heaven-touching Babel. Of course, your secret adoration of Manhattan, the greatest wild poem ever begotten by the heart of man, is not readily transmissible. You will stammer something of what it means to climb upward from the subway on a spring morning and see that golden figure over Fulton Street spreading its shining wings above the new day. And they will smile gently, that knowing, amiable Philadelphia smile.

We were false to our credo in that we went via the P. R. R., but we were compensated by a man who was just behind us at the ticket window. He asked for a ticket to Asbury Park. "Single, or return?" asked the clerk. "I don't believe I'll ever come back," he said, but with so unconsciously droll an accent that the ticket seller screamed with mirth.

There was something very thrilling in strolling again along Chestnut Street, watching all those delightful people who are so unconscious of their characteristic qualities. New York has outgrown that stage entirely: New Yorkers are conscious of being New Yorkers, but Philadelphians are Philadelphians without knowing it; and hence their unique delightfulness to the observer. Nothing seemed to us at all changed—except that the trolleys have raised their fare from five cents to seven. The Liberty Toggery Shop down on Chestnut Street was still "Going Out of Business," just as it was a couple of years ago. Philip Warner, the famous book salesman at Leary's Old Book Store, was out having lunch, as usual. The first book our eye fell upon was *The Experiences of an Irish R. M.*, which we had hunted in vain in these parts. The only other book that caught our eye particularly was a copy of "Patrins," by Louise Guiney, which we saw a lady carrying on the campus of the University of Pennsylvania.

But perhaps New York exerts its own fascination upon Philadelphians, too. For when we returned we selfishly persuaded a friend of ours to ride with us on the train so that we might imbibe some of his ripe orotund philosophy, which we had long been deprived of. He is a merciless

Celt, and all the way over he preached us a cogent sermon on our shortcomings and backslidings. Faithful are the wounds of a friend, and it was nice to know that there was still someone who cared enough for us to give us a sound cursing. Between times, while we were catching breath, he expatiated upon the fact that New York is death and damnation to the soul; but when we got to Manhattan Transfer he suddenly abandoned his intended plan of there catching the next train back to the land of Penn. A curious light began to gleam in his mild eyes; he settled his hat firmly upon his head and strode out into the Penn Station. "I think I'll go out and look round a bit," he said. We wonder whether he has gone back yet?

## II

THE OTHER DAY we had a chance to go to Philadelphia in the right way—by the Reading, the P. and R., the Peaceful and Rapid. As one of our missions in life is to persuade New York and Philadelphia to love one another, we will tell you about it.

Ah, the jolly old Reading! Take the 10 o'clock ferry from Liberty Street, and as the *Plainfield* kicks herself away from the slip with a churning of cream and silver, study Manhattan's profile in the downpour of morning sun. That winged figure on the Tel and Tel Building (the loveliest thing in New York, we insist) is like a huge and queerly erect golden butterfly perched momently in the blue. The 10:12 train from Jersey City we call the Max Beerbohm Special because there are Seven Men in the smoker. No, the Reading is never crowded. (Two more men did get on at Elizabeth.) You can make yourself comfortable, put your coat, hat, and pipecleaners on one seat, your books, papers, and matches on another. Here is the stout conductor whom we used to know so well by sight, with his gold insignia. He has forgotten that we once travelled with him regularly, and very likely he wonders why we beam so cheerfully. We flash down the Bayonne peninsula, with a glimpse of the harbour, Staten Island in the distance, a schooner lying at anchor. Then we cross Newark Bay, pure opaline in a clear, pale blue light. H. G. Dwight is the only other chap who really enjoys Newark Bay the way it deserves to be. He wrote a fine poem about it once.

But we had one great disappointment. For an hour or so we read a rubbishy novel, thinking to ourself that when the Max Beerbohm Express reached that lovely Huntington Valley neighbourhood, we would lay down the book and study the scenery, which we know by heart. When we came to the Neshaminy, that blithe little green river, we were all ready to be thrilled. And then the train swung away to the left along the cut-off to Wayne Junction and we missed our bright Arcadia. We had wanted to see again the little cottage at Meadowbrook (so like the hunting lodge in the forest in "The Prisoner of Zenda") which a suasive real-estate man once tried to rent to us. (Philadelphia realtors are no less ingenious than the New York species.) We wanted to see again the old barn, rebuilt by an artist, at Bethayres, which he also tried to rent to us. We wanted to see again the queer "desirable residence" (near the gas tanks at Marathon) which he did rent us. But we had to content ourself with the scenery along the cut-off, which is pleasant enough in its way—there is a brown-green brook along a valley where a buggy was crawling down a lane among willow trees in a wealth of sunlight. And the dandelions are all out in those parts. Yes, it was a lovely morning. We found ourself pierced by the kind of mysterious placid melancholy that we only enjoy to the full in a Reading smoker, when, for some unknown reason, hymn tunes come humming into our head and we are alarmed to notice ourself falling in love with humanity as a whole.

We could write a whole newspaper page about travelling to Philly on the Reading. Consider those little back gardens near Wayne Junction, how delightfully clean, neat, domestic, demure. Compare entering New York toward the Grand Central, down that narrow frowning alleyway of apartment house backs, with imprisoned children leaning from barred windows. But as you spin toward Wayne Junction you see acres and acres of trim little houses, each with a bright patch of turf. Here is a woman in a blue dress and white cap, busily belabouring a rug on the grass. The bank of the cutting by Wayne Junction is thick with a tangle of rose-bushes which will presently be in blossom; we know them well. Spring Garden Street: if you know where to look you can catch a blink of Edgar Allan Poe's little house. Through a jumble of queer old brick chimneys and dormers, and here we are at the Reading Terminal, with its familiar bitter smell of coal gas.

Of course we stop to have a look at the engine, one of those splendid Reading locos with the three great driving wheels. Splendid things, the big Reading locos; when they halt they pant so cheerfully and noisily, like huge dogs, much louder than any other engines. We always expect to see an enormous red tongue running in and out over the cowcatcher. Vast thick pants, as the poet said in "Khubla Khan." We can't remember if he wore them, or breathed them, but there it is in the poem; look it up. Reading engineers, too, always give us a sense of security. They have gray hair, cropped very close. They have a benign look, rather like Walt Whitman if he were shaved. We wrote a poem about one of them once, Tom Hartzell, who used to take the 5:12 express out of Jersey City.

Philadelphia, incidentally, is the only large city where the Dime Museum business still flourishes. For the first thing we see on leaving the Terminal is that the old Bingham Hotel is now The World's Museum, given over to Ursa the Bear Girl and similar excitements. But where is the beautiful girl with slick dark hair who used to be at the Reading terminal news-stand?

How much more we could tell you about travelling on the Reading! We would like to tell you about the queer assortment of books we brought back with us. (There were twelve men in the smoker, coming home.) We could tell how we tried to buy, without being observed, a magazine which we will call *Foamy Fiction*, in order to see what the new editor (a friend of ours) is printing. Also, we always buy a volume of Gissing when we go to Philly, and this time we found *In the Year of Jubilee* in the shop of Jerry Cullen, the delightful bookseller who used to be so red-headed, but is getting over it now in the most logical way. We could tell you about the lovely old whitewashed stone farmhouses (with barns painted red on behalf of Schenk's Mandrake Pills) and about the famous curve near Roelofs, so called because the soup rolls off the table in the dining car when they take the curve at full speed; and about Bound Brook, which has a prodigious dump of tin cans that catches the setting sunlight——

It makes us sad to think that a hundred years hence people will be travelling along that road and never know how much we loved it. They will be doing so to-morrow, too; but it seems more mournful to think about the people a hundred years hence.

When we got back to Jersey City, and stood on the front end of the ferryboat, Manhattan was piling up all her jewels into the cold green dusk. There were a few stars, just about as many as there are passengers in a Reading smoker. There was one big star directly over Brooklyn, and another that seemed to be just above Plainfield. We pondered, as the ferry slid toward its hutch at Liberty Street, that there were no stars above Manhattan. Just at that moment—five minutes after seven—the pinnacle of the Woolworth blossomed a ruby red. New York makes her own.

# BROAD STREET
# STATION

**B**ROAD STREET STATION is to me a place of extraordinary fascination. Among the cloudy memories of early childhood it stands solidly, a home of thunders and shouting, of gigantic engines with their fiery droppings of coal and sudden jets of steam. It was a place in which a delightful sense of adventure was closely mixed with fear. I remember being towed along, as a very small urchin, among throngs of hasty feet and past the prodigious glamour of those huge wheels and pistons. (Juvenile eyes are very close to the ground.) Then, arrived within, the ramping horses carved opposite the head of the stairs and the great map on the northern wall were a glorious excitement to my wondering gaze. Nowadays, when I ramble about the station its enchantment is enhanced by the recollection of those early adventures. And as most people, when passing through a station, are severely intent upon their own problems and little conscious of scrutiny, it is the best of places to study the great human show. Mr. Joseph Pennell, in a thrilling drawing, has given a perfect record of Broad street's lights and tones that linger in the eye—the hurdling network of girders, the patterning files of passengers, the upward eddies of smoke.

A sense of baffling excitement and motion keeps the mind alert as one wanders about the station. In the dim, dusky twilight of the trainshed this is all the more impressive. A gray-silver haze hangs in the great arches. Against the brightness of the western opening the locomotives come gliding in with a restful relaxation of effort, black indistinguishable profiles. The locomotives are the only restful things in the scene—they and the red-capped porters, who have the priestly dignity of oracles who have laid aside all

129

earthly passions. Most of the human elements wear the gestures of eagerness, struggle and perplexity. The Main Line commuters, it is true, seem to stroll trainward like a breed apart, with an air of leisurely conquest and assurance. They have the bearing of veterans who have conquered the devils of transportation and hold them in leash. But this superb carelessness is only factitious. Some day their time will come and they will fall like the rest of us. They will career frantically to and fro, dash to information desk and train bulletin, rummage for tickets and wipe a beaded brow. What gesture, incidentally, is so significantly human as that of mopping the forehead? If I were a sculptor at work on a symbolic statue of Man I would carve him with troubled and vacant eyes, dehydrating his brow with a handkerchief.

Take your stand by the train gate a few moments before the departure of the New York express. What a medley of types, and what a common touch of anxiety and wistfulness makes them kin! Two ladies are bidding each other a prolonged farewell. "Now, remember, 7 Howland street, Cambridge," says the departer. "Be sure to write!" A feverish man rushes back from the train, having forgotten something, and fights his way against the line which is filing through the gate. Another man hunts dismally through all his pockets for his ticket, rocking gently and thoughtfully on his heels. The ticket seems to have vanished. He pushes his hat back on his forehead and says something to the collector. This new posture of his hat seems to aid him, for in another half minute the ticket appears in a pocket that he has already gone through several times. The official cons his watch every five seconds. A clerk, apparently from one of the ticket windows, rushes up with a long strip ticket. There is some question about a sailor with a furlough ticket to Providence. Has he gone through? Haven't seen him. The gateman claps the gate to and switches off the light. Three other men come dashing up and are let through by the kindness of the usher. Then comes the sailor galloping along with a heavy suitcase. "Here he is! Here's your ticket!" Again the gate is opened and the navy man tears down the platform. The train is already moving, but he just makes it. Far out, in the bright sunlight beyond the station, the engine can be seen pulling out, ejecting a stiff spire of smoke and horizontal billows of steam.

At the same time rumbles in the hourly express from New York. Watch the people come out. Here is the brisk little man with a brown bag, who always leads the crowd. The men from the smoker are first, puffing pipes or cigars. They all seem to know exactly where they want to go and push on relentlessly. After the main body of travelers come the Pullman passengers, usually followed by porters. Here is a girl in a very neat blue suit. Her porter carries an enormous black hat-box painted with very swagger stripes of green. She is pretty, in a rather frank way, but too dusty with powder. An actress, one supposes. A tall young man steps out from the crowd, something very rakish about him, too. She looks surprised. "Nice of me to meet you, wasn't it?" he says. They walk off together, and one notices the really admirable hang of her blue skirt, just reaching her fawn spats. Sorry she uses so much powder. Curious thing; the same young chap was back again an hour later, this time to meet a man on the next New York train. They both wore brightly burnished brown shoes and seemed to have completely mastered life's perplexities. All these little dramas were enacted to a merry undertone of constant sound: the clear chime of bells, the murmur and throb of hissing steam, the rumble of baggage trucks, the slither of thousands of feet.

There is not much kissing done when people arrive from New York, but if you will linger about the gate when the Limited gets in from Chicago you will see that humanity pays more affectionate tribute to friends arriving from that strange country. There was one odd little group of three. A man and a woman greeted another lady who arrived on the

Chicago train. The two women kissed with a luxurious smacking. Then the man and the arrival kissed. The Chicago lady wore an enormous tilted hat with plumes. "Well, I'm here," she said, but without any great enthusiasm. The man was obviously frightfully glad to see her. But stand how he would, she kept the slant of her hat between her face and him. He tried valiantly to get a straight look at her. She would not meet his gaze. He put his head on one side astonishingly like a rooster, and his whole attitude expressed an earnest desire to please. When he spoke to her she answered to the other woman. She handed him her baggage checks without looking at him. Then she pointed to a very heavy package at her feet. With a weary resignation he toted it, and they moved away.

Inside the station the world is divided sharply into two halves. On the trainward side all is bustle and stir; the bright colors of news-stands and flower stalls, brisk consultation of timetables at the information desk, little telephone booths, where lights wink on and off. In one of these booths, with the door open for greater coolness, a buyer is reporting to his home office the results of an out-of-town trip. "He offered me a lot—pretty nice leather— he wanted seventy-five—well, listen, finally I offered him sixty-five—Oh, no, no, no, he claims it's a dollar grade— well, I don't know, it might be ninety cent maybe."

But abaft the big stairway a quiet solemnity reigns. The long benches of the waiting room seem a kind of Friends' meeting. Momently one expects to see some one rise and begin to speak. But it is not the peace of resignation; it is the peace of exhaustion. These are the wounded who have dragged themselves painfully from the onset, stricken on the great battlefield of Travel. Here one may note the passive patience of humanity, and also how pathetically it hoards its little possessions. A lady rises to get a drink of water. With what zealous care she stacks all her impediments in a neat pile—umbrella, satchel, handbag, shawl, suitcase, tippet, raincoat and baby—and confides them to her companion. A gust of that characteristic railroad restaurant odor drifts outward from the dining room—a warm, soupy blend of browned chicken-skin and crisp roll-crust. On one end of the bench are three tall bronzed doughboys, each with two service stripes and the red chevron. They have bright blue eyes and are carefully comparing their strip tickets, which seem nearly a yard long. A lady in very tight black suede slippers stilts out of the dining room. Like every one else in the waiting room she walks as though her feet hurt her. The savor of food is blown outward by electric fans. The doughboys are conferring together. They have noticed two lieutenants dining at one of the white-draped tables. This seems to enrage them. Finally they can stand it no longer. Their vast rawhide marching boots go clumping into the dining room. Every now and then the announcer comes to the head of the stairway and calls out something about a train to Harrisburg, Altoona, Pittsburgh and Chicago. There is a note of sadness in his long-drawn wail, as though it would break his heart if no one should take this train, which is a favorite of his. A few weary casuals hoist themselves from the benches, gather their belongings anew and stagger away.

## ELEGY IN A RAILROAD STATION
(Broad Street, Philadelphia, obiit 1952)

I've always been in love with railroad stations:
By no means least of man's superb creations.
Particularly I rate high
Old London termini,
Liverpool Street (cathedral of catarrh)
Where antique bathtubs in the cellar are;
And you may know
Altars of the great gods To and Fro
At Paddington, Euston, King's Cross, Gare du Nord,

133

## CHRISTOPHER MORLEY'S PHILADELPHIA

La Salle Street in Chicago, Windsor Montreal,
The Lackawanna on Hoboken shore,
The B & O beloved Mount Royal, Baltimore.
Even little Roslyn, on fish-shaped Paumanok,
Where the Long Island falters, still in hock—
Too many I love, to list, but of them all
None ever gave me quite such sublimation
As Broad Street Station.
Maybe tops of all I rank it
Because it was there, by jeepers,
Walt climbed aboard the Pullman Palace Sleepers
And tucked his noble beard outside the blanket.

I repeat your glory, Broad Street Station!
The proper shrine, the true Main Line,
Of Immortality the Intimation;
Such offsteam blowing,
Such bells, and hells of coming and going,
Suburban cowcatchers' dainty snouts,
Beautiful barytone *All abooaard* shouts,
Drive wheels, and firebox glowing.
Nothing was so holy as the Local to Paoli
(15 and 45) when we were youngalive
For Wynnewood, Ardmore, Haverford, Bryn Mawr
Or anywhere along the P.R.R.
Then, as child, boy, student, family man,
We were too self-occupied to scan
That gigantic arch of joys and pains
When trains were really trains.

There beneath tall wheels, fierce jets of steam,
We guessed the bulk and power of a dream;
To shorten space and anguish to appease
The engine rests at crouch and purrs at ease.
People cry God bless you's and So long's,
Gates contract or widen like lazy-tongs—
Goodbye, Goodbye! No wonder I
Preserve in pure imagination
My memory of Broad Street Station.

134

# NEIGHBORHOODS

# LITTLE ITALY

THERE ARE three gentlemen with whom I have been privileged, on happy occasions, to take travels in Philadelphia. The first is the Mountaineer, a tall vagabond, all bone and gristle, member emeritus of the Hoboes' Union, who can tramp all day on seven cents' worth of milk chocolate, knows the ins and outs of every queer trade and is a passionate student of back alleys and mean streets. Pawnshops, groggeries, docks and factories make his mouth water with the astounding romance of every day.

The second is the Soothsayer, an amiable visionary whose eye dotes on a wider palette. Soothsayer by profession, artist and humanitarian at heart, he is torn and shaken on every street by the violent paradoxes of his lively intellect. A beggar assaults his sense of pity—but rags are so picturesque! A vast hotel, leaking golden flame at every window against the green azure of the dusk, fascinates his prismatic eyeball—but how about the poor and humble? Treading the wide vistas of the Parkway in a sunset flush he is transported by the glory of the vision. Scouting some infamous alley of smells he would blast the whole rottenness from the earth. He never knows whether the city is a sociological nightmare or an Arabian color-box.

And the third is the Epicure. In person very similar to Napoleon the Third, late emperor of the French, some mysterious tincture of the Mediterranean moves in his strictly Saxon blood. A man of riotous and ungovernable humor, frequently halting on the streets until his paroxysms of outrageous mirth will permit further locomotion, the only thing he never laughs at is food. He sees the city not as a vast social riddle, nor as a network of heavenly backalleys, but as a waste of irrelevant architecture, dotted here and there with oases of good meals. Mention some spot in the city and his eye will brighten like a newly sucked glass marble. "Oh, yes," he cries, "that's just round the corner from the Cafe Pancreas, where they have those admirable ortolans!" To eat a meal in company with the Epicure is like watching a great artist at work. He studies the menu with the bitter concentration of a sculptor surveying the block of marble from which the statue is to be chiseled. He does not assassinate his appetite at one swoop with mere sum total of victuals. He gently woos it to annihilation, so that he himself can hardly tell just at what point it dies. He eats with the skill and cunning of a champion chess player, forgoing a soup or an entree in the calculating spirit of Lasker or Marshall, sacrificing pawns in order to execute some coup elsewhere on the board. Waiters, with that subtle instinct of theirs, know as soon as they see that delicately rounded figure enter the salle à manger that here is a man to be reckoned with.

You may imagine, then, my privilege in being able to accompany the Epicure the other day to the Italian market at Ninth and Christian streets, where he purposed to look over the stalls. It was a day of entrancing sunlight, when all that lively district of Little Italy leaped and trembled in the fullness of light and appetizing fluent air. One saw a secret pathos in the effort to reproduce in the flat dull streets of a foreign city something of the color and mirth of Mediterranean soil. One often wonders what fantastic dream or illusion—was it only a steamship poster?—led so many citizens of the loveliest land on earth to forsake their blue hills and opal valleys to people the cheerless byways of American towns? What does Little Italy think of us and our climate in the raw, bitter days of a western winter? Well, now that the letters are speeding homeward telling of the unbelievable approach of prohibition, there will be few enough of those bright-eyed immigrants!

Christian street breathes the Italian genius for good food. After lunching in a well-known Italian restaurant on Catharine street, where the Epicure instructed me in the mysteries of gnocchi, frittura mista, rognone, scallopini al marsala and that marvelously potent clear coffee which seems to the uninstructed to taste more like wine than coffee, and has a curious shimmer of green round the rim of the liquid, we strolled among the pavement stalls of the little market. It seems to me, just from a cursory study of the exhibit, that the secret of Italian gusto for food is that they take it closer to nature, and also that they are less keen than we about meat. They do not buy their food already prepared in cardboard boxes. Fish, vegetables, cheese, fruit and nuts seem to be their chief delights. Fish of every imaginable kind may be seen on Christian street. Some of them, small, flattened, silver-shining things, are packed cunningly in kegs in a curious concentric pattern so that the glitter of their perished eyes gleams in hypnotizing circles. Eels, mussels, skates, shrimps, cuttlefish—small pink corpses, bathed in their own ink—and some very tiny ocean morsels that look like white-bait. Cheeses of every kind and color, some of them a dull yellow and molded in a queer gourd-like shape. But the vegetables and herbs are the most inscrutable. Even the gastrologer Epicure was unable to explain them all to me. Chopped bayleaves, artichokes, mushrooms, bunches of red and green peppers, little boxes of dried peas, beans, powdered red pepper, wrinkled olives and raisins, and strange-smelling bundles of herbs that smell only like straw, but which presumably possess some strange seasoning virtue to those who understand them. In the windows of the grocers' shops you will always find Funghi secchi della Liguria (Ligurian dried mushrooms) and Finocchio uso Sicilia (Fennel, Sicilian style), which names are poems in themselves. And, of course, the long Bologna sausages—and great round loaves of bread.

The Italian sweet tooth is well hinted at in the Christian street pasticcerias (pastry shops), where cakes, macaroons, biscuits and wafers of every color beckon to the eye.

Equally chromatic are the windows of the bookshops, where bright portraits of General Diaz, King Victor and President Wilson beam down upon knots of gossipers arguing on the sunny side of the street, and a magnificent edition of the *Divina Commedia* lies side by side with *Amore Proibito* and *I Sotterranei di New York*. Another volume whose title is legible even to one with scarcely any smattering of tongues is *Il Kaiser All'Inferno*!

Some of the shops in Little Italy seem to embrace a queer union of trades. For instance, one man announces his office as a "Funeral agent and detective bureau"; another, "Bookbinder and flower shop." In one window may be seen elaborate plans of Signor Menotti Nanni's Ocean Floating Safe, in which transatlantic passengers are recommended to stow their valuables. The ship may sink and likewise the passengers, but in the Ocean Floating Safe your jewels and private papers will float off undamaged and roam the ocean until some one comes to salve them. The Italian name for this ingenious device is Cassaforte Galleggiante, which we take to mean a swimming strong-box.

No account of Christian street would be complete without at least some mention of the theatres between Eighth and Seventh streets. The other afternoon I stopped in at one of them, expecting to see moving pictures, which are comprehensible in all languages; but instead I found two Italian comedians—a man and a woman—performing on an odd little stage to an audience which roared applause at every line. I was unable to understand a word, but the skill and grace of the performers were evident, also the suave and liquid versification of their lines. The manager walked continually up and down the aisles, rebuking every sound and movement other than legitimate applause with a torrential hiss. Every time a baby squalled—and there were many—the manager sibilated like a python. The audience took this quite for granted, so evidently it is customary. It is a salutary lesson in modesty to attend a performance conducted in a foreign language: there is nothing that so rapidly impresses upon one our stupid provincial ignorance of most tongues but our own.

Little Italy is only a few blocks away from Chestnut street, and yet I daresay thousands of our citizens hardly suspect its existence. If you chance to go down there about 1 o'clock some bright afternoon, when all the children are enjoying the school recess, and see that laughing, romping mass of bright-eyed young citizens, you will wonder whether they are to be congratulated on growing up in this new country of wonderful opportunity, or to be pitied for losing the beauty and old tradition of that storied peninsula so far away.

# THE RONALDSON
# CEMETERY

WHENEVER I feel weary of life, liberty and the pursuit of some one else's happiness, whenever some one tells me that the League of Nations is sure to be a failure, or reminds me that the American Press Humorists are going to hold their convention here next June and we shall all have to flog our lethargic brains into competition with all the twenty-one-karat drolls of this hemisphere—whenever, in short, life is wholly gray and oblique, I resort to Veranda's for lunch.

Veranda's, of course, is not its name; nor shall I tell you where it is. Eighteen months of faithful lunching and, perhaps, half a ton of spaghetti consumed, have given me a certain prestige in the bright eyes of Rosa, the demurest and most innocently charming waitress in Philadelphia. I do not wish to send competitors in her regard flocking to that quiet little Italian restaurant, where the table cloths are so white, the coffee so fragrant and where the liver and kidneys come to the board swimming in a rich brown gravy the reality of which no words can approach. And that Italian bread, so crisply crusted, so soft and absorbent within! A slab of Veranda's bread dipped in that kidney gravy atones for three speeches by Senator Sherman! And then when Rosa brings on the tall pot of marmalade, which another devotee and I keep there for dessert, and we light up our cigarettes and watch the restaurant cat sprawling in Oriental luxury by the steam pipes—then we come somewhere near the throne of human felicity mentioned by Doctor Johnson.

Veranda's is an outpost of Little Italy, which does not really begin until you get south of Lombard. And the other day, after lowering the level of the marmalade by several inches, it occurred to me to renew my acquaintance with Little Italy proper.

THE PLACID BY-WAY OF CLINTON STREET
by Frank H. Taylor. Courtesy Free Library of Philadelphia.

Ninth street is the best channel of approach to Philadelphia's Mediterranean colony. There is a good deal to distract attention before you cross the Alps of South street. If you have a taste for alleys you will be likely to take a side tour of a few versts in the quaint section of stables and little brick houses that lies just below Locust street and between Ninth and Tenth. Just now you will find that region liberally placarded with small neat notices announcing the loss (on January 8) of a large yellow and white Angora cat, having white face, breast and feet and answering to the name of Taffy. This struck at my heart, for I once owned a yellow Angora of the same name, which I smuggled home from Boston one Christmas Eve in a Pullman sleeper, against all railway rules, and I hope and trust that by this time Taffy has returned to his home at 260 South Ninth street, and to Mrs. Walter M. James, his bereaved mistress.

The little notice about the recreant Master Taffy was strangely appropriate for this queer little district of Hutchinson, Delhi, Irving and Manning streets, for it is just what in London would be known as a "mews." It is a strange huddle of old brick houses, full of stables and carpenters' workshops, with agreeable vistas of chimneys, attic windows, and every now and then a gentleman of color leisurely bestraddling a horse and clumping along the quiet pavements. Small brown dogs of miscellaneous heritage sit sunning themselves on doorsteps; on Hutchinson street a large cart was receiving steaming forkloads of stable straw. In the leisurely brightness of midafternoon, with occasional old clo' men chanting their litany down the devious alleyways, it seems almost village-like in its repose. A great place to lead a fat detective a chase! The next time George Gibbs or John McIntyre writes a tale of mystery and sleuthing, I hope he will use the local color of Delhi street. Why do our native authors love to lay the scenes of their yarns in Venice, Madrid, Brooklyn or almost anywhere except Philadelphia?

144

On Ninth street below Pine one comes upon a poem in a window which interested me because the author, Mr. Otis Gans Fletcher, has evidently had difficulty with those baffling words "Ye" and "Thou," which have puzzled even greater poets—such as Don Marquis. The poem is called "Welcome to Our Heroes," and begins:

> Welcome! home, Great Heroes,
> Nobly! hath thou fought

and continues,

> We know the price, the sacrifice
> That ye each paid to learn,

and by and by concludes:

> Welcome! thrice!!! welcome, Great Heroes,
>   Defenders of Humanity;
> The world now lives, on what thou didst give,
>   For the great spirit, De–moc–ra–cy.

After putting Lombard street behind the voyager becomes immediately aware of the Italian atmosphere. Brightly colored cans of olive oil wanton in the windows; the Tripoli Barber Supply Company, whose window shines with all manner of lotions and shampoos, offers the Vesuvius Quinine Tonic, which is said to supply "unrivaled neutrement" for the hair. Little shops appear displaying that curious kind of painting which seems to be executed on some metallic surface and is made more vivid by the insertion of small wafers of mother-of-pearl where the artist wants to throw in a note of high emotion. These paintings generally portray Gothic chapels brooding by lakes of ultramarine splendor; their only popular competitor is a scene of a white terrier with an expression of fixed nobility

145

watching over the bedside of a young female innocent who lies, clad in a blue dress, beneath a scarlet coverlet, her golden locks spread over a white pillow. The faithfulness of the animal and the secure repose of the child may be profitably studied in the length of time necessary to light a pipe. I feel sure that no kind-hearted footpad's home is complete without this picture.

The Ronaldson Cemetery, laid out in 1827 at Ninth and Bainbridge streets, comes as a distinct shock to a sentimental wayfarer already unmanned by the above appeal to the emotions. Mrs. Meredith, the kindly caretaker, admitted me through the massive iron gates, surprised and pleased to find a devotee of cemeteries. In the damp chill of a February afternoon the old graveyard is not the cheeriest of spots, but I was restored to optimism by this inscription:

> Passing stranger think this not
>   A place of fear and gloom:
> We love to linger near this spot,
>   It is our parents' tomb.

This, however, was carved some fifty years ago. I fear there is little lingering done in Ronaldson's Cemetery nowadays, for the stones are in ill repair, many of them fallen. According to Scharf and Westcott's history, it was once considered the finest cemetery in the country and "a popular place of burial." Just within the gateway are two little houses, in at least one of which a merry little family of children is growing up undepressed by the strange surroundings. One of these houses, according to Ronaldson's cautious plan, was "to have a room provided with a stove, couch, etc., into which persons dying suddenly might be laid and the string of a bell put into their hand, so that if there should be any motion of returning life the alarm bell might be rung, the keeper roused and medical help procured."

James Ronaldson was a Scotchman, as I had already

surmised from an obelisk erected, "Sacred to the memory
of Scottish Strangers," and possibly his cautiousness in the
matter of burying people alive may have suggested this
favorite theme to Edgar Allan Poe, who was living in
Philadelphia at the time when the magnificent new cemetery must have been the talk of the town. Scotchmen have
always been interested in cemeteries, and as I walked those
desolate paths among the graves I could not help thinking
of Stevenson's love of the old Grayfriars and Calton Hill
burying grounds in Edinburgh. A man was busy digging a
grave near the front gate, and a new oak casket lay at the
door of the keeper's house. It was strange to see the
children playing round happily in such scenes.

# THE *HAVERFORD*
# COMES HOME

PHILADELPHIA'S hands were tied in the matter of welcoming the *Haverford*. What a greeting we could have given her men if they had been permitted to parade through the center of the city, past Independence Hall—the symbol of all they fought for—and down the shining sweep of Broad street! And yet, although we were morosely forbidden to "come in contact with them" (it sounds rather like the orders given to citizens of Coblenz), what a fine human note there was in the mass of humbler citizens that greeted the transport at the foot of Washington avenue. I wish Mr. Baker might have been there—the scene would have made him more tender toward those loyal Philadelphians who don't quite see why most of the transports should dock at—well, at another Atlantic port!

But I hadn't intended to go down to see the *Haverford* come in. I have traveled on her myself and know her genial habits of procrastination. I shrewdly suspected she would arrive at her dock long after the hour announced. Days ago, when we were told she would arrive on the 27th, I smiled knowingly. When she was off the Capes and word was telegraphed of a "disabled steering gear," I chuckled. The jovial old ship was herself again! It is almost incredible that an enemy submarine should have dared to fire a tin fish at her. I should think a cautious, subaqueous commander would have sheered off and dived away in panic, fearing some devil's ruse. Surely no harmless vessel (he ought to have gutturaled to himself) would travel as leisurely as that! How many U-boat captains must have fled her dignified presence, suspecting her to be one of Beatty's trick fleet, sent out to lure innocent submarines to death by loitering blandly on the purple sea. This is no ill-natured jibe. Slow

148

ships are ever the best to travel on. Her unruffled, imperceptible progress across blue horizons is her greatest charm, and was undoubtedly her subtle security.

But passing along Pine street, about thirty tobacco whiffs after breakfast, I saw three maidens run out from the Peirce School in a high cackle of feminine excitement. Evidently they had been let off for the day. "What shall we do with these old books?" I heard one say. "Do we have to cart them round with us?" It was plain from their gleeful chatter that they were bound for Washington avenue. And then on Broad street I saw little groups of pedestrians hurrying southward. Over that spacious thoroughfare there was a feeling of suspense and excitement—the feeling of "something happening" that passes so quickly from brain to brain. I could not resist temptation to go down and join the throng.

Washington avenue is not a boulevard of pleasure. Most of it is a dreary expanse of huge factories and freight cars. But over the cobbles citizens of all sorts were hurrying with bright faces. Peddlers carried bundles of flags and knots of colored balloons, which tugged and eddied in the cold wind. In an Italian drug store at the corner of Sixth, under a sign, Telefono Pubblico per Qualsiasi Distanza, a distracted pretzel basket man, who had already sold out his wares, was calling up some distant base of supplies in the hope of replenishing his stock. Jefferson Square, brown and leafless, was packed with people. Down by the docks loomed up a tall, black funnel, dribbling smoke. "There she is!" cried an excited lady, leaping from cobble to cobble. For a moment I almost apologized to the good old *Haverford* for having misjudged her. Was she really docked already, on the tick of time? Then I saw that the vessel in sight had only two masts, and I knew that my old favorite had four.

The crowd at the lower end of Washington avenue was immense, held firmly in check by mounted police. Red

Cross ambulances and trucks were slowly butting their way down to the pier, envied by us humbler souls who had no way of getting closer. Perched on a tall wagon a group of girls, apparently factory hands, were singing merrily "Bring Back My Bonnie to Me." On every side I heard scraps of detached conversation. "He was wounded and gassed, and he says 'if they send me back to that stuff it'll be in a box.' " Sheltering behind a stout telephone pole, perhaps the very one which was flinging the peddler's anguished cry for more pretzels, I sought a light for my pipe and found myself gazing on a red-printed dodger: "WORKING CLASS, KNOW THE TRUTH. The workers of Russia have done away with the capitalistic, distroctive, parasitic sistem, which on one hand creates Millionaires and luxury and on the other hobos and misery."

The longest way round is usually the shortest way home, and it occurred to me that the graveyard of Old Swedes Church would be a useful vantage point. I found my way there down the quaint little vista of League street and the oddly named channel of Reckless street. Apparently the same thought had occurred to several other wise-acres, for I got to the gates just as the sexton was locking them. Ignoring the generous offer that the church makes on several signboards—"$10 Reward for Any Person Found Destroying the Church Property"—I took my stand at one corner of the churchyard, looking out over the docks and the thousands crowded along the pavements below. Reading the tombstones passed away the time for the better part of an hour.

One sad little inscription runs like this:

LIZZIE
affectionate daughter of———
died Dec. 24, 1857

When Christmas bells ring out their chime
And holly boughs and sprigs of thyme
    Were hung on many a wall,
Our LIZZIE in her beauty's prime
    Lay in our darkened hall.

Escaping the chilly wind that blew up from the river I spent some time studying the interior of the lovely little church and reading the epitaphs of the old Swedish pastors. Of Olaf Parlin, one of these, it is nobly written "And in the Last Combat, strengthened by Heavenly Succours, he Quit the Field not Captive but Conqueror."

But still there was no sign of the *Haverford*. I strolled up the waterfront, stopping by the barge *Victor* to admire a very fat terrier fondled by the skipper's wife. I was about to ask if I could step aboard, thinking that the deck of the barge would afford a rather better view of the hoped-for transport, when I saw the ferry *Peerless*, one of the three ancient oddities that ply between South street and Gloucester. And at the same moment the whistles down the river began to blow a deep, vibrant chorus. Obviously, the best way to see the *Haverford* was to take a deep sea voyage to Gloucester.

And so it was. When the *Peerless* pulled away from her slip the first thing we saw was the reception boat *City of Camden*, with the Mayor's committee aboard, backing upstream in a flutter of flags. And then we came right abreast of the big liner, which had just come opposite her pier. She stood very high in the water, and seems none the worse for the five months' ducking she is said to have had. Her upper decks were brown with men, all facing away from us, however, to acknowledge the roar of cheering from the piers. So they did not hear the feeble piping set up by the few intrepid travelers to Gloucester. A spinster next to me cried out entranced: "Oh, I would like to take each of those boys and hug them."

A ship is always a noble sight, and while the *Haverford* was never built for beauty, she has the serene dignity of one who has gone about many hard tasks in her own uncomplaining fashion. She has a large and solid stateliness. Hurricanes cannot hustle her, nor have all the hosts of Tirpitz marred her sturdy comelihood. Her funnel is too outrageously tall and lean, her bows too bluff, her beam too broad for her to take on any of the queenly grace of her slim and swagger sisters. She is a square-toed, useful kind of creature; just the sort of vessel the staid Delaware loves, with no swank or swagger. And yet, in the clear yellow light of the winter morning, she seemed to have a new and very lovely beauty. Her masts were dressed with flags, from the bright ripple of the Stars and Stripes at the fore to the deep scarlet of her own Red Ensign over the taffrail. Half a dozen tugs churned and kicked beside her as she swung slowly to the dock. Over the water came a continuous roar of cheering as the waiting thousands tried to say what was in their hearts. In the crude language of the Board of Health, her passengers had not been "disinfected" and we were not to be allowed "contact" with them; but they had traveled far and dared much; they had gone out hoping no gain; they had come back asking no glory. From the low deck of the *Peerless* we could see them waving their brown caps against the bright blue nothingness of the skyline. They were home again, and we were glad.

# THE ENCHANTED
# VILLAGE

IT WAS A warm morning. Everybody knew it was going to be hot later on and was bustling to get work well under way before the blaze of noon. The broad vista of Market street was dimmed by the summer haze that is part atmospheric and part gasoline vapor. And as I strolled up Sixth street I kept to the eastern side, which was still in pleasant shadow.

Sixth street has a charming versatility. Its main concern in the blocks north of Market street seems to be machinery and hardware—cutlery and die stamping and tools. But it amuses itself with other matters—printing and bookbinding, oysters and an occasional smack of beer. Like most of our downtown streets, it is well irrigated. It is a jolly street for a hot day, calling out many an ejaculation of the eye. For instance, I cannot resist the office window of a German newspaper. The samples of job printing displayed are so delightful a medley of the relaxations which make the world safe for democracy. Dance Program of the Beer Drivers' Union, Annual Ball of the Bellboys of Philadelphia, Russian Tea Party, First Annual Picnic of the Young People's Socialist League, Banquet of the Journeymen Barbers' Union— who would not have found honest mirth (and plenty of malt and hot dogs) at these entertainments! Just so we can imagine Messrs. Lenine and Trotzky girding their seidels for a long midsummer day's junket with the Moscow Soviet. There also are the faded announcement cards for some address by Mme. Rosika Schwimmer (of Budapest), secretary of the International Woman Suffrage Alliance. Dear me, what has happened to the indefatigable Rosika since she and Henry Ford and others went bounding and bickering on a famous voyage to Stockholm? As some steamship

153

company used to advertise, "In all the world, no trip like this."

At Race street I turned east to St. John's Lutheran Church. The church stands between Fifth and Sixth. In front of it, in a little semi-circle of sun-bleached grass, stands the family vault of Bohl Bohlen. In this vault lie Brigadier General W. Henry C. Bohlen, killed in action at Freeman's Ford on the Rappahannock River, August 22, 1862, and his wife, Sophie. It is interesting to remember that they were the grandparents of the present Herr Krupp.

The little burying ground behind St. John's is one of the most fascinating spots in Philadelphia. I found George Hahn, the good-natured sexton, cutting the grass, and he took me round to look at many of the old tombstones, now mostly unreadable. Several Revolutionary veterans came to their resting in that little acre, among them Philip Summer, who died in 1814, and who is memorable to me because his wife was called Solemn. Solemn Summer—her name is carved on the stone. If I were an artist I should love to picture the quaint huddle of tawny red brick overlooking St. John's churchyard, the vistas of narrow little streets, the corners and angles of old houses. The sunny walls of the burying ground are a favorite basking place for cats of all hues—yellow, black and gray. I envy George Hahn his quiet hours of work in that silent inclosure, but he assured me that the grass is rank and grows with dreadful speed. The somewhat desolate and forgotten air of the graveyard, with its broken stones and splintered trees, adds greatly to the wistfulness of its charm.

Behind the churchyard is a kind of enchanted village. Summer street bounds the cemetery, and from this branch off picturesque little lanes—Randolph street, for instance, with its row of trim little red houses, the white and green shutters, the narrow cobbled footway. It was ironing day and, taking a furtive peep through basement doors, I could see the regular sweep of busy sad-irons on white boards.

Children abound, and I felt greatly complimented when one infant called out *Da-Da,* as I passed. Parallel with Randolph street run Fairhill and Reese—tiny little byways, but a kind of miniature picture of the older Philadelphia. Snowy clothes were fluttering from the lines and pumps gushing a silver stream into washtubs. Strong white arms were sluicing and lathering the clothes, sousing them in the bluing-tinted water. Everywhere children were playing merrily in the overflow. And there were window-boxes with bright flowers.

At the corner of Reese and Summer streets is a little statuary workshop—a cool dim place, full of white figures and an elderly man doing something mysterious with molds. I would have liked to hear all about his work, but as he was not very questionable I felt too bashful to insist.

If I were a sketcher I would plant my easel at the corner of Summer and Randolph streets and spend a long day puffing tobacco and trying to pencil the quaint domestic charm of that vista. The children would crowd round to watch and comment and little by little I would learn—the drawing would be only a pretext for learning—something of their daily mirth and tears. I would hear of their adventurous forays into the broad green space of Franklin Square, only a few yards away. Of scrambles over the wall into St. John's churchyard when George Hahn isn't looking. Of the sweets that may be bought for a penny at the little store on the corner. I should say that store sells more soap than anything else. Randolph street simply glistens with cleanliness—all except the upper end, where the city is too lazy to see that the garbage is carried away. But then a big city is so much more concerned with parades on Broad street than removing garbage from the hidden corners where little urchins play.

Round the corner on Fifth street is the quaint cul de sac of Central place, which backs up against Reese street, but does not run through. It is a quiet little brick yard, with three green pumps (also plopping into washtubs) and damp garments fluttering out on squeaky pulley lines from the upper windows. The wall at the back of the court is topped with flowers and morning-glory vines. On one of the marble stoops a woman was peeling potatoes and across the yard a girl with a little dress was washing clothes. It seemed to me like a scene out of one of Barrie's stories.

Who is the poet or the artist of this little village of ruddy brick behind St. John's graveyard? Who will tell me how the rain lashes down those narrow passages during a summer storm, when the children come scampering home from Franklin Square? Who will tell me of the hot noons when the hokey-pokey man tolls his bright bell at the end of the street and mothers search their purses for spare pennies? Or when the dripping ice wagon rumbles up the cobbles with its vast store of great crystal and green blocks of chill and perhaps a few generous splinters for small mouths to suck? I suppose poets may have sung the songs of those back streets. If they haven't they are very foolish. The songs are there.

# TRAILING
# MRS. TROLLOPE

THE MOUNTAINEER has lent us a copy of *Domestic Manners of the Americans*, in which Mrs. Trollope, the mother of Anthony, recorded her numerous chagrins during a three-year tour among the barbarians in 1827–30.

She visited Philadelphia in the summer of 1830, and remarks as follows upon some scenes familiar to us:

> "The State House has nothing externally to recommend it . . . there is a very pretty inclosure before the Walnut street entrance, with good, well-kept gravel walks. . . . Near this inclosure is another of much the same description, called Washington Square. Here there was an excellent crop of clover; but as the trees are numerous, and highly beautiful, and several commodious seats are placed beneath their shade, it is, in spite of the long grass, a very agreeable retreat from heat and dust. It was rarely, however, that I saw any of these seats occupied; the Americans have either no leisure or no inclination for those moments of *délassement* that all other people, I believe, indulge in. Even their drams, so universally taken by rich and poor, are swallowed standing, and, excepting at church, they never have the air of leisure or repose. This pretty Washington Square is surrounded by houses on three sides, but (lasso!) has a prison on the fourth; it is, nevertheless, the nearest approach to a London square that is to be found in Philadelphia."

Even after nearly ninety years there is a certain pang in learning that while Madam Trollope found nothing comely about the exterior of Independence Hall, she proclaimed New York's City Hall as "noble."

Trying to imagine that we were Mrs. Trollope, we took a stroll up Ninth street in the bright April sun. It was chilly and the burly sandwich-man of Market street, the long-haired, hatless philosopher so well known by sight, was leaning shivering in his shirt-sleeves against an arc light standard trying to wrap his advertising boards around him like an overcoat. "Why don't you walk up and down a bit?" we asked him, after he had rebuked the thermometer with a robust adjective which would have caused Mrs. Trollope to call for hartshorn and ammonia.

"Can't do it," he said. "I've got a bum job today. Got to stand on this corner, advertising a new drug store; 7:30 to 12:30 and 1:30 to 5:30. It's a long day, I'll say so."

Ninth street above Market is a delightful and varied world in itself. At the corner of Filbert we found the following chalked on a modest blackboard:

Irish Stew
Pot Roast
2 Vegatables
15c

Within, a number of citizens were taking those standing drams Mrs. Trollope deprecated. We were reminded by these social phenomena that we had not lunched. In a neighboring beanery we dealt with a delightful rhubarb pie, admiring the perfection of the waitress's demeanor. Neither too condescending nor too friendly, she laid the units of our repast upon the marble table with a firm clank which seemed to imply that our eating there meant nothing to her; yet she hoped we might find nourishment enough not to die on her hands.

The assorted attractions of North Ninth street never fail the affectionate stroller. Novelty shops where mysterious electric buzzers vibrate and rattle on the plate-glass panes, and safety razors reach bottomless prices that would tempt even a Russian statesman to unbush. Picture shops, where such really delightful sentimental engravings as "The End of the Skein" cause soft-hearted bystanders to fly home and write to dear old grandmother; wine shops where electric bulbs shimmer all day long within pyramids of gin bottles. "Stock Up Before July First!" cries the vintner. "There's a Bad Time Coming!" And he adds:

> We know a man who sells a
> quart of water with a little
> cheap whiskey in it
> VERY CHEAP
> Morale!
> If you really want a highball
> buy our, etc.

The animal shops always attract the passers-by. One window was crowded with new-hatched chicks, tender yellow balls of fluff that cause grizzled bums to moralize droopingly on the sweetness of youth and innocence. They (the chicks) were swarming around their feeding pans like diplomats at the Hotel Crillon in Paris.

These feeding pans are made like circular mousetraps, with small holes just large enough for the chicks to thrust in their heads. One ambitious infant, however, a very Trotzky among chicks, had got quite inside the pan, and three purple-nosed Falstaffs on the pavement were waiting with painful agitation to see whether he would emerge safely. In a goldfish bowl above, spotted newts were swimming, advertised at fifteen cents each as desirable "scavengas." Baby turtles the size of a dollar piece were crawling over one another in a damp tray. Bright-eyed rabbits twitched their small noses along the pane.

Then came Louis Guanissno, the famous balloon man, moving along in a blaze of color, his red and blue and yellow balloons tugging and gleaming in the sunny air. Louis is a poem to watch, a polychrome joy to behold. And such graceful suavity! "Here's health and prosperity, and

God bless you," he says, his kindly rugged face looking down at you; "and when you want any little balloons"—

On a sunny afternoon there are sure to be many browsers picking over the dusty volumes in the pavement boxes of that little bookshop near the old archway above Filbert street. Down the dark alley that runs under the archway horses stand munching their nosebags, while a big yellow coal wagon, lost in the cul-de-sac, tries desperately to turn around. The three big horses clatter and crash on the narrow paving. A first edition of *Rudder Grange* for fifteen cents wasn't a bad find. (I saw it listed in a recent bookseller's catalogue for $2.50.) By prying up a flyleaf that had been pasted down I learned that "Uncle George" had given it to Helen L. Coates for "Xmas, 1880."

Up at the Arch street corner is the famous Dumont's Minstrels, once the old Dime Museum, where Frank Dumont's picture stands in the lobby draped in black. Inside, in the quaint old auditorium, the interlocutor sits on his throne and tosses the traditional jest back and forth with the end men, Bennie Franklin and Alf Gibson, clad in their glaring scarlet frock-coats. The old quips about Camden are still doing brave service. Then Eddie Cassady comes on in his cream-colored duds and sings a ditty about Ireland and freedom while he waves the banner with the harp. Beneath the japes on prohibition there is an undertone of profound sadness. Joe Hamilton sings a song which professes to explain that July 1st will be harder on the ladies than any one else. "Good-by, Wild Women, Good-by," it is demurely called. Joe Horitz gets "Come Back to the Farm" over the footlights, a plaintive tenor appeal, in which the church steeple chimes 3 (a. m.) and all the audience can hear the cows lowing out in Manayunk and Marcus Hook. We are all nigh to tears for the little sister gone astray in the bad mad city; but here come Burke and Walsh in a merry little duo about whistle-wetting. "We took this country from the Indians," sings Burke. "We'll give it back after the 1st of July," replies Walsh in his dulcet barytone. Then, to show they really don't care so much, they wind up with a jovial bit of dancing.

Dumont's famous "timely burlesques" still keep pace with the humors of the town. The "Drug Store Telephone Fight" reduces the audience to cheery hysteria. Joe Hamilton or some body gets Saint Peter on the wire; the rival demonstrator gets connected with "the other place." The problem is whether the Jazzbo Phone Company or its rival can locate the whereabouts of Mr. William Goat, who (it appears) is the father of the interlocutor, the dignified interlocutor in his purple dress suit, who is writhing in embarrassed distress on his throne. And then, as we are already trespassing on the preserve of the dramatic editor, comes what the program calls "intermission of several minutes, to enable the ladies to powder their noses."

# RIDGE AVENUE

ONE OF THE odd things about human beings is that wherever they happen to live they accept it as a matter of course. In various foreign cities I have often been amused (as every traveller has) to see people going about their affairs just as though it were natural and unquestionable for them to be there. It is just the same at home. Everyone I see on the streets seems to be not at all amazed at living here instead of (let us say) Indianapolis or Nashville. I envy my small Urchin his sense of the extreme improbability of everything. When he gets on a trolley car he draws a long breath and looks around in ecstasy at the human scenery. I am teaching him to say in a loud, clear tone, as he gets on the car, "Look at all the human beings!" in the same accent of amazement that he uses when he goes to the Zoo. Perhaps in this way he will preserve the happy faculty of being surprised.

It is an agreeable thing to keep the same sense of surprise in one's home town that one would have in a strange city. You will find much to startle you if you keep your eyes open. Yesterday, for instance, I was lucky enough to meet a gentleman who had stood only a few feet away from Lincoln when he made the Gettysburg Speech. Then I found that in a certain cafeteria which I frequent the price you pay for your lunch is always just one cent less than that punched on the check. The cashier explained that this always gives a pleasant surprise to the customers, and has proved such a good advertising dodge that the proprietor made it a habit. And I saw, in a clothing dealer's window on Ninth Street, some fuzzy caps for men, mottled purple and ochre, that proved that the adventurous spirit has not died in the breast of the male sex.

There is much to exercise the eye in a voyage along

162

Ridge Avenue. Approaching by way of Ninth Street, one sees in the window of a barber shop the new contract that the employing barbers have drawn up with their journeymen. This agreement shows a sound sense of human equities, proclaiming as it does that "the owner must not do no act to enjure the barber personal earnings." It suddenly occurred to me, what I had not thought of before, how the barbers of Great Britain must have grieved when a London newspaper got up (some years ago) an agitation in favour of every man in England raising a beard in memory of King Edward. The plan was that the money thus saved was to be devoted to building—I had almost said "growing"—a battleship, to be named after the Merry Monarch. Of course, one should not speak of raising a beard, but of lowering it. However——

Ridge Avenue begins at Ninth and Vine, in a mood of depression. Perhaps the fact that it runs out toward the city's greatest collection of cemeteries has made it morbidly conscious of human perishability. At any rate, it starts among pawnshops, old clothing and furniture, and bottles of Old Virginia Bitters, the Great Man Restorer. The famous National Theatre at Callowhill Street has become a garage: it is queer to see the old proscenium arch and gilded ceiling dustily vaulted over a fleet of motortrucks. After a wilderness of railway yards one comes to a curious bit in the 1100 block; a little brick tunnel that bends around into a huddle of backyards and small houses, where a large green parrot was stooping and nodding on a pile of old boxes. This little scene is overlooked by the tall brown spires of the Church of the Assumption on Spring Garden Street.

There is matter for tarrying at the Spring Garden Street crossing. Here is an ambitious fountain built by the bequest of Mary Rebecca Darby Smith, with the carving by J. J. Boyle picturing another Rebecca (she of Genesis XXIV, 14) giving a drink to Abraham's servant and his camels. It is carved in the bronze that the donor gave the fountain "To refresh the weary and thirsty, both man and beast," so it is disconcerting to find it dry, as dry as the inns along the way. The horse trough is boarded over and thirsting equines go up to Broad Street for a draught. The seat by the fountain was occupied by a man reading the New York *Journal*, always a depressing sight.

Across from the fountain is one of the best magazine and stationery shops in the city. Here I overheard a conversation which I reproduce textually. "What you doing, reading?" said one to another. "Yes, reading about the biggest four-flusher in the Yew-nited States," said he, looking over an afternoon paper which had just come in. "Who do you mean?" "Penrose. Say if it was a Republican in the White House, theyda passed the treaty long ago." The proprietor of this shop is a humorist. Someone came in asking for a certain brand of cigarettes. He does not sell tobacco. "Next door," he said, and added: "And you'll find some over on the fountain."

Ridge Avenue specializes in tobacco shops, where you will find many brands that require a strong head. Red Snapper, Panhandle Scrap, Pinch Hit, Red Horse, Brown's Mule, Jolly Tar, Penn Statue Cuttings, Nickel Cross Cut, Cotton Ball Twist. In the shop windows you will see the photographs illustrating current events, the two favourites just now being a picture of Mike Gilhooley, the famous stowaway, gazing plaintively at the profile of New York, and "Jack Dempsey Goes the Limit," where Jack signs up for a $1,000 war-savings certificate. One wonders if Jack's kind of warfare is really so profitable after all.

There are a number of little side excursions from the avenue that repay scrutiny. Lemon Street, for instance, where in a lane of old brown wooden houses some children were playing in an empty wagon, with the rounded tower of the Rodef Shalom synagogue looming in the background. Best of all is Melon Street and its modest tributary, Park

Avenue—stretches of quiet little brick homes with green and yellow shutters and mottled gray marble steps. These little houses have the serene and sunny air so typical of Philadelphia byways. Through their narrow side entrances one sees glimpses of green in backyards. In the front windows move the gently swaying faces of grandmothers, lulled in the to and fro of a rocking chair. There are shining brass knobs and bell-pulls; rubber plants on the sills, or perhaps a small bowl of goldfish with a white china swan floating. In one window was a sign "Vacancies." Over it hung a faded service flag with a golden star. Who could phrase the pathos of these two things, side by side?

At Broad Street, Ridge Avenue leaps up with a spurt of high life. In the window of a hotel dining room a gentleman sat eating his lunch, stevedoring a buttered roll with such gusto that one felt tempted to applaud. There are the white pillars of a bank and the battleship gray of the Salvation Army headquarters. Beyond Broad, the avenue spruces up a bit and enters upon a vivacious phase. Dogs are frequent: white bull terriers lie sunning in the shop windows. Offers to lend money are enticing. There is a fascinating slate yard at 1525, where great gray slabs lie in the sun, a temptation to urchins with a bit of chalk. In the warm bask of the afternoon there rises a pleasing aroma of fruits and vegetables piled up in baskets and crates on the pavement. Grapes give off a delectable savour in the golden air. Elderly ladies are out in force to do the marketing, and their eyes are bright with the bargaining passion. Round the windows of a ten-cent store, most fascinating of all human spectacles, they congregate and compare notes. A fruit dealer has an ingenious stunt to attract attention. On his cash register lies a weird-looking rotund little fish—a butter fish, he calls it— which has a face not unlike that of Fatty Arbuckle. Either this fish inflates itself or he has blown it full of air in some ingenious manner, for it presents a grotesque appearance, and many ladies stop to inquire. Then he spoofs them gently. "Sure," he says, "it's a jitney fish. It lives on the cash register. It can fly, it can bite, it can talk, and it likes money."

At the corner of Wylie Street stands an old gray house with a mansard roof and gable windows. Against it is a vivid store of fruit glowing in the sun, red and purple and yellow. Here, or on Vineyard Street, one turns off to enter the quaint triangular settlement of Francisville.

# WILDEY STREET

I SET OUT for a stroll with the Mountaineer, who knows more about Philadelphia than any one I ever heard of. He is long and lean and has a flashing eye; his swinging easy stride betrays the blood of southern highlands. He tracks down distant streets and leafy glimpses with all the grim passion of a Kentucky scout on the trail of a lynx or some other varmint. No old house, no picturesque corner or elbow alley escapes his penetrant gaze. He has secret trails and caches scattered through the great forests of Philadelphia, known to none but himself. With such a woodsman for guide good hunting was a matter of course.

The first game we bagged was a tattooing studio at 814 Summer street. Let no one say that war means a decline of the fine arts, for to judge by the photographs in the window there are many who pine to have the Stars and Stripes, the American eagle and the shield of the food administration frescoed on their broad chests. Professor Al E. Walters, the craftsman, proclaims himself artistic and reliable in this form of embroidery and the sitter has "1500 up-to-date designs to choose from." The Mountaineer and I peered through the window and were interested to see the professor's array of tools laid out on his operating table.

Passing by an imposing bust of Homer, which we found in front of a junk shop at 528 Noble street, the Mountaineer led me to see the old Hoboes' Union headquarters at Fifth and Buttonwood streets. The war may have given tattooing a fillip, but it seems that it has been the decline and fall of philosophic hoboism, for the vagrants' clubhouse is dusty and void, now used as some sort of a warehouse. Work or fight and high wages have done for romantic loafing. The Mountaineer pointed out to me the kitchen in which the boes held their evening symposia over a kettle of hot stew.

The house was donated through the munificence of J. Eads Howe, the famous millionaire hobo, and the Mountaineer admitted that he had spent many an entertaining evening there discussing matters of intellectual importance. "How did you get the entree to such an exclusive circle?" I asked enviously. "I was a member of the union," he said, with just the least touch of vainglory.

The Mountaineer led me north on Fourth street to where Wildey street begins its zigzag career. We found that the strip between Germantown avenue and Front street was buzzing with preparations for a "block party" in honor and benefit of its boys in service. All down the gay little vista flags were hanging out, Chinese lanterns had been strung on wires across the street, shop windows were criss-crossed with red, white and blue streamers and booths were going up on the pavement swathed in tricolored tissue paper. At one end of the block the curbstones had been whitewashed. We stopped to ask an elderly lady when the fun would begin.

"Tonight and tomorrow night," she said. (It was then Friday afternoon.) "Our boys are fighting for us and we want to do everything we can to help. I was at my summer residence when I heard about this party, and I came back at once. We've got to help as best we can."

The sky was clouding over and the Mountaineer and I expressed the hope that rain wouldn't spoil the festivity.

"Oh, I hope not," she said. "It doesn't seem as though the Lord would send rain when we're working for a good cause. We've hired a string band for the two nights—that's $60—and we're going to have dancing in the street. You'd better come around. It's going to be a great time."

Everybody in the street was busy with preparations for the jollification, and I was deeply touched by this little community's expression of gratitude and confidence in its boys who are fighting. That is the real "stuff of triumph" of which the President spoke. And one has only to pass along Wildey street to see that it is fine old native stock. It is an all-American street, of pure native breed, holding out stiffly and cleanly against the invasion of foreign population. The narrow side alleys look back into patches of vivid green; there are flower boxes and vines, and the pavements and marble steps are scrubbed as clean as water and soap will make them. A little further along we found a tavern dispensing Wildey street's favorite drink—pop and porter— and we halted to drink health to the block party.

Beyond Shackamaxon street we struck into the unique silence and quiet cleanliness of "Fishtown." The quietness of those streets of quaint little houses is remarkable: in the golden flood of a warm afternoon they lay with hardly an echo to break the stillness. The prevailing color scheme is green and red: many of the houses are neat cottages built of wood; others are the old parti-colored brick that comes down from ancient days. Almost every house has its little garden, often outlined with whitened shells. It seems like a New England fishing village in the heart of the city. An occasional huckster's wagon rumbles smoothly along the asphalt paving; an occasional tinkle of a piano in some cool, darkened parlor. That is all. I can imagine no haunt of ancient peace more drowsy with stillness and the treble chirp of birds than the tangled and overgrown cemetery at Thompson street and Columbia avenue, in the hush of a hot summer siesta.

There is a note of grace and comeliness in Wildey street life that one attributes to the good native stock of the inhabitants. The children are clean and rounded and goodly. The little girls have plump calves and crisp gingham dresses and blue eyes; they sit in their little gardens playing with paper dolls. Their brothers, with the mischief and errant humor that one expects of small boys, garnish walls and hoardings with whimsical legends scrawled in chalk. *The old family toothbrush that laid on the floor* was one such that amused me. Another was a regrettable allegation that

169

a (presumably absent) playmate was afflicted with "maines." The Mountaineer and I, after studying the context, came to the conclusion that the scourge hinted at was "mange!"

Most thrilling of all, Wildey street becomes more and more maritime. Over the roofs of the houses one sees the masts of ships—always a sight to make the eager heart leap up. Cramps' shipyard is at hand, and many of the front windows display the starred service cards of the United States Shipping Board. On Richmond street, parallel to Wildey, are ship chandlers' stores, with windows full of brass pulleys and chocks and cleats, coils of rope and port and starboard lanterns. We hurried down toward the waterfront and peeped through the high board fence to see a steamer in drydock for a coat of camouflage. Great stripes of black and blue and white were being laid along her hull.

Penn Treaty Park, at the foot of Columbia avenue, would deserve an essay of its own. Here, under a pavilion, the Mountaineer and I sat surrounded by the intoxicating presence of water and boats, watched the police patrol launches being overhauled, watched a little schooner loading lumber (I couldn't read her name, but she came from Hampton, Va.), watched the profile of Camden shining dimly through the rain. For a very smart rainstorm had come up and we sat and felt a pang of sympathy for the good people of Wildey street, whose Chinese lanterns and tricolored tissue paper would be ruined by the wet. We watched the crew of the tug *Baltic* getting ready for supper and dinghies nosing the piers and bobbling with the rise and fall of the water, and we saw how the gleam of rain and mist on the roofs of Camden looked exactly like a fall of snow. Fishtown uses Penn Treaty Park as a place for lounging and smoking under the peeling sycamores and watching the panorama of the river.

P. S.: I thought a great deal about the block party on Wildey street that night and hoped that the rain would not have spoilt it. So the next morning I got off the 8:13 at Columbia avenue and walked down past that deep violin note of the Columbia avenue sawmills to see how things were going. I found the same old lady on the sidewalk, hopefully renewing her red, white and blue tissue, and I noticed that all the children were wearing fantastic patriotic caps made of shirred and fluted paper. "Well," I said, "how did things go?" "Oh," she replied, "the rain hurt things a bit, but tonight's going to be the big night. It's going to be a great time: you'd better come around."

The stuff of triumph!

# PENN TREATY PARK

DOWN BY THE wharf in old Penn Treaty Park
The trees are all a canopy of green—
The staunch policeboat *Stokley*, ancient craft,
Is purring with a gentle push of steam
That whispers in her valves. Along the pier
The water clucks and sags. Two river cops
Sit smoking pipes outside their small caboose,
Above them looms a tragic rusty bow,
The *Roald Amundsen*, Norwegian tanker,
She that caught fire last winter at Point Breeze
While loading oil. The river cops will tell you
How all the Schuylkill was a hell of flame
And ten men lost their lives. The good old *Stokley*
Dredged the river afterward for bodies.

At sunset time in old Penn Treaty Park
The children sprawl and play: the tawny light
Pours through the leafy chinks in sifted gold
And turns the middle-stream to level fire.
Then, after that red sunset comes the dusk,
The little park is steeped in living shadow,
And Cupid pairs the benches by the pier.
But there's one girl who always sits alone.
Coming at dark, she passes by the shaft
That marks the treaty ground of William Penn.
Too dusk for reading, yet how well she knows
The words carved in the stone: *Unbroken Faith*.

Mary, of Wildey street, had met Alf Larsen
Up at a picture show on East Girard.
Her father was a hard one: he said fiercely
No girl of his should run around with sailors,

No girl of his should play with bolsheviks.
Alf was Norwegian, and a decent fellow,
A big blond youngster with a quiet eye;
He loved the girl, but old man Morton swore
All Scandinavians were the same as Russians,
And every Russian was a bolshevik.

Mary was stubborn; all her blood was willful;
At twilight, by the old Penn Treaty stone,
She used to wait for Alf, or he for her.
And in some whim of Celtic flame and fancy
The carven words became her heart's own motto,
And there they pledged their love: *Unbroken Faith*.

Oh, golden evening there along the river!
    When all the tiny park was Eden land—
Oh, eager hearts that burn and leap and shiver,
    Oh, hand that mates with hand!
And they would cross the Shackamaxon ferry,
    Or walk by Cramps' to see the dry-docked ships
Or in a darkened movie house make merry
    With sudden lips on lips—

And half their talk was tremulous with yearning,
    And half was of their future, shrewdly planned—
How Alf would leave the sea, and soon be earning
    Not less than thirty in a job on land;
Between their kisses they would talk of saving,
    Between their calculations, kiss anew,
And she would say that he must be behaving
    While she described a little house for two.

With Alf at sea, the girl would still go down
To see the very bench where they had sat,
The tidy *Stokley* moored beside the pier,
The friendly vista of the Camden shore,

The stone where they had locked their hearts in one.
So time went by. The armistice came on,
And Mary radiant, for her lad no more
Would run the gauntlet of the submarines,
And he had heard a chance to get a job
As watchman up at Cramps'. Just one more voyage
He planned; then he would quit and they'd begin.
So, late one night, in the familiar park
They said good-by. It was their last good-by,
As Mary said: his ship was due to sail
Day after next, and he would have no chance
To come again. She turned beside the stone
To fix in view that place of happy tryst,
The quiet leafless park with powdered frost,
The lamps of the policeboat, red and green.

The *Roald Amundsen* was Larsen's ship.
She lay at the refinery, Point Breeze,
Taking on oil for Liverpool. The day
She was to sail, somehow she caught on fire.
A petaled rose of hell, she roared in flame—
The burning liquid overflowed her decks,
The dock and oil-scummed river blazing, too.
Her men had little chance. They leaped for life
Into the river, but the paraffin
Blazing along the surface, hemmed them in.
They either burned or drowned, and Alf was one.

The irony of fate has little heed
For tenderness of hearts. The blistered hulk,
Burnt, sunk and raised, with twisted, blackened plates,
A gaunt and gutted horror, seared and charred,
Was towed upstream, and, to be sold for junk,
Was moored beside the *Stokley*. Where her bow,
All scarred and singed with flame and red with rust,
Must almost overhang the very bench

Of love and happy dreams, the *Roald* lay.
And Mary, coming down to that old haunt
Where all her bliss and heartbreak were most near,
Found the dead ship, approached, and read the name.

Well, such a tale one cannot tell in full;
Heart's inmost anguish is the heart's alone.
But night by night the girl is sitting there,
Watching the profile of that ship of death,
Watching the *Stokley*, and the kindly men
Who fought the fire and grappled in the ooze
And did not find the thing she hoped and feared.
And still her only consolation lies
In those two words cut on the trysting stone,
*Unbroken Faith*. Her faith unbroken still
She sits in shadow near their meeting place:
She will not fail him, should he ever come.
She watches all the children at their play,
And does not fear to dream what might have been,
And half believes, beneath the summer roof,
To see, across the narrow strip of park,
His ruddy face, blond head and quiet eyes.
Yet not until the kindly dusk has come
And fills the little park with blue that heals
Does she go down. She cannot bear to see
The sunset sheet the river o'er with flame.

# CATTERINA OF SPRING
# GARDEN STREET

SPRING GARDEN STREET is a pleasant thoroughfare for wandering on a cool summer morning about eight-thirty of the clock. It has been my diversion, lately, to get off the Reading train at the Spring Garden Station and walk to the office from there instead of pursuing the too familiar route from the Terminal. Try it some day, you victims of habit. To start the day by a little variation of routine is an excellent excitement for the mind.

That after-breakfast period, before the heat begins, has a freshness and easy vigor of its own. Housewives are out scrubbing the white marble steps; second-hand furniture dealers have spread their pieces on the pavement for better inspection and sit in their morris chairs by the curb to read the morning paper. Presumably the more ease and comfort they show the more plainly the desirability of a second-hand morris chair will be impressed on the passer-by; such is the psychology of their apparent indolence. A fire engine with maroon chassis and bright silver boiler rumbles comfortably back to its station after putting out a fire somewhere. The barbers are out winding up the clock-work that keeps their red and white striped emblems revolving. And here and there on the pavement, reclining with rich relish where the sunlight falls in white patches, are gray and yellow cats.

The cats of Spring Garden street are plump and of high cheer and they remind me of the most famous cat that ever lived in that neighborhood. She was a big tortoise-shell puss called Catterina (Kate for short) and she lived in a little three-story brick cottage on Brandywine Street, which is just off Seventh street behind the garage that now stands on the northwest corner of Seventh and Spring Garden.

176

Catterina played a distinguished, even a noble, part in American literature. I am the gladder to celebrate her because I do not believe any one has ever paid her a tribute before. You see, she happened to be the particular pet and playmate of Mr. and Mrs. Edgar Allan Poe.

It is curious that Philadelphia pays so little honor to that house on Brandywine street, which is associated with the brief and poignant domestic happiness of that brilliant and tragic genius. Poe lived in Philadelphia from 1838 until 1844, and during the last two or three years of his stay he occupied the little brick house on Brandywine street. One of those who visited it then described it as "a small house, in one of the pleasant and silent neighborhoods far from the center of the town, and though slightly and cheaply furnished everything in it was so tasteful and so fitly disposed that it seemed altogether suitable for a man of genius." What is now only a rather dingy back yard was then a little garden full of roses, grapevine and creepers. Perhaps the pear tree that is still the most conspicuous feature of the yard was growing in Poe's tenancy. It was a double tree, with twin trunks, one of which was shattered by lightning quite recently.

Mrs. William Owens, who has lived in the house for eight years, was kind enough to take me through and showed me everything from attic to cellar. The house is built against a larger four-story dwelling which fronts on Seventh street, now numbered as 530. In Poe's day the two houses were separate, the larger one being the property of a well-to-do Friend who was his landlord. Since then doors have been pierced and the whole is used as one dwelling, in which Mrs. Owens takes several boarders. It would interest Poe perhaps (as he was once in the army) to know that a service flag with three stars hangs from the front of the house. The stars represent John Pierce, Harry Bernhardt and Dominic Dimonico, the first of these being, as I understand, a foster son of Mr. and Mrs. Owens.

177

It is not hard to imagine the charm of this snug little house as it may have been in the days when Poe (in his early thirties) and his sylphlike young wife and heroic mother-in-law, Mrs. Clemm, faced the problem of living on the irregular earnings of editing and writing. Spring Garden was then near the northern outskirts of the city: the region was one of sober ruddy brick (of that rich hue dear to Philadelphia hearts) and well treed and gardened. Until very recent years an old lady was living, a neighbor of Mrs. Owens, who remembered how Virginia Poe used to sit at the window and play her harp.

The house is well and solidly built; the door opening toward Brandywine street still has its original old-fashioned bolt lock, which Poe's hand must have fastened many and many a time. The little dining room has a fireplace, now filled in with a stove. In one of the rooms upstairs (according to local tradition) "The Raven" was written; and there are two bedrooms with casement windows in the attic. Some of Poe's finest work was done in this house, among other tales probably "The Murders in the Rue Morgue," "The Gold Bug" and "The Black Cat." And here a curious coincidence may be noted. It will be remembered that in the story of "The Black Cat" Poe describes how some very unpleasant digging was done in a cellar. In cleaning the cellar of the Brandywine street house Mrs. Owens discovered recently a place where the bricks in the flooring had been removed and a section of planking had been put in. Is it possible that this circumstance suggested to Poe the grisly theme of his story? Just for fun I would very much like to explore under those boards. They are old and have evidently been there a long time.

Imagination likes to conjure up the little household: the invalid Virginia Poe (it was in this house that she broke a blood vessel while singing), the stout-hearted and all-sacri-ficing mother-in-law—"Muddy," as the poet affectionately called her—the roses that grew over the wall, and (let us

178

not forget her) Catterina, the cherished pet. Catterina was very much a member of the family. In April, 1844, when Poe and his wife moved to a boarding house in New York, where they found the table amazingly cheap and plentiful, he wrote to Mrs. Clemm:

"The house is old and looks buggy. The cheapest board I ever knew. I wish Kate could see it—she would faint. Last night, for supper, we had the nicest tea you ever drank, strong and hot—wheat bread and rye bread—cheese—tea cakes (elegant), a great dish (two dishes) of elegant ham and two of cold veal, piled up like a mountain—three dishes of the cakes and everything in the greatest profusion. No fear of starving here."

Poor Catterina (or Kate, as they sometimes called her)! Does not this suggestion of her swooning imply that she may have had to go on rather short commons in the little home on Brandywine street? But after all, there must have been mice in the cellar, unless the ghost of the Black Cat frightened them away.

In the same letter, written from New York the day after the Poes had gone there to look for better fortune, he says "Sissy [his wife] had a hearty cry last night because you and Catterina weren't here."

But it was in the winter of 1846–47, when Mrs. Poe lay dying of consumption in the cottage at Fordham, that Catterina came to her highest glory. The description of that scene touches upon a human nerve of pity and compassion that must give the most callous a pang. Poe himself, harassed by poverty, pride and illness, had to witness the sufferings of his failing wife without ability to ease them. This is the description of a kind-hearted woman who saw them then:

"There was no clothing on the bed but a snow-white counterpane and sheets. The weather was cold and the sick lady had the dreadful chills that accompany the hectic fever of consumption. She lay on the straw bed, wrapped in her

179

husband's great-coat, with a large tortoise-shell cat in her bosom. The wonderful cat seemed conscious of her great usefulness. The coat and the cat were the sufferer's only means of warmth."

Perhaps Philadelphia will some day do fitting honor to the memory of that ill-starred household that knew its best happiness in the little house on Brandywine street. Mr. Owens, who is a druggist, has whimsically set up in the front parlor one of the big scarlet papier-mâché ravens that are used to advertise Red Raven Splits. But it seems to me that Philadelphia might go just a little further than that in honoring the house where "The Raven" may have been written.

# THE INDIAN POLE

E VERY STREET has a soul of its own. Somewhere in its course it will betray its secret ideals and preferences. I like to imagine that the soul of Callowhill street has something to do with beer. Like a battered citizen who has fallen upon doleful days, Callowhill street solaces itself with the amber.

Between Tenth and Fourth streets Callowhill numbers at least a dozen pubs, not to enumerate a score of "cider saloons." A soft breath of hope seems to haunt the air, and the trucks unloading kegs into cellars give promise of quenchers to come. Generally one may meet along those pavements certain rusty brothers who have obviously submitted themselves to the tramplings of the brewer's great horses, as Homer Rodeheaver's anthem puts it.

Callowhill street, like so much of Philadelphia's old and gentle beauty, is in a downward pang, at any rate so far as the picturesque is concerned. It is curious to see those comely old dwellings, with their fluted dormer windows, their marble facings and dusty fanlights, standing in faded dignity and wistfulness among factories, breweries and railroad spurs. Down their narrow side alleys one may catch a glimpse of greenery (generally the ailanthus, that slummish tree that haunts city back yards and seems to have such an affinity for red brick). If one has a taste for poking and exploring, he will find many a little court or cul-de-sac where hardly a stone or a window has changed for a hundred years. One does not need to travel abroad to find red walls with all the mellow stain that one associates with Tudor manors. There is an old wagon yard on the north side of Callowhill, near Fifth, where an artist might trance himself with the plain lines of old houses, the clear sunlight falling athwart the flattened archways and the decrepit vehicles with their weary wheels.

It is a perpetual delight to wander in such byways, speculating on the beauty of those rows of houses in days gone by. What a poetry there is in the names of our streets—Nectarine, Buttonwood, Appletree, Darien, Orianna! Even the pawnbrokers are romantics. There is a three-ball establishment on Ninth street where the uncle keeps a great rookery of pigeons in his back yard. They coo seductively to embarrassed wanderers. I can hardly keep my watch in my pocket when I hear their soft suggestions. What a city of sober dignity and clean comfort Philadelphia must have been in the forties—say when Mr. and Mrs. James Russell Lowell came to the northeast corner of Fourth and Arch on their honeymoon, in 1845. "My cheeks are grown so preposterously red," wrote Lowell, "that I look as if I had rubbed them against all the brick walls in the city."

As I turned off Callowhill street, at the oblique junction of York avenue, leaving behind the castellated turrets of a huge brewery, I came upon an interesting sight. Where Wood street cuts York avenue and Fourth street there stands a tall white flagpole, surmounted by an enormous weather-vane representing an Indian with bow and quiver, holding one arm outstretched. At its foot stands an iron drinking fountain of the S.P.C.A., dated 1868, and on the other side another water basin (now dry) with a white marble slab behind it. I thought that this might offer some inscription, but it is pasted over with a dodger commending "The coolest theatre in town." The Indian figure engaged my curiosity and I made for a nearby tobacconist to inquire. (I always find tobacconists genial people to supply information.) He referred me to Mr. William Renner, the maker of flags and awnings round the corner at 403 Vine street, and from Mr. Renner I learned many things of interest.

Startling pleasures accrue to the wanderer who starts upon his rambles in total ignorance of what he is going to find. Let me frankly confess that I know nothing of the history and topography of Philadelphia; I am learning it as I go. Therefore when I discover things they give me the vivid delight of a totally fresh experience. The Indian Pole, as it is called, may be an old story to many citizens; to me it was entirely new.

Mr. Renner, who has taken the landmark under his personal protection, tells me that the weathervane was erected many years ago to commemorate the last Indian "powwow" held in Philadelphia, and also that it is supposed to have been a starting place for the New York stage coaches. However that may be, at any rate the original pole was replaced or repaired in 1835, and at that time a sheet of lead (now kept by the Historical Society) was placed at the top of the pole bearing the names of those who had been instrumental in the restoration. The work was done at the expense of the "United States" Fire Engine Company, that being the day of the old volunteer fire departments.

Apparently the Indian Pole became a kind of rallying point for rival fire engine companies, and there was much jealous competition, when steam fire apparatus was introduced, to see which company should first project a stream of water over the top of the staff. This rivalry was often accompanied by serious brawls, for Mr. Renner tells me that when the Indian figure was repaired recently it was found to be riddled with bullet holes. This neighborhood has been the scene of some dangerous fighting, for St. Augustine's Church, which was destroyed in the riots of 1844, stands only a few yards away down Fourth street.

In 1894 the pole again became dangerous, not as a brawling point, but on account of age. It was removed by the city, but at the instance of Mr. Howard B. French, of Samuel H. French & Company, the paint manufacturers on Callowhill street, the Indian figure and the ball on which it revolved were kept and a new pole was erected by Mr. French and four other merchants of the neighborhood, T.

Morris Perot, Edward H. Ogden, John C. Croxton and William Renner (the father of the present Mr. Renner). That pole, which is still standing, is eighty-five feet from ground to truck. The Indian figure is nine and one-half feet high; it stretches nine feet from the rear end of the bow to the outstretched hand. The copper ball beneath it is sixteen inches in diameter. Mr. Renner says the figure is of wood, several inches thick, and sheathed in iron. He thinks that the hand alone would weigh 150 pounds. He thinks it quite remarkable that though many church steeples in the neighborhood have been struck by lightning the Indian has been unscathed. On holidays Mr. Renner runs up a large flag on the pole, twenty-one by thirty-six feet.

When I remarked that this was a pretty big flag I touched Mr. Renner in a tender spot. Probably there is no man who knows more about big flags than he, for he told me that in 1911 he had made in his workroom on Vine street a Stars and Stripes which is supposed to be the largest flag ever made. It measured 75 by 150 feet. It was flown in Chestnut Hill Park that summer and the next year was hung in a park in Bridgeport, Conn. It was hung on a wire cable between two masts, each 125 feet high and 780 feet apart. Mr. Renner was to have taken it to Panama to be exhibited there when the canal was opened, but unfortunately it was damaged in a fire in Bridgeport. What has become of it since he does not know. The flag was made of standard wool bunting and weighed half a ton. It was sold for $2500.

We are not thought to be very sentimental about our flag, but Mr. Renner tells me that a few years ago, when he was hoisting a very large flag at Chestnut Hill Park, he had an amusing experience which sounds more Parisian than Philadelphian. He had been sitting in a "bosun's chair" at the top of the staff while the flag was pulled up and his face was black with soot from the smoke of the nearby scenic railway. Descending from the pole he was leaning against a pavilion looking up at the flag, when an old lady who had been watching rushed up, threw her arms round his neck and embraced him. Mr. Renner still blushes modestly when he recalls the ordeal.

It is a pleasant thing for any community to have some relic or trophy of its own that fosters local pride. Those who live in the neighborhood of Fourth and Callowhill streets are proud of the Indian Pole, which the city once consigned to the dump heap, but which they rescued and have cherished as an interesting landmark. And there are other matters thereabout to invite imagination: The bright blue laboratory of a certain dandruff nostrum; inns named "The Tiger" and "The Sorrel Horse," and a very curious flatiron-shaped house that stands just behind the flagstaff.

I thought the Indian Pole was quite an adventure for one morning, but at Fifth and Arch I met another. Passing the grave of Ben and Deborah Franklin I noticed that it was being swept.

"Do you do that every day?" I asked the sexton.

"Every day," he said. "I like to keep it clean."

I think that Deborah, who was a good housewife, would be glad to know that her plain Quakerish tombstone is dusted every day. The good man who does it is Jacob Schweiger and he lives at 221 Noble street.

# MADONNAS OF THE CURB

A LITTLE GIRL—she can't have been more than twelve years old—stood up gravely and said: "The meeting will please come to order. The secretary will read the minutes of the last meeting."

The gathering of small females—some ragged, some very trim, ranging in age from eight to fourteen—sat expectant. A child in a clean pink dress with neatly braided blonde hair advanced seriously and read the minutes of the previous meeting.

"Are there any corrections?" said the president.

There were none and the meeting proceeded to business. On a long table in the schoolroom was a large laundry basket, a small quilted mattress, sheets, blankets and other accessories. There was a baby there, a life-size doll, amazingly realistic. The business of the meeting was the discussion, under the guidance of Miss Matilda Needle, the teacher, of the proper way of making a baby's bed, putting him to sleep in the basket and ventilating the room. It was the Little Mothers' League of the Vare School, on Morris street, holding its weekly meeting.

Miss Needle took the chair. "I saw something the other day," she said to the children, "that pleased me very much. I was coming down the street and I saw Elsie Pulaski holding a baby like this." (She illustrated by picking up the doll, letting its head sag, and all the Little Mothers looked very grave.) "I was about to speak to her when Bertha Fitz ran across the street and said to her: 'You mustn't hold the baby like that. You'll hurt him.' And Bertha showed her the right way to hold him. Now can any of you show me the way Bertha did it?"

Thirty small arms waved frantically in the air. There was

a furious eagerness to show how the luckless Elsie should have held her baby brother.

"Well, Mary," said the teacher, "you show us how the baby should be picked up."

Blushing with pride, Mary advanced to the table and with infinite care inserted one arm under the large doll. But in her excitement she made a false start. She used the right arm where the position of the artificial infant demanded the left. This meant that her other arm had to pass diagonally across the baby in an awkward way. Immediately several of the juvenile audience showed signs of professional disgust. Hands vibrated in air. Another member of the Little Mothers' League was called upon, and poor Mary took her seat in discomfiture.

They passed to another topic. One of the members demonstrated the correct way of making the baby's bed. With proud correctness she disposed the mattress, the rubber sheeting, the sheets and blankets, showing how each should be tucked in, how the upper sheet should be turned down over the top of the blanket, so that the wool would not irritate the baby's chin. The others watched her with the severity of judges on the bench.

The teacher began to ask questions.

"Who should the baby sleep with?" she said.

One very small girl, carried away by the form of the question, cried out, "His mother!" The others waved their hands.

"Well, who *should* he sleep with?" said Miss Needle.

"Himself!" cried several triumphantly.

"Why should he sleep by himself? Rose, you tell us."

Rosa stood up. She was a dark-eyed little creature, with hair cropped short—we will not ask why. Her face worked with the excitement of putting her thoughts into language.

"If he sleeps with his mother she might lay on him and smother him."

They all seemed to shudder. It was as though the unfortunate infant was perishing before their very eyes.

The Little Mothers' Leagues are groups of small girls, ranging in age from eight to fourteen, who are being taught the essentials of caring for babies, under the direction of the Child Federation. By the kindness of the Federation and Miss O'Neill, the supervisor of public school playgrounds, I was privileged to visit four of these classes the other afternoon. In three of the schools the children were learning how to put the baby to bed; in one they were sitting around a small bathtub studying the technique of the baby's bath. Some of the girls had brought babies with them, for almost all of them are at least partly responsible for the care of one or more children. There was a moving pathos in the gravity with which these matrons before their time discussed the problems of their craft; and yet it was also the finest kind of a game and they evidently enjoyed it heartily. Many of them come from ignorant homes where the parents know next to nothing of hygiene. Their teachers tell of the valiant efforts of these children to convert their mothers to more sanitary ways—efforts which are happily often successful. In one home, where the father was a tailor, the baby was kept in a room where the pressing was done, the air was hot and heavy with steam. The small daughter, who was a member of the Little Mothers' League, insisted on the baby being removed to another room. Two children in another school, who had been told of the importance of keeping the baby's milk on ice, tried to make home-made ice-boxes, which their fathers, becoming interested, promised to finish for them.

One wishes that all this might be only an enchanting game for these children, and that it would not be necessary for them to put it into practice every day, with tired little arms and aching backs. He must be stiff-hearted indeed who can watch these gatherings, their tousled little heads and bare legs, their passionate intentness, their professional enthusiasm, without something of a pang. They know so much of the problems, and they are so pathetically small. There is a touching truth in the comment of one teacher in her report: "The girls who had no babies at home seemed to take greater interest than those that did have." But this is not always so, for nothing could be more enthusiastic than the little essays written by the children themselves, describing what they have learnt. I cannot resist a few quotations:

> No one can be healthy unless she is extremely clean. Baby will want his bath daily, with soap and warmish water. You should not put to much soap on the baby's face as it get in the baby's eyes. They likes to kick the water as long as support his head. Before starting on this swimming expedition, you should have all, her or him clothes, warm, by you, and he expects a warm flannel on your knees to lie on. You must carefully dry all the creases in his fat body for him, with a soft towel. (Ruth Higgins, Fifth Grade.)

> The Little Mothers' League has helped me a good bit in dressing my little baby sister and I have enjoyed it very much and I think it is a very sencible society. I have learnt how to dress the baby in winter and summer. And after it is done with the bottle it should be boiled. (Helen Potter.)

> A baby is not to be made to walk to soon because he might become bollegged. Some mothers think it is nice to see the baby walk soon. You should never listen to what your neighbor says when your baby is sick, but take him to a doctor. (Anna Mack, Sixth Grade.)

> In washing a baby you should have a little tub to bath it in and when you hear the doorbell ring you should never let your baby in the tub while you go because many of them get drowned, and you should use castial soap because that is the best. (Marie Donahue, Seventh Grade, age 12.)

But perhaps most eloquent of all is what little Mary Roberts says. Mary is in the Sixth Grade at the Boker School:

"The melancholy days are come
The saddest of the year,"

Is what we all think when the time comes when The Little Mothers' League has to break up for the year. For seven weeks we have listened eagerly to what Miss Ford has told us. We all hope Miss Ford will come back to Boker School next fall and teach us how to care for infants.

# IN WEST
# PHILADELPHIA

CLIMBING ABOARD car No. 13—ominously labelled "Mt. Moriah"—I voyaged toward West Philadelphia. It was a keen day, the first snow of winter had fallen, and sparkling gushes of chill swept inward every time the side doors opened. The conductor, who gets the full benefit of this ventilation, was feeling cynical, and seeing his blue hands I didn't blame him. Long lines of ladies, fumbling with their little bags and waiting for change, stepped off one by one into the windy eddies of the street corners. One came up to pay her fare ten blocks or so before her destination, and then retired to her seat again. This puzzled the conductor and he rebuked her. The argument grew busy. To the amazement of the passengers this richly dressed female brandished lusty epithets. "You Irish mick!" she said. (One would not have believed it possible if he had not heard it.) "That's what I am, and proud of it," said he. The shopping solstice is not all fur coats and pink cheeks. If you watch the conductors in the blizzard season, and see the slings and arrows they have to bear, you will coin a new maxim. The conductor is always right.

It is always entertaining to move for a little in a college

atmosphere. I stopped at College Hall at the University and seriously contemplated slipping in to a lecture. The hallways were crowded with earnest youths of both sexes—I was a bit surprised at the number of co-eds, particularly the number with red hair—discussing the tribulations of their lot. "Think of it," said one man, "I'm a senior, and carrying twenty-three hours. Got a thesis to do, 20,000 words." On a bulletin board I observed the results of a "General Intelligence Exam." It appears that 1,770 students took part. They were listed by numbers, not by names. It was not stated what the perfect mark would have been; the highest grade attained was 159, by Mr. (or Miss?) 735. The lowest mark was 23. I saw that both 440 and 1124 got the mark of 149. If these gentlemen (or ladies) are eager to play off the tie, it would be a pleasure to arrange a deciding competition for them. The elaborate care with which the boys and girls ignore one another as they pass in the halls was highly delightful, and reminded me of exactly the same thing at Oxford. But I saw the possible beginning of true romance in the following notice on one of the boards:

> WANTED: Names and addresses of ten nice American university students who must remain in Philadelphia over Christmas, away from home, to be invited to a Christmas Eve party to help entertain some Bryn Mawr College girls in one of the nicest homes in a suburb of Philadelphia.

Certainly there is the stage set for a short story. Perhaps not such a short one, either.

Naturally I could not resist a visit to the library, where most of the readers seemed wholly absorbed, though one student was gaping forlornly over a volume of Tennyson. I found an intensely amusing book, *Who's Who in Japan*, a copy of which would be a valuable standby to a newspaper paragrapher in his bad moments. For instance:

SASAKI, TETSUTARO: One of the highest taxpayers of Fukushima-ken, President of the Hongu Reeling Partnership, Director of the Dai Nippon Radium Water Co.; brewer, reeler; born Aug., 1860.

SAKURAI, ICHISAKU: Member of the Niigata City Council; Director of the Niigata Gas Co., Niigata Savings Bank. Born June, 1872, Studied Japanese and Chinese classics and arithmetic. At present also he connects with the Niigata Orphanage and various other philanthropic bodies. Was imprisoned by acting contrary to the act of exposive compound for seven years. Recreations: reading, Western wine.

Relying on my apparent similarity to the average undergrad, I plunged into the sancta of Houston Hall and bought a copy of the *Punch Bowl*. What that sprightly journal calls "A little group of Syria's thinkers" was shooting pool. The big fireplaces, like most fireplaces in American colleges, don't seem to be used. They don't even show any traces of ever having been used, a curious contrast to the always blazing hearths of English colleges. The latter, however, are more necessary, as in England there is usually no other source of warmth. A bitter skirmish of winds, carrying powdered snow dust, nipped round the gateways of the dormitories and Tait MacKenzie's fine statue of Whitefield stood sharply outlined against a cold blue sky. I lunched at a varsity hash counter on Spruce Street and bought tobacco in a varsity drug store, where a New York tailor, over for the day, was cajoling students into buying his "snappy styles" in time for Christmas. There is no more interesting game than watching a lot of college men, trying to pick out those who may be of some value to the community in future— the scientists, poets, and teachers of the next generation. The well-dressed youths one sees in the varsity drug stores are not generally of this type.

The Evans School of Dentistry at Fortieth and Spruce is a surprising place. Its grotesque gargoyles, showing (with true medieval humour) the sufferings of tooth patients, are the first thing one notices. Then one finds the museum, in which is housed Doctor Thomas W. Evans's collection of paintings and curios brought back from France. Unfortunately there seems to be no catalogue of the items, so that there is no way of knowing what interesting associations belong to them. But most surprising of all is to find the travelling carriage of the Empress Eugénie in which she fled from France in the fatal September days of 1870. She spent her last night in France at the home of Doctor Evans, and there is a spirited painting by Dupray showing her leaving his house the next morning, ushered into the carriage by the courtly doctor. The old black barouche, or whatever one calls it, seems in perfect condition still, with the empress's monogram on the door panel. Only the other day we read in the papers that the remarkable old lady (now in her ninety-fourth year) has been walking about Paris, revisiting well-known scenes. How it would surprise her to see her carriage again here in this University building in West Philadelphia. The whole museum is delightfully French in flavour; as soon as one enters one seems to step back into the curiously bizarre and tragic extravagance of the Second Empire.

One passes into the dignified and placid residence section of Spruce and Pine streets, with its distinctly academic air. Behind those quiet walls one suspects bookcases and studious professors and all the delightful passions of the mind. On Baltimore Avenue the wintry sun shone white and cold; in Clark Park, Charles Dickens wore a little cap of snow, and Little Nell looked more pathetic than ever. There is a breath of mystery about Baltimore Avenue. What does that large sign mean, in front of a house near Clark Park—THE EASTERN TRAVELLERS? Then one comes to the famous shop of S. F. Hiram, the Dodoneaean Shoe-maker he calls himself. This wise coloured man has learned the advertising advantages of the unusual. His placard reads:

> Originator of that famous Dobrupolyi System of repairing.

When one enters and asks to know more about this system, he points to another placard, which says:

> It assumes the nature and character of an appellative noun, and carries the article The System.

His shop contains odd curios as well as the usual traffic of a cobbler. "The public loves to be hoodwinked," he adds sagely.

# THE UNIVERSITY AND
# THE URCHIN

SUNDAY AFTERNOON is by old tradition dedicated to the taking of Urchins out to taste the air, and indeed there is no more agreeable pastime. And so, as the Urchin sat in his high chair and thoughtfully shovelled his spoon through meat chopped remarkably small and potatoes mashed in that curious fashion that produces a mass of soft, curly tendrils, his curators discussed the question of where he should be taken.

It was the first Sunday in March—mild and soft and tinctured with spring. "There's the botanic garden at the University," I suggested. The Urchin settled it by rattling his spoon on the plate and sliding several inches of potato into his lap. "Go see garden!" he cried. With the generous tastes of twenty-seven months he cares very little where he is taken; he can find fascination in anything; but something about the word "garden" seemed to allure him. So a little later when he had been duly habited in brown leggings, his

196

minute brown overcoat, and white hat with ribbons behind it, he and his curators set out. The Urchin was in excellent spirits, for he had been promised a ride on a trolley car—a glorious adventure. In one pocket he carried his private collection of talismans, including a horse-chestnut and a picture of a mouse. Also, against emergencies, a miniature handkerchief with a teddy bear embroidered in one corner and a safety pin. The expedition may be deemed to have been a success, as none of these properties were called upon or even remembered.

The car we boarded did not take us just where we expected to go, but that made little difference to the Urchin, who gazed steadfastly out of the window at a panorama of shabby streets, and offered no comment except one of extreme exultation when we passed a large poster of a cow. Admirably docile, he felt confident that the unusual conjunction of both arbiters of destiny and an impressive trolley car would in the end produce something extremely worth while. We sped across Gray's Ferry bridge—it seems strange to think that region was once so quiet, green, and rustic—transferred to another car on Woodland Avenue, past the white medley of tombstones in Woodland Cemetery, and got off at the entrance to the dormitory quadrangles at Thirty-seventh Street. We entered through the archway—the Urchin's first introduction to an academic atmosphere. "This is the University," I said to him severely, and he was much impressed. As is his way, he conducted himself with extreme sobriety until he should get the hang of this new experience and see what it was all about. I knew from the serene gold sparkle of his brown eyes that there was plenty of larking spirit in him, waiting until he knew whether it was safe to give it play. He held my hand punctiliously while waiting to see what manner of place this University was.

A college quadrangle on a Sunday afternoon has a feeling all its own. Thin tinklings of mandolins eddy from open windows, in which young men may be seen propped up against bright-coloured cushions, always smoking, and sometimes reading with an apparent zeal which might deceive a few onlookers. But the slightest sound of footfalls on the pavement outside their rooms causes these heads to turn and scan the passers. There is always a vague hope in these youthful breasts that some damsel of notable fairness may have strayed within the bastions. Groups of ladies of youth and beauty do often walk demurely through the courts, and may be sure of hearing admiring whistles shrilled through the sunny air. When a lady walks through a college quadrangle and hears no sibilation, let her know sadly that first youth is past. Even the sedate guardianship of Scribe and Urchin did not forfeit one Lady of Destiny her proper homage of tuneful testimonial. So be it ever!

One who inhabited college quadrangles not so immeasurably long ago, and remembers with secret pain how massively old, experienced, and worldly wise he then thought himself, can never resist a throb of amazement at the entertaining youthfulness of these young monks. How quaintly juvenile they are, and how oddly that assumption of grave superiority sits upon their golden brows! With what an inimitable air of wisdom, cynicism, ancientry, learned aloofness and desire to be observed do they stroll to and fro across the quads, so keenly aware in their inmost bosoms of the presence of visitors and determined to grant an appearance of mingled wisdom, great age, and sad doggishness! What a devil-may-care swing to the stride, what a nonchalance in the perpetual wreath of cigarette smoke, what a carefully assumed bearing of one carrying great wisdom lightly and easily casting it aside for the moment in the pursuit of some waggish trifle. "Here," those very self-conscious young visages seem to betray, "is one who might tell you all about the Holy Roman Empire, and yet is, for the moment, diverting himself with a mere mandolin." And yet, as the Lady of Destiny shrewdly observed, it is a

pity they should mar their beautiful quadrangles with orange peel and scraps of paper.

We walked for some time through those stately courts of
Tudor brick and then passed down the little inclined path
to the botanic garden, where irises and fresh green spikes
are already pushing up through the damp earth. A pale
mellow sunlight lay upon the gravel walks and the Urchin
resumed his customary zeal. He ran here and there along
the byways, examined the rock borders with an air of
scientific questioning, and watched the other children playing by the muddy pond. We found shrubbery swelling with
buds, also flappers walking hatless and blanched with talcum, accompanied by Urchins of a larger growth. Both
these phenomena we took to be a sign of the coming
equinox.

Returning to the dormitory quadrangles, we sat down on
a wooden bench to rest, while the Urchin, now convinced
that a university is nothing to be awed by, scampered about
on the turf. His eye was a bright jewel of roguishness, for
he thought that in trotting about the grass he was doing
something supremely wicked. He has been carefully
trained not to err on the grass of the city square to which
he is best accustomed, so this surprising and unchecked
revelry quite went to his head. Across and about those wide
plots of sodden turf he trotted and chuckled, a small, quaint
mortal with his hat ribbons fluttering. Cheering whistles
hailed him from open windows above, and he smiled to
himself with grave dignity. Apparently, like a distinguished
statesman, he regarded these tributes not as meant for
himself, but for the great body of childhood he innocently
represents, and indeed from which his applauders are not
so inextricably severed. With the placid and unconscious
happiness of a puppy he careered and meandered, without
motive or method. Perhaps his underlying thought of a
university, if he has any, is that it is a place where no one
says "Keep Off the Grass," and, intellectually speaking,

that would not be such a bad motto for an institution of learning.

I don't know whether Doctor Tait McKenzie so intended it, but his appealing and beautiful statue of Young Franklin in front of the University gymnasium is admirably devised for the delight of small Urchins. While their curators take pleasure in the bronze itself, the Urchin may clamber on the different levels of the base, which is nicely adapted for the mountaineering capacity of twenty-seven months. The low brick walls before the gymnasium and the University museum are also just right for an Urchin who has recently learned the fascination of walking on something raised above the ground, provided there is a curator near by to hold his hand. And then, as one walks away toward the South Street bridge an observant Urchin may spy the delightful spectacle of a freight train travelling apparently in midair. Some day, one hopes, all that fine tract of open space leading from the museum down to the railroad tracks may perhaps be beautified as a park or an addition to the University's quadrangle system. I don't know who owns it, but its architectural possibilities must surely make the city-planner's mouth water.

By this time the Urchin was beginning to feel a bit weary, and was glad of a lift on a parental shoulder. Then a Lombard Street car came along and took us up halfway across the bridge. So ended the Urchin's first introduction to a university education.

# THE URCHIN
# AT THE ZOO

I DON'T KNOW just what urchins think about; neither do they, perhaps; but presumably by the time they're twenty-eight months old they must have formed some ideas as to what is possible and what isn't. And therefore it seemed to the Urchin's curators sound and advisable to take him out to the Zoo one Sunday afternoon just to suggest to his delightful mind that nothing is impossible in this curious world.

Of course, the amusing feature of such expeditions is that it is always the adult who is astounded, while the child takes things blandly for granted. You or I can watch a tiger for hours and not make head or tail of it—in a spiritual sense, that is—whereas an urchin simply smiles with rapture, isn't the least amazed, and wants to stroke the "nice pussy."

It was a soft spring afternoon, the garden was thronged with visitors and all the indoor animals seemed to be wondering how soon they would be let out into their open-air inclosures. We filed through the wicket gate and the Urchin disdained the little green go-carts ranked for hire. He preferred to navigate the Zoo on his own white-gaitered legs. You might as well have expected Adam on his first tour of Eden to ride in a palanquin.

The Urchin entered the Zoo much in the frame of mind that must have been Adam's on that original tour of inspection. He had been told he was going to the Zoo, but that meant nothing to him. He saw by the aspect of his curators that he was to have a good time, and loyally he was prepared to exult over whatever might come his way. The first thing he saw was a large boulder—it is set up as a memorial to a former curator of the garden. "Ah," thought the Urchin, "this is what I have been brought here to admire." With a shout of glee he ran to it. "See stone," he cried. He is an enthusiast concerning stones. He has a small cardboard box of pebbles, gathered from the walks of a city square, which is very precious to him. And this magnificent big pebble, he evidently thought, was the marvelous thing he had come to examine. His custodians, far more anxious than he to feast their eyes upon lions and tigers, had hard work to lure him away. He crouched by the boulder, appraising its hugeness, and left it with the gratified air of one who has extracted the heart out of a surprising and significant experience.

The next adventure was a robin, hopping on the lawn. Every child is familiar with robins, which play a leading part in so much Mother Goose mythology, so the Urchin felt himself greeting an old friend. "See Robin Redbreast!" he exclaimed, and tried to climb the low wire fence that bordered the path. The robin hopped discreetly underneath a bush, uncertain of our motives.

Now, as I have no motive but to attempt to record the truth, it is my duty to set down quite frankly that I believe the Urchin showed more enthusiasm over the stone and the robin than over any of the amazements that succeeded them. I suppose the reason for that is plain. These two objects had some understandable relation with his daily life. His small mind—we call a child's mind "small" simply by habit; perhaps it is larger than ours, for it can take in almost anything without effort—possessed well-known classifications into which the big stone and the robin fitted comfortably and naturally. But what can a child say to an ostrich or an elephant? It simply smiles and passes on. Thereby showing its superiority to some of our most eminent thinkers. They, confronted by something the like of which they have never seen before—shall we say a League of Nations or Bolshevism?—burst into shrill screams of panic abuse and flee the precinct! How much wiser the level-headed Urchin! Confronting the elephant, certainly an appalling sight to so small a mortal, he looked at the curator, who was carrying him on one shoulder, and said with an air of one seeking gently to reassure himself, "Elphunt won't come after Junior." Which is something of the mood to which the Senate is moving.

It was delightful to see the Urchin endeavor to bring some sense of order into this amazing place by his classification of the strange sights that surrounded him. He would not confess himself staggered by anything. At his first glimpse of the emu he cried ecstatic, "Look, there's a—," and paused, not knowing what on earth to call it. Then rapidly to cover up his ignorance he pointed confidently to a somewhat similar fowl and said sagely, "And there's another!" The curious moth-eaten and shabby appearance that captive camels always exhibit was accurately recorded in his addressing one of them as "poor old horsie." And after watching the llamas in silence, when he saw them nibble at some grass he was satisfied. "Moo-cow," he stated positively, and turned away. The bears did not seem to interest him until he was reminded of Goldylocks. Then he remembered the pictures of the bears in that story and began to take stock of them.

The Zoo is a pleasant place to wander on a Sunday afternoon. The willow trees, down by the brook where the otters were plunging, were a cloud of delicate green. Shrubs everywhere were bursting into bud. The Tasmanian devils, those odd little swine that look like small pigs in a high fever, were lying sprawled out, belly to the sub-warmed earth, in the same whimsical posture that dogs adopt when trying to express how jolly they feel. The Urchin's curators were at a loss to know what the Tasmanian devils were and at first were led astray by a sign on a tree in the devils' inclosure. "Look, they're Norway maples," cried one curator. In the same way we thought at first that a llama was a Chinese kinkgo. These errors lead to a decent humility.

203

There is something about a Zoo that always makes one hungry, so we sat on a bench in the sun, watched the stately swans ruffling like square-rigged ships on the sparkling pond, and ate biscuits, while the Urchin was given a mandate over some very small morsels. He was much entertained by the monkeys in the open-air cages. In the upper story of one cage a lady baboon was embracing an urchin of her own, while underneath her husband was turning over a pile of straw in a persistent search for small deer. It was a sad day for the monkeys at the Zoo when the rule was made that no peanuts can be brought into the park. I should have thought that peanuts were an inalienable right for captive monkeys. The order posted everywhere that one must not give the animals tobacco seems almost unnecessary nowadays, with the weed at present prices. The Urchin was greatly interested in the baboon rummaging in his straw. "Mokey kicking the grass away," he observed thoughtfully.

Down in the grizzly-bear pit one of the bears squatted himself in the pool and sat there, grinning complacently at the crowd. We explained that the bear was taking a bath. This presented a familiar train of thought to the Urchin and he watched the grizzly climb out of his tank and scatter the water over the stone floor. As we walked away the Urchin observed thoughtfully, "He's dying." This somewhat shocked the curators, who did not know that their offspring had even heard of death. "What does he mean?" we asked ourselves. "He's dying," repeated the Urchin in a tone of happy conviction. Then the explanation struck us. "He's drying!" "Quite right," we said. "After his bath he has to dry himself."

We went home on a crowded Girard Avenue car, thinking impatiently that it will be some time before we can read *The Jungle Book* to the Urchin. In the summer, when the elephants take their bath outdoors, we'll go again. And the last thing the Urchin said that night as he fell asleep was, "Mokey kicking the grass away."

204

# DAY TRIPS

# WILLOW GROVE

SPEAKING AS A foreigner—every man is a foreigner in Philadelphia until he has lived here for three generations—I should say that no place is more typical of the Philadelphia capacity for enjoying itself in a thoroughly genteel and innocent way than Willow Grove. Cynics have ascribed the placid conduct of Willow Grove's merrymakers to the fact that eighty minutes or so standing up in a crowded trolley blunt human capacity for abandonment and furious mirth. Physiologists say that the unprecedented quantity of root beer and hard-boiled eggs consumed at the Grove account for the staid bearing of the celebrants. Be that how it may, Willow Grove has the genial and placid flavor of a French amusement park. Contrary to popular theory the French, like ourselves, are comely behaved on an outing. People to whom enjoyment is a habit do not turn their picnics into an orgy.

It takes practically as long to get to Willow Grove as it does to Atlantic City, but the sunburn does not keep one awake all night and asleep at the office the next day. That rolling watershed where the creeks run alternately into the Delaware and the Schuylkill is well hilled, watered and aired. There is no surf, it is true; but a superb panorama of the white combers of the sky, the clouds. And fields of plumed and tasseled corn, flickering in the wind, are no mean substitute for sand beaches. Let us be practical; no one can eat the surf! And the most important matter in a picnic is to have plenty of food.

Let me state, in passing, that the ideal picnic lunch is always packed in a shoebox; there should be included an opener for root-beer bottles, and doughnuts calculated on a basis of three for each adult. Inside the ring of each doughnut should be packed a hard-boiled egg. Each party should include one person (preferably an aunt) of prudent instincts, to whom may be entrusted the money for return carfares, Ada's knitting bag, Ada's young man's wrist watch and registration card in draft Class 4A, father's spare cigar for the home voyage, grandmother's pneumatic cushion and Cousin Janet's powder-papers and copy of Spumy Stories. This prudent person will form a headquarters and great general staff, a strong defensive position upon which the maneuvers of the excursion will be based.

The first thing that always strikes me at Willow Grove is how amazingly well dressed everybody is. The frocks, hats and ankles of the young ladies are a vision of rapture. The young men, too, are well dressed, in the best possible style, which is, of course, the uniform of Uncle Sam. The last time I was there it was a special celebration day for the marines. Several hundred of them were loping about in their *café-au-lait* khaki, fine, tall, lean chaps, with that curious tautness of the trousers that makes the devil dogs look stiff-kneed. Bronzed, handsome fellows, with the characteristic tilt of the Stetson that must flutter the hearts of French flappers. And as for the girls, if Willow Grove on a Saturday afternoon is a fair cross-section of Philadelphia pulchritude, I will match it against anything any other city can show.

Willow Grove, of course, is famous for its music, and at dusk the Marine Band was to play in the pavilion. That open-air auditorium, under the tremulous ceiling of tall maples and willows and sycamores, with the green and silver shimmer of the darkening lake at one side, is a cheerful place to sit and meditate. I had a volume of Thoreau with me, and began to read it, but he kept on harping upon the blisses of solitude which annoyed me when I was enjoying the mirths and moods of the crowd. Nowhere will you find a happier, more sane and contented and typically American crowd than at Willow Grove. Perhaps in wartime we take our pleasures a little more soberly than of old. Yet there seemed no shadow of sadness or misgiving on all those happy faces, and it was a good sight to see tall marines romping through the "Crazy Village" arm in arm with bright-eyed girls. Those boys in the coffee-and-milk uniform will see crazier villages than that in Champagne and Picardy.

The last arrows of sunlight were still quivering among the upmost leaves when the Marine Band began to play, and the great crowd gathered under the trees was generous with affectionate enthusiasm. And then, at a bugle call, the rest of the sea-soldiers charged shouting down the dusky aisles, climbed the platform, and sang their war songs with fine pride and spirit. "America, Here's My Boy"; "It's a Long, Long Way to Berlin, But We'll Get There, by Heck"; "Goodby, Broadway: Hello, France" and "There's a Long, Long Trail" were the favorites. And then came the one song that of all others has permeated American fiber during the last year—"Over There." There is something of simple gallantry and pathos in it that I find genuinely moving. The clear, merry, audacious male voices made me think of their brothers in France who were, even at that very moment, undergoing such fiery and unspeakable trial. The great gathering under the trees seemed to feel something of this, too; there was a caught breath and a quiver of secret pain on every bench. "Over There," unassuming ditty as it is, has caught the spirit of our crusade with inspiration and truth. It is the informal anthem of our great and dedicated resolve.

As we walked back toward the station the rolling loops and webbed framework of the scenic railway were silhouetted black against a western sky which was peacock blue with a quiver of greenish crystal still eddying in it. The bullfrogs were drumming in the little ponds enameled with green scum. And from the train window, as we rattled down that airy valley, we could see the Grove's spangles and festoons of light. Philadelphia may take her amusements placidly, but she knows how to enjoy them.

209

# HOG ISLAND

My only regret was that my friend John Fitzgerald didn't take Rudyard Kipling or William McFee or Philip Gibbs down to Hog Island, instead of a humble traveler whose hand can never do justice to that marvelous epic of human achievement. It would be worth Mr. Kipling's while to cross the Atlantic just to see the Island.

Far across the low-lying meadows the great fringe of derricks rises against the sky. Along a beautiful solid highway, over the Penrose Ferry drawbridge and past the crumbled ramparts of old Fort Mifflin, motors and trolley cars now go flashing down to the huge shipyard, where eighteen months ago a truck struggled along a miry country road carrying enough lumber to put up a timekeeper's shack. The story of that great drama of patient courage and effort lies behind and underneath all one sees at Hog Island. As we walked along the marvelous stretch of fifty shipways, each carrying a vessel in course of construction, and as Fitz and I stood on the bridge of the *Saluda*, one of the eleven steamers now getting their finishing touches at the seven huge piers, one had a vision of the Island as it was during that first winter. Engineers and laborers wrestled with frozen swamp and blizzard snows. Workmen were brought from Philadelphia day by day, roped in like sardines in open trucks, arriving numbed to the bone. Perhaps some day there will come some poet great enough to tell the drama of Hog Island as it ought to be told. The men who gritted their teeth and put it through will never tell. They are of the old stalwart breed that works with its hands. As they talk you can divine something of what they endured.

I don't believe there is a more triumphant place on earth than Hog Island these days. Ships are the most expressive creatures of men's hands, and as I stood with Fitz on the bridge of the *Saluda* and looked out through a driving rain on the comely gray hulls of those 7500-ton cargo carriers, it was hard to resist the thought that each of them had a soul of her own and was partaking in the general exultation. Eight ships now going about their business on the world's waters, eleven at the outfitting piers getting ready to smell blue water, and fifty on the ways—the Island is launching one every Saturday—that is the record. Smoke was drifting from the funnels of several, whose turbine engines were getting their tuning up.

These thousand-foot piers, each of which can accommodate four 8000-ton ships at a time, will one day make Philadelphia one of the world's greatest ports. And the thought that every lover of seafaring will bring away with him is that these fabricated ships, built according to a set plan with interchangeable parts, are beautiful ships. Humble cargo carriers, but to an untutored eye they have much of the loveliness of form of some of the stateliest liners. Looking into the newly finished chartroom, wheelroom and other deckhouses of the *Saluda*, I envied her future master.

We climbed down steep steel ladders to look at the engine and boiler rooms. No grimy stokehold on these ships—they are oil-burners. One of the furnaces was lit, and through the half-open door one could see a roaring glow of flame. In the engine room quiet and skillful workmen were doing mysterious things to a huge turbine. The shining cylinders and huge pistons of the old reciprocating engine were missing; in their place a bewildering complex of wheels and valves and asbestos covered piping. Looking down from above the engine room was a vast echoing cavern, spotted with orange electric bulbs, with the occasional groan and humming of electric motors and men in overalls moving quietly about their tasks. The quietness of Hog Island is one of its curiously impressive features. It is not a wilderness of roaring, frenzied machinery. Everything moves with efficient docility. Even the riveting guns that echo inside the hollow caves of unfinished hulls are hardly as clamorous as I had expected. In the plate and angle shops vast traveling cranes swing overhead with the ease and silence of huge dark birds. Acetylene torches, blowing dainty little wisps of blue-gold flame, slice through half-inch steel plates while the dissolving metal dribbles down in yellow bubbles and streamers and a shower of brilliant sparks flies off gently and quietly. Great wedges descend on flat plates and bend them into right angles with only a soft crunch.

Scaling tall scaffolds we clambered over one of the half-finished hulls, a naked shell of steel echoing with sudden fierce outbursts of riveting. As it was raining the out-of-door riveting had ceased, as whenever there is danger of water getting under the flange of the rivet there is a liability of the work not being quite watertight. But between decks some of the men were hard at work. Across the deck red-hot rivets came flying through the air from the brazier; these were deftly caught in a metal cone by the passer. With a long pair of tongs he inserts the glowing finger of metal in the hole; the backer-up holds it rigid with a compressed-air hammer, while the riveter, on the other side of the plates, mushrooms down the shining stalk of the rivet with his air gun. It is fascinating to watch the end of the rivet flattening under the chattering blows of the gun. An expert riveting team can drive several hundred rivets a day, and when paid on piecework the team gets six and one-half cents per rivet. This is divided among the team, usually in the proportion of 40 per cent to the riveter, 30 per cent to the backer-up and 15 per cent each to heater and passer. Many expert riveters can earn as much as $60 a week.

We crawled under the bottom of the *Schoodic* which is to be launched tomorrow morning. She had just had her first coat of paint, and her tall, graceful bow loomed high in air on the slanting shipway. Mr. White, the engineer in charge of the launchings, was kind enough to show me the ingenious system of shores, packing and "sandjacks" which holds up the hull on the ways and the special Hog Island grease which is used to ease the ship's slide toward the water. The cunning manipulation by which the ship's great weight is thrown off the shores onto the "sandjacks," and then lowered by removing the sand from these iron boxes, would require an essay in itself. Not one of Hog Island's launchings—and they have had nineteen—has been marred by any hitch. Mr. White told me that his gang of 120 men can put through a launching in two hours and half from the time they first begin work.

In the training school, where about 200 men are learning the various shipbuilding trades, 92 per cent of the pupils are former soldiers and sailors. They are all men of powerful physique, but many of them were in sedentary clerical occupations before the war. Many a man who has served in the army has no taste now to re-enter a trade that will keep him indoors eight or ten hours a day. I must confess to an envy of those brawny fellows who were learning to drive rivets. And after the army pay of $30 or so a month it must seem good to get $20 a week while learning the job.

Hog Island is a poem, a vast bracing chant of manly achievement in every respect, that is, save the names of the ships they are building down there. I don't think Hog Island workmen will ever quite forgive Mrs. Wilson for the names she chose for their cherished and beautiful ships! *Quistconck, Saccarappa, Sacandaga, Saguache, Sapinero, Sagaporack, Schoodic, Saugus, Schroon*—what will homely sailormen make of these odd Indian syllables? As one said to me, whimsically, "Think of some wireless operator, calling for help, trying to get that name across!"

We must assume, however, that no Hog Island ship will ever be in distress, from her own fault at any rate. The experiment of "fabricated" ships was watched with eagerness by all shipping experts, some of whom didn't believe it could be successful. The first chapter of Hog Island's epic closes fitly with this cablegram, received the other day from the American International Shipbuilding Corporation's representative in Rome:

> Rome, March 16.—Quistconck arrived March 8th, Savona. Excellent voyage. Has been inspected by representatives of government, steamship companies and banks. Opinion favorable. Hope you will be able to send more of that type.

Hog Island men have accomplished what they have partly because they go about their work with such a sense of humor. There are more grins to the square acre down there than any place I ever visited. The Hog Islander who drove me down was grumbling because the man driving the car in front didn't give the usual signal when turning across our path. "Why doesn't he hold out his hand?" he muttered. "Must be afraid a flivver will run up his arm." That's the jovial spirit of Hog Island.

# UP THE WISSAHICKON

THE SOOTHSAYER is a fanatical lover of Fairmount Park. His chief delight is to send his car spinning along the Lincoln Drive about the time the sun drops toward setting; to halt at a certain hostelry (if the afternoon be chilly) for what Charles Lamb so winningly describes as "hot water and its better adjuncts"; and then, his stormy soul for the moment at armistice with life, to roll in a gentle simmer down gracious byways while the Park gathers her mantle of dusk about her. Sometimes he halts his curricle in some favorite nook, climbs back into the broad, well-cushioned tonneau seat and lies there smoking a cigarette and watching the lights along the river. The Park is his favorite relaxation. He carries its contours and colors and sunsets in the sparc locker of his brain, and even on the most trying day at his office he is a little happier because he knows the Wissahickon Drive is but a few miles away. Wise Soothsayer! He should have been one of the hermits who came from Germany with Kelpius in 1694 and lived bleakly on the hillsides of that fairest of streams, waiting the millennium they expected in 1700.

The Soothsayer had long been urging me to come and help him worship the Wissahickon Drive, and when luck and the happy moment conspired I found myself carried swiftly past the Washington Monument at the park entrance and along the margin of the twinkling Schuylkill. At first there was nothing of the hermit in the Soothsayer's conversation. He was bitterly condemning the handicraft of a certain garage mechanic who had done something to his "clutch." He included this fallacious artisan in the class of those he deems most degraded: The People Who Don't Give a Damn. For intellectual convenience, the Soothsayer tersely ascribes all ills that befall him to Bolshevism. If the waitress is tardy in delivering his cheese omelet, she is a bolshevixen. If a motortruck driver skims his polished fender, he is a bolshevik. In other words, those who Don't Give a Damn are bolsheviks.

The Soothsayer lamented that I had not been in the Park with him two weeks ago, when the autumn foliage was a blaze of glowing color. But to my eye the tints (it was the first of November) were unsurpassably lovely. It was a keen afternoon, the air was sharp, the sky flushing with rose and massed with great banks of cloud the bluish hue of tobacco smoke. When we neared the corner of Peter's Island the sun slid from under a cloudy screen and transfused the thin bronze-yellow of the trees with a pale glow which sparkled as the few remaining leaves fluttered in the wind. Most of the leafage had fallen and was being burnt in bonfires at the side of the road, where the gusts tossed and flattened the waving flames. But the trees were still sufficiently clothed to show a rich tapestry of russet and orange and brown, sharpened here and there by wisps and shreds of yellow. And where the boughs were wholly stripped (the silver-gray beeches, for instance) their delicate twigs were clearly traced against the sky. I think one hears too much of the beauty of October's gold and scarlet and not enough of the sober, wistful richness of November buffs and duns and browns.

The Wissahickon Drive is the last refuge of the foot and the hoof, for motors are not allowed to follow the trail up the ravine, which still remains a haunt of ancient peace— much more so, indeed, than in former years, when there must have been many and many a smart turnout spanking up the valley for supper at the Lotus Inn. Over the ruins of this hostelry the Soothsayer becomes sadly eloquent, recalling how in his salad days he used to drive out from town in a chartered hansom and sit placidly on a honeysuckled balcony over chicken and waffles served with the proper flourish by a colored servitor named Pompey. But we must take things as we see them, and though my conductor rebuked me for thinking the scene so lovely—I should have been there not only two weeks ago to see the autumn colors, but ten years ago to see Pompey and the Lotus Inn—still, I was marvelously content with the dusky beauty of the glades. The cool air was rich with the damp, sweet smell of decaying leaves. A tiny murmur of motion rose from the green-brown pools of the creek, ruffled here and there with a milky bubble of foam below some boulder. In the feathery tops of evergreen trees, blackly outlined against the clear arch of fading blue, some birds were cheeping a lively squabble. We stopped to listen. It was plainly an argument, of the kind in which each side accuses the other of partisanship. "Bolshevism!" said the Sooth-sayer.

It is wonderfully still in the Wissahickon ravine in a pale November twilight. Overhead the sky darkened; the sherry-brown trees began to shed something of their rich tint. The soft earth of the roadway was grateful underfoot to those too accustomed to pavement walking. Along the drive came the romantic thud of hoofs: a party of girls on horseback perhaps returning from tea at Valley Green. What a wonderful sound is the quick drumming of horses' hoofs! To me it always suggests highwaymen and Robert Louis Stevenson. We smoked our pipes leaning over the wooden fence and looking down at the green shimmer of the Wissahickon, seeing how the pallor of sandy bottom shone up through the clear water.

And then, just as one is about to sentimentalize upon the beauty of nature and how it shames the crass work of man, one comes to what is perhaps the loveliest thing along the Wissahickon—the Walnut Lane Bridge. Leaping high in air from the very domes of the trees, curving in a sheer smooth superb span that catches the last western light on its concrete flanks, it flashes across the darkened valley as nobly as an old Roman viaduct of southern France. It is a thrilling thing, and I scrambled up the bank to note down the names of the artists who planned it. The tablet is dated 1906, and bears the names of George S. Webster, chief engineer; Henry H. Quimby, assistant engineer; Reilly & Riddle, contractors. Many poets have written verses both good and bad about the Wissahickon, but Messrs. Reilly & Riddle have spanned it with a poem that will long endure.

We walked back to the Soothsayer's bolshevized car, which waited at the turning of the drive where a Revolutionary scuffle took place between American troops and a detachment of redcoats under a commander of the fine old British name of Knyphausen. As we whirred down to the Lincoln Drive and I commented on the lavender haze that overhung the steep slopes of the glen, the Soothsayer said: "Ah, but you should have seen it two weeks ago. The trees were like a cashmere shawl!"

I shall have to wait fifty weeks before I can see the Wissahickon in a way that will content the fastidious Soothsayer.

# UP TO VALLEY GREEN

MADRIGAL HAD a bad cold, and I was trumpeting with hay fever; and we set off for consolation in a tramp along the Wissahickon. In the drowsy stillness of a late August afternoon, with a foreboding of autumn chill already in the air, we sneezed and coughed our way along the lovely ravine. Those lonely glades, that once echoed to the brisk drumming of horses' hoofs, rang with our miserable sternutations. The rocky gullies and pine-scented hillsides became for one afternoon the Vallombrosa of two valetudinarians. Thoughts of mortal perishment lay darkly upon us. We had lunched gorgeously with a charming host who was suffering with sciatica, and had described this affliction to us as a toothache as long as your leg. Then the Ridge avenue car carried us between two populous cities of the dead—Laurel Hill and Mount Vernon Cemeteries. Was this (we thought) the beginning of the end?

The Ridge avenue car set us down at the mouth of Wissahickon creek. We each got out a clean handkerchief from a hip pocket and determined to make a brave fight against the dark angel. Under the huge brown arches of the Reading Railway, which have all the cheering gayety of an old Roman aqueduct, we entered the valley of enchantment. At this point it occurred to us that the ancient Romans were really prohibitionists at heart, since it was on aqueducts that they lavished the fullness of their structural genius. They never bothered with vinoducts.

Perhaps Philadelphians do not quite realize how famous the Wissahickon valley is. When my mother was a small girl in England there stood on her father's reading table a silk lampshade on which were painted little scenes of the world's loveliest beauty glimpses. There were vistas of Swiss mountains, Italian lakes, French cathedrals, Dutch canals, English gardens. And then, among these fabled glories, there was a tiny sketch of a scene that chiefly touched my mother's girlish fancy. She did not ever expect to see it, but often, as the evening lamplight shone through it, her eye would examine its dainty charm. It was called "The Wissahickon Drive, Philadelphia, U. S. A." Many years afterward she saw it for the first time, and her heart jumped as hearts do when they are given a chance.

The lower reach of the creek, with its placid green water, the great trees leaning over it, the picnic parties along the western marge, and the little boats splashing about, is amazingly like the Thames at Oxford. I suppose all little rivers are much the same, after all; but the likeness here is so real that I cannot forebear to mention it. But one has an uneasy sense, as one walks and watches the gleaming motors that flit by like the whizz of the Ancient Mariner's crossbow, that the Wissahickon has seen better days. The days when the horse was king, when all the old inns were a bustle of rich food and drink, and the winter afternoons were a ringle-jingle of sleigh chimes. Then one turns away to the left, into the stillness of the carriage drive, where motors are not allowed, and the merry clop-clop of hoofs is still heard now and then. Two elderly gentlemen came swiftly by in a bright little gig with red wheels, drawn by a spirited horse. With what a smiling cheer they gazed about them, innocently happy in their life-long pastime! And yet there was a certain pathos in the sight. Two old cronies, they were living out the good old days together. Only a few paces on was the abandoned foundation of the Lotus Inn. And I remembered the verses in which Madrigal himself, laureate of Philadelphia, has musicked the spell of the river drive—

> On winter nights ghost-music plays
> (The bells of long-forgotten sleighs)

Along the Wissahickon.
And many a silver-headed wight
Who drove that pleasant road by night
Sighs now for his old appetite
    For waffles hot and chicken.
And grandmas now, who then were belles!
How many a placid bosom swells
At thought of love's old charms and spells
    Along the Wissahickon.

"But my dear fellow," said one of these silver-headed wights to Madrigal when he had written the poem—"it wasn't chicken, it was catfish that was famous in the Wissahickon suppers." "All right," said Madrigal, "will you please have the name of the creek changed to Wissahatfish to fit the rhyme?" The necessities of poets must be consulted, unless we are to go over, pen, ink and blotter, to the blattings of vers libre.

But a plague on the talk about "the good old days!" Certainly in those times the road along the creek was never such a dreaming haunt of quietness as it is today. An occasional proud damsel, cantering on horse, accompanied by a sort of Lou Tellegen groom; a rambling carriage or two, a few children paddling in the stream, and a bronzed fellow galloping along with eager face—just enough movement to vary the solitude. The creek pours smoothly over rocky shelves, churning in a white soapy triangle of foam below a cascade, or slipping in clear green channels through an aisle of buttonwoods and incredibly slender tulip-poplars. Here and there is a canoe, teetering gently in a nook of shade, while Colin and Amaryllis are uttering bashful pleasantries each to other—innocent plagiarisms as old as Eden, that seem to themselves so gorgeously new and delicious. The road bends and slopes under cliffs of fern and evergreen, where a moist pungency of balsam and turpentine breathes graciously in the nose of the sneezer. Gushing springs splash on the steep bank.

221

Already, though only the end of August, there was a faint tinge of bronze upon the foliage. We were at a loss to know whether this was truly a sign of coming fall, or some unnatural blight withering the trees. Can trees suffer from hay fever? At any rate we saw many dead limbs, many great trunks bald and gouty on the eastern cliffs and a kind of pallor and palsy in the color of the leaves. The forestry of the region did not seem altogether healthy, even to the ignorant eye. We have seen in recent years what a plague has befallen one noble species of tree: it would be a sorry thing if Philadelphia's dearest beauty spot were ravaged by further troubles.

Talking and sneezing by turns, we came to Valley Green, where a placid caravanserai sits beside the way, with a broad, white porch to invite the traveler, and a very feminine barroom innocently garnished with syphons of soda and lemons balanced with ladylike neatness on the necks of grape-juice bottles. Green canoes were drawn up on the river bank; a grave file of six small yellow ducklings was waddling toward the water; a turkey (very similar in profile to Mr. Chauncey Depew) was meditating in the roadway. A bantam cock and his dame made up in strut what they lacked in stature, and a very deaf gardener was trimming a garden of vivid phlox. Here was a setting that cried loudly for the hissing tea urn. Yet to think again of refreshment seemed disrespectful to the noble lunch of a noble host, enjoyed only four hours earlier, and we passed stoically by, intending to go as far as Indian Rock, a mile further. But at a little waterfall, by the Wises Mill road, we halted with a common instinct. We turned backward and sought that gracious veranda at Valley Green. There, in a pot of tea and buttered toast with marmalade, we forgot our emunctory woes.

We set match to tobacco and strode upward on Springfield road, through thickets where the sunlight quivered in golden shafts, toward the comely summits of Chestnut Hill.

Let Madrigal have the last word, for he has known and
loved this bonniest of creeks for forty years:

> There earliest stirred the feet of spring,
> There summer dreamed on drowsy wing;
> And autumn's glories longest cling
>    Along the Wissahickon!

# ON THE WAY TO
# BALTIMORE

THE OTHER DAY we had occasion to take a B. and O. train down to Baltimore. We had to hurry to catch the vehicle at that quaint abandoned château at Twenty-fourth and Chestnut, and when we settled down in the smoker we realized that we had embarked with no reading matter but a newspaper we had already read. We thought, with considerable irritation, that we were going to be bored.

We were never less bored in our life than during that two-hour ride. In the first place, the line of march of the B. and O. gives one quite a different view of the country from the course of the P. R. R., with which we are better acquainted. From the Pennsy, for instance, Wilmington appears as a smoky, shackish and not too comely city. In the eye of the genteel B. and O. it is a quiet suburb, with passive shady lawns about a modest station where a little old lady with a basket of eggs and black finger-gloves got gingerly on board. There were a number of colored doughboys in the car, just landed in New York and on their way to southern homes. "Oh, boy!" cried one of these as we left Wilmington, "de nex' stop's Baltimuh, an' dat's wheah mah native home at." Every ten minutes a fawn-tinted minion from some rearward dining car came through with a tray of ice-cream cones, and these childlike and amiable darkies cleaned out his stock every time. They had all evidently just bought new and very narrow-toed cordovan shoes in New York; there was hardly one who did not have his footgear off to nurse tortured members. The negro soldier has a genius for injudicious purchase. We saw some of them the other day in a "pawn-brokers' outlet" on Market street laying down their fives and tens for the most preposterous gold watches, terrible embossed and flashy engines of

224

inaccuracy, with chains like brass hawsers, obviously about as reliable as a sundial at night.

It was a gray and green day, quite cool—for it was still early forenoon—and we looked out on vanishing woodlands and bosky valleys with a delight too eager to express. Why (we thought) should any sane being waste his energy bedeviling the Senate when all a lifetime spent in attempting to describe the beauty of earth—surely an innocent ambition—would be insufficient? Statesmen, we thought, are but children of a smaller growth; and with a superbly evacuated mind we gazed upon the meadows and dancing streams near Leslie, just over the Maryland border. There were glimpses of that most alluring vista known to man: a strip of woodland thin enough to let through a twinkle of light from the other side. What a mystery there is about the edge of a wood, as you push through and wonder just what you may be coming to. In that corner of Cecil county there are many Forest of Arden glimpses, where the brown and velvety cows grazing in thickets seem (as the train flies by) almost like venison. There are swelling meadows against the sky, white with daisies and Queen Anne's lace; the lichened gray fences, horses straining at the harrow and white farmhouses sitting back among the domes of trees.

Then comes the glorious Susquehanna—that noble river that caught the fancy of R. L. S., you remember. He once began a poem with the refrain, "Beside the Susquehanna and along the Delaware." Olive-green below the high railway bridge, the water tints off to silver in the pale summer haze toward Port Deposit. The B. and O. bridge strides over an island in midstream, and looking down on the tops of the (probably) maples, they are a bright yellow with some blossom-business of their own. A lonely fisherman was squatting in a gray and weathered skiff near the bridge. What a river to go exploring along!

It is quaint that men who love to live in damp and viewless hollows always select the jovial and healthy spots to bury themselves in. Just beyond the Susquehanna, on the south side of the track, we pass a little graveyard in quite the most charming spot thereabouts, high on a hill overlooking the wide sweep of the river. And then again the green rolling ridges of Harford county, with yellow dirt roads luring one afoot, and the little brooks scuttling down toward Chesapeake through coverts of fern and brambles. We remembered the lovely verse of the Canadian poet, Charles G. D. Roberts:

> Comes the lure of green things growing,
> Comes the call of waters flowing—
>    And the wayfarer desire
> Moves and wakes and would be going.

What a naughtiness of pagan temptation sings to one across that bewitching country; what illicit thoughts of rolltop desks consumed in the bonfire, of the warm dust soft under the bootsoles, and the bending road that dips into the wood among an ambush of pink magnolias. If the train were to halt at one of those little stations—say Joppa, near the Gunpowder river—there might be one less newspaper man in the world. I can see him, dropping off the train, lighting his pipe in the windless shelter of a pile of weather-beaten ties, and setting forth up the Gunpowder valley to discover the romantic hamlets of Madonna and Trump, lost in that green paradise of Maryland June. Or the little town of Loreley, on the other side of the stream! Think of the fireflies and the honeysuckle on a June evening in the village of Madonna! Ah, well, of what avail to imagine these things? The train, unluckily, does not stop.

And Baltimore itself, with its unique and leisurely charm, its marvelously individual atmosphere of well-being and assured loveliness and old serenity, how little it realizes how enchanting it is! Baltimore ought to pay a special

226

luxury tax for the dark-eyed and almost insolent beauty of its girls, who gaze at one with the serene candor of unquestioned divinity. But that is a topic that belongs to Baltimore chroniclers, and we may not trespress on their privileges.

At any rate, we got our fishing rod, which is what we went for.

# THE PAOLI LOCAL

IT IS ALWAYS puzzling to the wayfarer, when he has traveled to some sacred spot, to find the local denizens going about their concerns as though unaware that they are on enchanted ground. It used to seem a hideous profanation to the Baedeker-stained tourist from Marsupial City, Ind., to step off the train at Stratford and find the butcher's cart jogging about with flanks and rumps. And even so does it seem odd to me that people are getting aboard the Paoli local every day, just as though it were the normal thing to do instead of (what it really is) an excursion into Arcadia.

Some day a poet will lutanize the Paoli local as it ought to be done, in a tender strain—

> Along that green embowered track
> My heart throws off its pedlar's pack
> In memory commuting back
>    Now swiftly and now slowly—
> Ah! lucky people, you, in sooth
> Who ride that caravan of youth
>    The Local to Paoli!

The 2:15 train is a good one to take, for it affords an interesting opportunity to observe those who may be called sub-commuters: the people who come in town in the morning, like honest working folk, but get back to the country after lunch. These, of course, are only half-breed commuters. They are the silver-chevron suburbanites, deserving not the true golden stripes of those who moil all day. They are teachers, schoolboys, golfomaniacs and damsels from the home of Athene, Bryn Mawr. They are mere cherubim and seraphim, not archangels. Stern and grizzled veterans, who go home on the Hjw6:05 ("H" Will not run New Year's, Memorial, Independence, Thanksgiving and

Christmas Days; "j" will not run Saturdays June 7 to Sept. 27, both inclusive; "w" No baggage service), speak of them scornfully as "Sam Browne belt commuters."

One who was nourished along the line of the Paoli local, who knew it long before it became electrified with those spider-leg trolleys on its roof and before the Wynnewood embankments were lined with neat little garages, sometimes has an inner pang that it is getting a bit too civilized. And yet no train will ever mean to us what that does! The saying that was good enough for Queen Mary and Mr. Browning is good enough for me. When I die, you will find the words PAOLI LOCAL indelibled on my heart. When the Corsican patriot's bicentennial comes along, in 1925, I hope there will be a grand reunion of all the old travelers along that line. The railroad will run specially decorated trains and distribute souvenirs among commuters of more than forty years' standing. The campus of Haverford College will be the scene of a mass-meeting. There will be reminiscent addresses by those who recall when the tracks ran along Railroad avenue at Haverford and up through Preston. An express agent will be barbecued, and there will be dancing and song and passing of the mead cup until far into the night.

The first surprise the Paoli local gives one never fails to cause a mild wonder. Just after leaving West Philadelphia Station you see William Penn looming up away on the right. As you are convinced that you left him straight behind, and have not noticed any curve, the sensation is odd. At Fifty-second street rise the shallow green slopes of George's Hill, with its Total Abstinence fountain. Nearer the track are wide tracts of vacant ground where some small boys of the sort so delightfully limned by Fontaine Fox have scooped military dug-outs, roofed over with cast-off sheets of corrugated iron, very lifelike to see.

At Overbrook one gets one's first glimpse of those highly civilized suburbs. It is a gloriously sunny May afternoon.

Three girls are sitting under a hedge at the top of the embankment reading a magazine. The little iron fences, so characteristic of the Main Line, make their appearance. A lady tubed in a tight skirt totters valiantly down the road toward the station, and the courteous train waits for her. If the director general of railroads were a bachelor perhaps he would insert a new footnote in his time-tables: "Sk," will not wait for ladies in hobble skirts. The signal gives its blithe little double chirp and we are off again.

Toward Merion we skirt a brightly sliding little brook under willow trees, with glimpses of daintily supervised wilderness. It is all so trimly artificed that one is surprised to see that the rubbery stalks of the dandelion have evaded the lawn-mower just as they do in less carefully razored suburbs. Honeysuckles sprawl along the embankments, privet hedges bound neat gardens. There is a new station at Merion. In old bucolic days the Main Line station masters lived and kept house in the depots, and if one had to wait for a train one could make friends with the station master's little girl and pet cat. But all those little girls are grown up now and are Bryn Mawr alumnae.

At Narberth one sees clustered roofs embowered in trees, in the hollow below the railway, and a snatch of plowed land. Now one is really in the country. Narberth, Wynne-wood, Ardmore, Haverford—so it runs, like a chapter of begats. At Wynnewood, if you are sitting on the right, you see an alluring vista of a long alley through sunspeckled greenery. The baggage agent has nailed an old chair seat to a little wooden box which provides a meditating throne for such small leisure as a Main Line baggage agent gets. Ardmore—strange to think that it used to call itself Athens-ville—doesn't quite know whether it is a suburb or a city. Clumps of iris look upon busy freight yards; back gardens with fluttering Monday linen face upon a factory and a gas tank. And then, in a flash, one is at Haverford, the goal of pilgrimage.

Haverford is changed as little as any of the suburbs since the days when one knew it by heart. Yet Mr. Harbaugh has moved his pharmacy to a new building and it can never be quite the same! The old stuffed owl sits bravely in the new window, but the familiar drug-scented haunt where we drank our first soda and bought our first tobacco is empty and forlorn. But the deep buttercup meadow by the Lancaster pike is still broad and green, with the same fawn-colored velvety cow grazing.

And there is one thing that they can never change: the smell of the Haverford lawns in May, when the grass is being mowed. A dazzling pervasion of sunlight loiters over those gentle slopes, draws up the breath of the grass, blue space is rich with its balmy savor. Under the arches of the old maples are the white figures of the cricketers. In the memorial garden behind the library the blue phlox is out in pale masses. The archway of the beech hedge looks down on the huge prostrate mock-orange tree. Under the hemlocks (I hope they're hemlocks) by the observatory is that curious soft, dry, bleached grass which is so perfect to lie on with a book and not read it. And here comes Harry Carter careering over the lawns with his gasoline mowing machine. Everything is the same at heart. And that is why it's the perfect pilgrimage, the loveliest spot on earth, then, now and forever!

# TO LEAGUE ISLAND
# AND BACK

YESTERDAY afternoon the American Press Humorists visited League Island. When the party boarded a Fifteenth street car I was greatly excited to see a lady sitting with a large market basket in her lap and placidly reading *The American Marriage*. "You see," I said to Ted Robinson, the delightful poet from Cleveland, "we have a genuine culture in Philadelphia. Our citizens read Meredith on the trolleys as they return from shopping." "That's nothing," said Ted. "I always read Meredith on the cars at home. I've often read the greater part of a Meredith novel on my way to the office in the morning." So perhaps the Cleveland transits aren't any more rapid than our own.

The rain came down in whirling silver sheets as we crossed the flats toward League Island, but after a short wait at the end of the car line the downfall slackened. Under the guidance of three courteous warrant officers we were piloted about the navy yard.

Nothing is ever so thrilling as a place where ships are gathered, and the adventurousness of a trip to the navy yard begins as soon as one steps off the car and finds great gray hulls almost at one's side. It seems odd to see them there, apparently so far inland, their tall stacks rising up among the trees. The *Massachusetts* and the *Iowa* were the first we passed, and we were all prepared to admire them heartily until told by our naval convoy that they are "obsolete." Passing by a pack of lean destroyers, leashed up like a kennel of hounds, we gazed at the gray profile of the *Nevada*. The steep chains perpending from her undercut prow we were told were for the use of the paravanes, and I think the ladies of the party were pleased not to be paravanes. The older destroyers—such as the *Wainwright*—are very small compared with the newer models; but it is curious that the outmoded types of battleship appear to the civilian eye more massive and towering than the latest superdreadnoughts. The *Ohio*, the *Connecticut*, the *New Hampshire*, all older vessels, loomed out of the water like cliffs of stone; their two and three high funnels out-topping the squat single stack of the new oil-burners.

The word submarine has become a commonplace of our daily life, but there is always a tingle of excitement on seeing these strange human fishes. The O-16, one of the American undersea craft that operated from the Azores base during the war, was lying awash at her pier. I would have given much to go aboard, but as the officer guiding us said, "It pretty nearly takes an act of Congress to get a civilian aboard a submarine."

In a vast dry-dock, like small minnows gasping for breath in a waterless hollow, lay four diminutive submarines of the K type. Men were hosing them with water, as though to revive them. Their red plates made them look absurdly like goldfish; the diving rudders, like a fish's tail, and the little fins folded pathetically upon their sides toward the bow, increased the likeness. Their periscopes were stripped off, and through openings in the hull workmen were clambering inside. One tried to imagine what the interior of these queer craft might be like. Of all the engines of man they are the most mysterious to the layman. Their little brass propellers seemed incongruously small to drive them through the water. At their noses we could see the revolving tubes to hold the four torpedoes.

We passed, alas too fast, the great air-craft factory, with its delicious glimpses of clean and delicate carpentry, the steamboxes for bending the narrow strips of wood, the sweet smell of banana oil which I suppose is used in some varnishing process. A little engine came trundling out of a shed, pulling a shining gray fuselage on a flat-car. Its graceful lines, its sensitive and shining metal work, its sleek, clean body, all were as beautiful and tender as the works of a watch. Overhead roared an older brother, a flying hydroplane with tremendous sweep of wing, singing that deep hum of unbelievable motor power.

In the recreation hall we stopped for orange soda and salted peanuts. Sailors in white ducks were playing pool. The sailor soda-tender passed out his iced bottles from a huge chest under the counter. In the old days of naval tradition one doubts whether a sailors' bar would have been a place where a party, including ladies and children, could have tarried with such satisfaction. In the Y. M. C. A. building next door marines in their coffee-and-milk uniforms were writing letters; a band was tuning up some jazz in preparation for a theatrical show; a copy of *Soldiers Three* lay on a table. Oilskins lying along the benches gave a nautical touch. There was something characteristically American about the sharp, humorous, nonchalant features of the men. Everywhere one saw sturdy, swing-strided marines whose shoulders would have thrilled a football coach.

At one of the wharves along the Delaware side was the new destroyer *Tattnall*, just taking on her equipment—coils of yellow, creaky rope; fenders, cases of electric bulbs, galvanized buckets, cases of heavy sea boots. It was a tale of adventure just to study her lean, crisp, flaring bow with its concave curves, her four slender funnels, her tall glass-screened bridge, the sternward slant of her hull. Even in the mild swell and swing of Delaware water she rode daintily as a yacht, lifted and caressed by the flow and wash of the water. How she must leap and sway in the full tumble of open seas. She seemed an adorable toy. Who would not go to war, with such delicious playthings to covet and care for! And beside her on the pier lay a clumsier and grimmer-seeming engine. Three great gun-mounts for Admiral Plunkett's naval railroad battery, that carried the fourteen-inch guns that dropped shells into Metz from

twenty-eight miles away. On one of these huge steel cais-
sons I saw that some member of the A. E. F. had scratched
his doleful message: *George W. Moller, a soldier of St. Nazaire,*
*France, who wishes to go home toot sweet.*

The lively little tug *Betty* curtsied up to the pier and took
us on board. Harry Jones, her friendly skipper, steamed us
down past the green mounts of old Fort Mifflin, past the
long tangle of Hog Island's shipways and the wet-basins
where the *Scantic,* the *Pipestone County* and other of Hog
Island's prides were lying, one of them kicking up a white
smother with her propeller in some engine test. Then we
turned upstream. It had been raining on and off all afternoon. From the Jersey shore came the delicious haunting
smell of warm, wet pinewoods, of moist tree-trunks and the
clean whiff of sandy soil and drenched clover fields.

Our Humorist visitors admitted that they had never realized that Philadelphia is a seaport. The brave array of
shipping as we came up the river was an interesting sight.
Among several large Dutch steamers lying in the stream
below Kaighn's Point I noticed the *Remscheid,* which bore
on her side in large white letters the inscription:

WAFFENSTILLSTAND—ARMISTICE

Waffenstillstand is the German for armistice. This struck
me as particularly significant. Probably the cautious Dutch
owner of the *Remscheid,* sending his ship to sea soon after
November 11, feared there might still be U-boats at large
that had not learned of the truce and would not respect a
neutral flag.

Among other ships we noticed the *Edgemoor* and *Westfield*
of Seattle, the four-masted schooner *Charles S. Stanford* of
Bangor, the *Naimes* of London, the *Meiningen* of Brest, the
*Perseveranza* of Trieste, and *Iskra* of Dubrovnik (which W.
M. explains to me is the Slavic name for Ragusa). Thus, in
the names on the sterns along Philadelphia piers one reads

echoes of the war. And most appealing of all the ships we passed was the little white Danish bark *Valdivia*, just such a craft as used to be commanded by the best-known sea captain of modern years, Joseph Conrad.

It must be a brave life to be a tugboat skipper. To con the *Betty* up the shining reaches of the Delaware in a summer dusk, the soft flow of air keeping one's pipe in a glow, that good musk of the Jersey pines tingling in the nostril. Then to turn over the wheel to the mate while one goes below to tackle a tugboat supper, with plenty of dripping steak and fried murphies and coffee with condensed milk. And a tugboat crew sleep at home o' nights, too. Think of it—a sailor all day long, and yet sleep in your own bed at home!

# ALONG THE GREEN
# NESHAMINY

THERE ARE SCENES so rich in color, so flooded with sunlight, that the hand hardly knows how to set them down. They seem to yearn for expression in what is called poetry, yet one fears to submit them to the bending and twisting of rhyme. For when one embarks on the ecstatic search for words in tune with one another he may find bright and jovial cadences, but rarely does he say just what was in his heart. How, then, may one order the mysterious mechanism that gears brain with forefinger so that the least possible color and contour be lost in transmission?

The other day I rowed up Neshaminy Creek. It is a bright little river seventeen miles or so from Philadelphia, a stripling of the great-hearted Delaware. Its wooded and meaded banks are a favored pleasuring ground for pavement-keeping souls, who set up a tent there in the summertime and cruise those innocent waters in canoes. It is a happy stream, beloved of picnic parties. Millions of hard-boiled eggs and ice cream cones have perished in the grove above the dam, and a long avenue of stately poplar trees has grown up to commemorate them. The picnicking point is known as Neshaminy Falls, though the falling is done mostly by high-spirited flappers on the entertaining toboggan chute, down which they launch themselves in a cheering line. The river falls tamely enough over a small dam; Niagara's prestige is nowhere menaced.

There is a kind of emergency fleet corporation doing a bustling traffic at the little plank landing stage. The chief navigating officer was toting a roll of bills larger than I can face with comfort. From him one hires a vessel of sorts, propelled by bright red oars, and then one sets forth up the stream. Most of the voyagers are content after passing the island, for the current, though sluggish, is persistent. But it is well to keep on. Neshaminy shows her rarest charms to those who woo her stoutly.

Above the island there is a long strip of thick woodland on both banks. The treetops, rising steeply into the bright air, keep tossing and trembling in the wind, but the stream itself is entirely still. Along the bank, where the great bleached trunks climb out of the water, there hangs the peculiar moist, earthy, pungent smell of a river that runs among woods. Every freshwater bather must know that smell. It has in it a dim taint as of decay, a sense of rotting vegetation. Yet it is a clean odor and a cool one. It is a smell particularly dear to me, for it recalls to my eager nostril the exact scent of the old bathing place on the Cherwell at Oxford, quaintly known as Parson's Pleasure. How vividly I remember that moist, cool corner of turf, the afternoon sunlight stabbing it with slanting arrows of gold, the enigmatic old Walt Whitman (called Cox) handing out damp towels from his dingy hutch, and the clean white bodies poised against green willows! Would it hurt Neshaminy's feelings if I were to confess that the poignance of its appeal to me was partly due to its kinship with the Oxford Cher?

A little farther up, the creek has the good sense to throw off its mantle of woods. Wide meadows come to the water's edge; hills of a friendly sort are folded down about it, showing a bare line of upland against the sky. A clean line of hill against the emptiness of blue is a sight that never tires. A country road crosses the stream on a flimsy bridge that leans on stout old stone piers. The road bends away uphill, among a wilderness of blackberry bushes, winding among pastures where the cows are grazing. That is a good kind of road; the sort of road one associates with bare feet and hot dust sifting between boyish toes.

Above this bridge the creek shallows. Through the clear water one sees the bottom humped with brown stones. Many of the larger boulders bear a little white paint stain on their upward ridges, showing where a venturesome excursionist has bumped one of the transports of the emergency fleet corporation. Dragonflies gleam like winged scarfpins. Under the boat flashes the bright shape of a small perch or sunfish. On the willow trunks that lean along the bank an occasional fisherman is watching his float. The current moves faster here, dimpling and twisting in little swirls. The water shines and glows: it seems to have caught whole acres of living sunlight. Far above a great hawk is lazily slanting and sliding, watching curiously to see the mail plane from Bustleton that passes up the valley every afternoon.

There is no peace like that of a little river, and here it is at its best.

At last we reached the point where, if the boat is to go further, it must be propelled by hand, the pilot walking barefoot in the stream. Easing her round sharp reefs, pushing through swift little passages where the current spurts deeply between larger stones, she may be pushed up to a huge tree trunk lying along the shore, surrounded by the deliciously soft and fluid mud loved by country urchins, the mud that *schloops* when one withdraws the sunken foot. Here, the world reduced to "a green thought in a green shade," one may watch the waterbirds tiptoeing and teetering over the shallows, catch the tune of the little rapids scuffling round the bend and eat whatever sandwiches are vouchsafed by the Lady of the White Hand. High above treetops and framing the view stands the enormous viaduct of the Trenton cutoff. A heavy freight train thundering over it now and then keeps one in touch with the straining world.

In the swift sparkle that bickers round the bend one may get a dip and a sprawl in the fashion that is in favor with those who love the scour of lightly running water over the naked flesh. That corner of the stream is remote and screened. There is a little gap between two shouldery

stones where the creek pours itself chuckling and vehe-
ment. The bottom is grown with soft, spongy grasses that
are very pleasant to squat upon. I presume that every man
in the world takes any opportunity he can to wallow in a
running brook. It is an old tradition, and there cannot be
too much of it.

The little rivers are excellent friends of man. They are
brisk, cheerful and full of quiet corners of sun. They are
clear and clean, the terror of dark unknown waters is not in
them. I have known and loved many such, and I hope to
make friends with more. When I look back and reckon up
the matters that are cause for regret there will not stand
among them my private and pagan sluice in the bright
waters of Neshaminy.

# STONEHOUSE LANE
# AND THE NECK

IT HAD BEEN a very hot day. At seven o'clock the rich orange sunshine was still flooding straight down Chestnut street. The thought occurred to me that it would be a splendid evening to see the sunset over the level fens of The Neck, that curious canal-country of South Philadelphia which so few of us know.

You take the Fourth street car to Fifth and Ritner. The wide space of Mifflin Square is full of playing children. Here you halt to light a pipe. This is advisable, as you will see in a moment. A couple of blocks south brings you to one of the most noxious areas of dump heaps and waste litters in the world. An expanse of evil-smelling junk smokes with a thin haze of burning. Queer little wooden shacks, stables, pig-pens, sit comfortably in a desert of tin cans and sour rubbish. You will need your tobacco if you are squeamish. In the shadow of mountains of outcast scrap are tiny homes under dusty shade, where a patient old lady was sitting in a wheel-chair reading a book.

A winding track, inconceivably sordid, leads through fields of rank burdock, ashes, broken brick, rusty barrel hoops. Two ancient horses were grazing there, and there seemed a certain pathos in a white van I encountered at the crossing where Stonehouse lane goes over the freight tracks. *The Brown Company*, it said, *Removers of Dead Animals*.

But once across the railway you step into a new world, a country undreamed of by the uptown citizen. Green meadows lie under the pink sunset light. One-story white houses, very small, but with yards swept clean and neat whitewashed fences, stand under poplars and willows. It is almost an incredible experience to come upon that odd little village as one crosses a wooden bridge and sees boys fishing hopefully in a stagnant canal. At the bend in the lane is a trim white house with vivid flowers in the garden, beds patterned with whited shells, an old figurehead—or is it a cigar-store sign?—of a colored boy in a blue coat, freshly painted in the yard. It is like a country hamlet, full of dogs, hens, ducks and children. In the stable yards horses stand munching at the barn doors. Some of the little houses are painted red, brown and green. A girl in a faded blue pinafore comes up the road leading two white horses; a solitary cow trails along behind.

Like every country village, Stonehouse lane has its own grocery store, a fascinating little place where one can sit on the porch and drink a bottle of lemon soda. This tiny shop is stuffed with all manner of provisioning; it has one of the old-fashioned coffee grinders with two enormous flywheels. In the dusk, when the two oil lamps are lit and turned low on account of the heat, it shines with a fine tawny light that would speak to the eye of a painter. A lamplighter comes along kindling the gas burners, which twinkle down the long white lane. A rich essence of pig steeps in the air, but it is not unpalatable to one accustomed to the country. As one sits on the porch of the store friendly dogs nose about one, and the village children come with baskets to do the evening purchasing.

A map of the city gives one little help in exploring this odd region of The Neck. According to the map one might believe that it is laid out and built up in rectilinear streets. As a matter of fact it is a spread of meadows, marshes and scummy canals, with winding lanes and paths stepping off among clumps of trees and quaint white cottages half hidden among rushes, lilies and honeysuckle matting. Off to the east rise the masts and wireless aërials of League Island. It is a strange land, with customs of its own, not to be discerned at sight. Like all small communities, sharply conscious of their own identity, it is proud and reserved. It is a native American settlement: the children are flaxen and sturdy, their skin gilded with that amazing richness and beauty of color that comes to small urchins who play all day long in the sun in scant garmenting.

Over another railway siding one passes into the fens proper, and away from the village of Stonehouse lane. (I wonder, by the way, what was the stone house which gave it the name? All the present cottages are plainly wood.) Now one is in a country almost Dutch in aspect. It is seamed with canals and was probably an island originally, for it is still spoken of as Greenwich Island. Along the canals are paths, white and dusty in the summer drought, very soft to walk upon. Great clumps of thick old willows stand up against the low horizon. The light grows less steep as the sun sinks in a powdery haze of rose and orange. In one of the canals, below a high embankment, half a dozen naked boys were bathing, attended by a joyous white dog. In that evening pinkness of light their bodies gleamed beautifully. Through masses of flowering sumac, past thick copses and masses of reeds, over broad fields of bird-song, narrow paths lead down to the river. In the warm savor of summer air it all seemed as deserted and refreshing as some Adirondack pasture. Then one stands at the top of a little sandy bank and sees the great bend of the Delaware. Opposite is the mouth of Timber Creek, Walt Whitman's favorite pleasure haunt. A little lower down is League Island.

One of the most fascinating dreams one could have is of all this broad fen-land as a great city playground. It is strange that Philadelphia has made so little use of the Delaware for purposes of public beauty. A landscape architect would go mad with joy if given the delightful task of planning The Neck as a park. It would take comparatively little effort to drain it properly and make it one of the noblest pleasure grounds in the world. Will this wonderful strip of river-bank be allowed to pass into slime and smoke as the lower Schuylkill has done?

The stream lap-laps against a narrow shelf of sandy beach, where there are a number of logs for comfortable sitting. A water rat ran quietly up the bank as I slid down it. A steamer passed up the river, her windows aflame with the last of the sunlight. Birds were merry in the scrub willows, and big dragon-flies flittering about. The light grew softer and grayer, while a concave moon swung high over the water. Motorboats chugged gently by, while a big dredge further upstream continued to clang and grind. By and by the river was empty. It had been a very hot day, and a great idea occurred to me. In the good old brownish water of the Delaware I had what my friend Mifflin McGill used to call a "surreptious" swim.

# VALLEY FORGE

A CURIOUS MAGIC moves in the air of Valley Forge. There is the same subtle plucking at heart and nerves that one feels when, coming home from abroad, passing up some salty harbor on a ship, he sees his own flag rippling from a home staff. It is a sudden inner vision of the meaning of America. It is a realization of the continuity of history, a sense of the imperishable quality of human virtue. And today, when this nation stands on the sill of a new era, ready to surrender for the sake of humanity some of the proud traditions ingrained by years of bitter struggle, what place could be a more fitting haunt of dreams and nursery of imagination? Here, on these wind-swept slopes where now the summer air carries the sweetness of fresh-cut hay, here in this vale of humiliation men met the arrows of despair. There is an old belief that it is the second summer that is the danger time in a baby's life. It was the second winter that was the cradle-crisis of the young republic—the winter of 1777–1778. It was then that began the long road that carries us from Valley Forge to Versailles.

Few of us realize, I think, what a vast national shrine Valley Forge has become under the careful hands of a few devoted people. There is little of winter and dearth in that spreading park as one views it on a July afternoon. In the great valley of the Schuylkill green acres of young corn ripple in the breeze. Sunlight and shadow drift across the hillsides as great rafts of cloud swim down unseen channels of the wind. There is no country in America lovelier than those quiet hills and vales of Montgomery and Chester counties, with their shadowed creeks, their plump orchards and old stone farmhouses. My idea of jovial destiny would be to be turned loose (about the beginning of the scrapple season) somewhere in the neighborhood of the King of

245

Prussia—no one but an idiot will ever call him by his new name of Ye Old King!—with a knapsack of tobacco, a knobby stick and a volume of R. L. S.

Coming down the road from Devon, the first thing one sees is the great equestrian statue of Anthony Wayne on its pink pedestal. It stands on a naked ridge, which was formerly groved with fine oaks. The Caliph who had me in charge told me with blood in his eye that the trees had been slaughtered in order to give a wider view of the statue. It seems a serious pity. Beyond this one comes to the National Arch, designed by Paul Cret, of the University of Pennsylvania, who has since so gallantly served his native France on fields of battle far more terrible than Valley Forge. From this arch, with its fine inscription by Henry Armitt Brown, there is a serene view across yellow fields of stubble where a big hay wagon was piled high with its fragrant load.

Mr. Weikel, the friendly guard on duty at this spot, a Civil War veteran, was kind enough to show us the hut which is his headquarters. It is one of the many scattered through the park, replicas of the original soldiers' huts, built of logs and chinked with clay. With its little smoke-stained fireplace and weathered roof, sitting on that hilltop in the sweet quick air, it seemed a pleasant place for meditation. Over the rough-hewn mantel was an old picture of George Washington and a badge belonging to some member of the American Press Humorists, dropped by one of these mad wags on their recent visit to the park.

But the chief glory of Valley Forge is the Washington Memorial Chapel, a place so startling in its beauty that it takes the breath away. Through a humble arched door—as lowly as the doorway of suffering through which the nation came to birth—one enters a shrine of color where the history of the republic is carved in stone. The tall windows blaze with blue and scarlet. A silk Stars and Stripes, hanging by the stone pulpit, waves gently in the cool wind that draws up from the valley and through the open door. The archway into the cloister frames a glimpse of green. In every detail this marvelous little Westminster Abbey of America shows the devoted thought of Dr. Herbert Burk, the man who has lavished his heart upon this noble symbol of our national life. With his brown eyes glowing with enthusiasm he will explain how the religion, the romance, the pathos and humor of a century and a half are woven into every line and tint of the fabric. The magnificent stained windows—windows that recall nothing less fine than the most splendid cathedrals of the middle ages— were planned by Doctor Burk and executed by Nicola D'Ascenzo. The marvelous oak carvings of the choir stalls and pews, the carved lead lamps, the organ, all were done here in Philadelphia.

This amazing poem in stone, endless in lovingly elaborated beauty, can no more be described than any great poem can be described. It is as perfect, as unique, as "The Eve of Saint Agnes"; as rich in color and as thrilling in meaning. On these hillsides, where men "tramped the snow to coral," hungry, shivering and unshod; where a great artist, wanting to paint the commander-in-chief, had to do it on bedticking; and where this same commander, worshiper as well as warrior, stole from the campfire to pray; on this field of doubt and suffering there has risen this monument of religious art, devised as a focus of patriotic inspiration for the whole republic. It is an altar of national worship, as though expressly conceived to give outward shape to the words uttered only yesterday by another commander-in-chief:

> The stage is set, the destiny disclosed. It has come about by no plan of our conceiving, but by the hand of God, who led us into this way. We cannot turn back. We can only go forward, with lifted eyes and freshened spirit, to follow the vision. It was of this that we dreamed at our birth.

Of the dreams of America's birth the Washington Memorial Chapel is the noble and fitting symbol. It is both a thanksgiving and a prophecy.

From no other lips than those of Doctor Burk himself can the story of this place be told. He will tell you how the chapel grew out of humility and discouragement. He will show you the plain little wooden chapel which he built first of all, before money could be raised for the present building. He will show you the gargoyle—the Imp of Valley Forge—which he says is emblematic of the spirit of the place because he can smile even in winter when his mouth is full of ice. The chapel goes back to the truest tradition of medieval art, when so much humor was carved into the stone ornaments of cathedrals. When the cornerstone was laid in 1903 Doctor Burk had only enough money on hand to pay for two loads of stone; he had only a piece of hemlock board to shelter the copper box that contained the relics to be inclosed in the foundations, and after the ceremony had to smuggle the box back to his home for safe-keeping. Standing in the beautiful little cloister, where the open-air pulpit looks out into the woodland cathedral (with Mount Vernon elms planted in the form of a cross), he says: "If the park were left alone it would be merely a picnic ground. It's the most spiritual spot in America: we must maintain its spiritual heritage."

It is one of the rector's regrets that only one President has ever visited Valley Forge. As one stands in the open-air pulpit looking out through the grove of elms and over the blue and green valley, one wishes that Mr. Wilson might visit the spot. There is no place in America of such peculiar significance just now; there would be no man so quick as Mr. Wilson to catch its spiritual echoes. Even the humblest of us hears secret whispers in the rustle of those trees.

# DARBY CREEK

THE OTHER DAY we had an adventure that gave us great joy, and, like all great adventures, it was wholly unexpected.

We went out to spend an evening with a certain Caliph who lives at Daylesford—how many Main Line commuters, by the way, know that it is named for Daylesford in Gloucestershire, the home of Warren Hastings?—and after supper the Caliph took us for a stroll round the twilight. In a green hollow below the house, only a few paragraphs away from the room where this Caliph sits and writes essays (he is the only author in Philadelphia who has never received a rejection slip), he showed us a delicious pool, fed by several springs and lying under great willows. From this pool tinkled a modest brook, splashing over a dam and winding away down an alluring valley. A white road ran beside it, through agreeable thickets and shubbery, starting off with a twist that suggested all manner of pleasant surprises for the wayfarer. It was just the kind of road to see spread before one at the cool outset of a long summer day.

"This," said the Caliph, "is the headwater of Darby creek."

Little did the Caliph, douce man, know what that simple statement meant to us. The headwaters of Darby! Darby creek, and its younger brother, Cobb's creek, were the Abana and Pharpar of our youth. We were nourished first of all on Cobb's, where we had our first swim and caught our first tadpoles and conducted our first search for buried treasure (and also smelt our first skunk cabbage). Then, in our teens, we ranged farther afield and learned the way to Darby, by whose crystal waters we used to fry bacon and read R. L. S. There will never be any other stream quite as dear to our heart.

Until the other evening at the Caliph's we had not seen the water of Darby creek for ten years; not such a long time, perhaps, as some reckon these matters, but quite long enough. And our mind runs back with unrestrained enthusiasm to the days when we lived only two miles away from that delicious stream. Darby creek is associated in our mind with a saw and cider mill that used to stand—and very likely still stands—where the creek crosses the West Chester pike. To that admirable spot, in the warm blue haze of an October afternoon, certain young men used to tramp. While the whirling blades of the sawmill screamed through green logs, these care-free innocents used to sit round a large vat where the juice of fresh apples came trickling through some sort of burlap squeezing coils, and where fat and groggy wasps buzzed and tottered and expired in rapture. These youths (who should not be blamed, for indeed they had few responsibilities and cares) would ply the flagon with diligence, merrily toasting the trolleys that hummed by on the way to West Chester. We will not give away their names, for they are now demure and respected merchants and lawyers and members of Rotary clubs and stock exchanges. But we remember one of these who was notably susceptible to cider. On the homeward path, as he flourished his intellect broadcast and quoted Maeterlinck and Bliss Carman, he was induced by his comrades to crawl inside a large terra-cotta pipe that lay by the roadside. Just how this act of cozening was accomplished we forget; perhaps it was a wager to see whether he, being proud of his slender figure, was slim enough to eel through the tube. At any rate, he vanished inside. The pipe lay at the top of a gentle hill, and for his companions it was the work of an inspired moment to seize the cylinder and set it rolling down the grade. Merrily it revolved for a hundred feet or more, at high velocity, and culbutted into a ditch. The dizzied victim emerged at length, quoting Rabelais.

The mile and a half along the creek above this sawmill—up to where an odd little branch railroad crosses the stream on a tottery trestle and Ithan creek runs in—was the pleasure haunt best known to us. It was approached through Coopertown, that rustic settlement which the Bryn Mawr squire has recently turned into a Tom Tiddler's ground. Across stubble fields and down an enchanting valley carpeted with moss we scoured on many and many an afternoon, laden with the rudiments of a meal. There was said to be a choleric farmer with a shotgun and an angry collie on the western marge of the stream, and it was always a matter of courage to send over an envoy (chosen by lot) to bag a few ears of corn for roasting. But for our own part we never encountered this enemy, though Mifflin once came throbbing back empty-handed and pale-faced, reporting that a charge of lead had sung past his ears. Above a small dam the creek backed up to a decent depth, five feet or so of cool green water, and here bathing was conducted in the ancient Greek manner. There were sun-warmed fence rails nearby for basking, and then a fire would be built and vittles mobilized. Tobacco pouches were emptied out into one common store, and by the time this was smoked out a white moonlight would be spilling over the autumn fields.

We grew so fond of this section of our Abana that we never explored the full length of the stream. It would be a lovely day's jaunt, we imagine, to set out from Darby (where Cobb's creek joins Darby creek) and walk up the little river to its source at Daylesford. (The original Daylesford, by the way, is also made lovely by the only other stripling stream that competes with Darby in our heart. This is the delicious Evenlode, an upper twig of the Thames.) It would be about twenty miles, which is a just distance for a walker who likes to study the scenery as he goes. Through the greater part of the trail the stream trots through open farming country, with old mills here and there—paper mills, flour mills and our famous shrine of sawdust and cider. The lower waters, from Darby down to Tinicum Island and the mouth at Essington, would probably be less walkable. We suspect them of being marshy, though we speak only by the map. Mr. Browning, we remember, wrote a poem about a bishop who ordered his tomb at Saint Praxed's. We, if we had a chance to lay out any blue-prints of our final rolltop, would like to be the Colyumist who ordered his tomb by Darby creek, and not too far away from that cider mill. And let no one think that it is a stream of merely sentimental interest. Hog Island, as all will grant, is a place of national importance. And what is Hog Island, after all? Only the delta of Darby creek.

# DARBY REVISITED

THE SOOTHSAYER owns a car, and tools passionately about the country, revisiting the vistas and glimpses that he thinks particularly lovely. But he is a stubborn partisan of such beauty spots as he has himself discovered, and bitterly reluctant to concede any glamour to places he hasn't visited. For a long time he has heard us raving about Darby creek, and always asserted furiously that we had never seen a certain road up Norristown way that was (he said) a far, far better thing than any place we would be likely to know about. But the other evening, somewhat stirred by our piteous babble about the old cider mill we hadn't visited for ten years, he got out his 'bus and we set forth.

We went out along the West Chester pike, and the manner of the Soothsayer was subtly supercilious. All the way out from Sixty-ninth street the road is in bad condition, and as he nursed his handsome vehicle over the bumps we could see that the Soothsayer thought (though too polite to say so) that we were leading him into a very bedraggled and ill-assorted region. Another very sinister rebuke was that he had left up the canopy top over the car, although it was a serene and lucid evening, flushed with quiet sunset. This seemed to imply that any tract of country we would lead him to would hardly be worth examining carefully. As we passed by the university astronomical observatory he made a last attempt to divert us from the haven of our desire. He suggested that we both go in and have a look at the moon through the big telescope. As it was then broad and sunny daylight we treated this absurd project with contempt.

Down a steep winding hill, and we came upon the historic spot with delightful suddenness. Our heart was uplifted. There it was, unchanged, the old gray building

253

standing among trees, with the clank and grind of the
water-wheels, the yellow dapple of level sun upon the
western wall.

But what was this? Under the porch-roof was a man
bending over iron plates, surrounded by a dazzle of pale
blue light. He was using an electric welder, and the groan
of a dynamo sounded from the interior of the old mill. "It's
probably a garage now," said the Soothsayer, "most of
these old places are."

But that was the Soothsayer's last flash of cynicism, for in
another moment the spell of the place had disarmed him.
We approached, and it seemed to us there was something
familiar in the face of the man operating the welder, as he
watched his dazzling blue flame through a screen. It was
Mr. Flounders, who has run the old mill for going on thirty
years, and who used to preside at the cider press in days
gone by, when we had many a pull at his noble juices. But
he hasn't made any cider for several years, he told us; the
sawmill shed is unused, and the old mill itself is being
fitted up with ice-making machinery. He says he went out
West for a while, but he came back to Darby creek in the
end. We don't blame him. The spell of that enchanting
spot may well keep its hold on all who have ever loved it.

The Soothsayer and his passenger got out their pipes and
brooded a while, watching the green swift water of the mill
race; the sunny flicker of the creek below as it darts on its
way through the meadows; the great oak tree steeped in
sunlight, and the old millstones that still lie about by the
front door. Inside the building the wooden beams and
levers and grooved wheels are just as they were when the
place was built as a flour and feed mill, in 1837. The
woodwork still has that clean, dusty gloss that is characteristic of a flour mill. By the sawing shed lie a number of
great logs, admirable site for a quiet smoke. The Soothsayer, tremendously impressed by this time, wandered
about with us and listened kindly to all our spasms of

reminiscence. We both agreed that the old mill, dozing in the sunlight, with the pale and tremulous shimmer of blue light in the porch where Mr. Flounders was working, was a fit subject for some artist's brush.

We did not fail to admire the remarkable old house across the road, where Mr. Flounders lives. It is built in three portions: a wooden lean-to, a very ancient section of white-washed logs (which must be some 200 years old) and then the largest part of the dappled stone of various colors so familiar to Pennsylvania ramblers. Nothing can be more delightful in the rich tint of afternoon light than that medley of brown, gray, yellow and ochre stonework. We pointed out the little side road that we were to follow, running up the valley of the creek, past reddening apple orchards and along the meadows past the swimming pool. And then the Soothsayer paid us a genuine compliment. "Let's take down the top," said he. "Then we can really see something!"

# THE HAPPY VALLEY

TWO FRIENDS, who may be called for present purposes Messrs. Madrigal and Doggerel, dismounted from the West Chester trolley at the crossing of Darby creek. Madrigal rolled a cigarette. Doggerel filled a pipe. They paid their respects to the old sawmill and Mr. Flounders, its presiding deity. Then they set off for a tramp up the valley.

It was a genial afternoon, after a night of thrashing rain and gale. The air was meek and placid; the sky a riotous blue. After the tumultuous washing of the storm all the heavenly linen was hung out to dry, bulging and ballooning in snowy clots along the upper dome. The tents of creek-side campers were sodden, and great branches lay scattered on the meadows, wrenched down by the wind. By Mr. Sanderson's farm at Brookthorpe a scoutmaster was breaking camp, preparing to take his boys home. They had only been there four days and the grieved urchins stood in miserable silence. The hurricane of the night before had nearly washed them away, and as everything was so wet their leader feared to let them sleep on the ground. The boys were heartbroken, but the scoutmaster said sagely: "I'd rather have the boys mad at me than their mothers."

In spite of the recent downpour, the walking was admirable. Roads were damp, easy underfoot, free from dust. Madrigal and Doggerel were gay at heart. They scrambled up the embankment of the deserted Delaware County Railroad, which is the most direct pathway toward the headwaters of Darby. It is possible to go along the bank of the creek, but underbrush was still drenched, and Mr. Sanderson uttered cryptic warning of a certain bull. On the grass-grown track of the antique railroad, treading gingerly over worm-eaten wooden trestles, the explorer enjoys perfect sunny tranquillity. It is only five miles from the city limits, but one moves in the heart of bird-song and ancient solitude. One freight train a day is the traffic of the forgotten line, and probably the director general of railroads never heard of it. It would not be surprising to meet Rip Van Winkle pacing thoughtfully along the mouldering ties. And as it is raised high above the valley, the walker gains a fair prospect over the green country of Darbyland. The creek, swollen with rain, brawled rapidly along its winding shallows. Cattle munched in the meadows. Goldenrod was minting its gold, a first faint suggestion of autumn breathed in the sleepy air. Madrigal tore off his linen collar, stuffed it in his pocket, and fell to quoting Keats. Doggerel, having uttered some painful words about the old cider traffic, now evaporated, Madrigal bestirred his memory of the Ode to Autumn. "Or by a cider press, with patient look, Thou watchest the last oozings, hours by hours." Madrigal is a man of well-stored mind, and as the wayfarers tripped nimbly along the ties, where wild flowers embroider the old cuttings and deserted farms stand crumbling among knotted apple trees, he beguiled the journey with varied speculation and discourse.

At a long-abandoned station known as Foxcroft—which is now only a quarry, and has the air of some mining settlement of the far West—the walkers began to understand something of the secret of this region. It is a fox-hunting country (according to the map, the next station on this mystic line was called The Hunt) and from here on they caught glimpses of the life of that picturesque person known as the "country gentleman." There were jumping barriers for horses erected in the meadows; rows of kennels, and a red-cheeked squire with a riding crop and gaiters striding along the road. Along that rolling valley, with whispering cornfields and fair white mansions lingering among trees, is the tint and contour of rural England, long-settled, opulent and serene. In one thing only does it lack English charm: there are no old ale-houses along the way.

No *King's Arms* or *Waggon and Horses* or *Jolly Ploughboy* where one may sit on a bench well-polished by generations of corduroyed hindquarters and shut out the smiling horizon with a tankard's rim. "Oh land of freedom!" cried Madrigal, ironically, clucking his tongue upon a drouthy palate.

From Foxcroft there is a tempting blue vista up a tributary valley toward Newtown Square, which would be well worth exploring; but Madrigal and Doggerel turned away through another covered bridge in order to keep along the trend of Darby. A detour along the road brought them back to the creek at a magnificent stone bridge of three arches. The man who designed that bridge was a true artist, and had studied the old English bridges. And at this corner stands a curious old house bearing the inscription *Ludwig's Lust* (Ludwig's Pleasure) *Built 1774, Remodelled 1910.* As the pedestrians stood admiring, a car drove up to the door, and the hapless Doggerel created some irritation by hopefully asking one of the motorists if the place were an inn.

After Ludwig's Lust came the most enchanting stretch of the journey. The road runs close by the creek, which foams along a stony course under an aisle of trees. Where Wigwam Run joins the creek is a group of farm buildings and a wayside spring of perfect water. It was sorry to see a beautiful old outhouse of dappled stonework being pick-axed into rubble. At this point is the fork of Darby and Little Darby. An old deserted mill is buried in greenery, the stones furred with moss. Just beyond, a little road dips off to the left, crossing both branches of the stream. Here, where Little Darby churns cascading among great boulders and tiny shelves of sand, one might well be in some mountain elbow of the Poconos. Madrigal and Doggerel gazed tenderly on this shady cavern of wood and water. If it had been an hour earlier, with the sunlight strong upon these private grottoes, a bathe would have been in order. But it was already drawing late.

The Berwyn road, on which the travelers now proceeded,

is full of surprises. Great houses crown the hilltops, with rows of slender poplars silhouetted against the sky. Here and there a field of tawny grain lifts a smooth shoulder against blue heaven. A little drinking fountain on a downward grade drops a tinkling dribble of cold water from a carved lion's mouth. Among old willows and buttonwoods stand comely farmhouses—one beside the road is tinted a rich salmon pink. A real estate agent's sign at the entrance to a fine tract says, "For Sale, 47 acres, with Runing Water." The walkers thought they discerned a message in that. For a *rune* means a mark of magic significance, a whisper, a secret counsel. And the chiming water of Darby has its own whispers of secret counsel as it runs its merry way, a laughing little river that preaches sermons unawares.

In the meadows near Old St. David's Church—built when Philadelphia itself was hardly more than a village—are Guernsey calves, soft as a plush cushion, with bright topaz eyes. Madrigal told how he had written a poem about Old St. David's when he was sixteen, in which he described the "kine" grazing by the stream, and in which (after the manner of poets in their teens) he besought merciful Death to come and take him. Death, one supposes, was sorely tempted, but happily refrained from reaping the tender bardling.

In the quiet graveyard of Old St. David's the travelers halted a while, to see the grave of Anthony Wayne and admire the thin trailers of the larches swinging in the golden flood of late sunlight that slanted down the valley. It was 6 o'clock, and they were beginning to doubt their ability to reach their destination on time. A party of motorists were just leaving the church, and both Madrigal and Doggerel loitered pointedly by the gate in hopes of a lift. But no such fortune. So they set valiantly upon the last leg of the afternoon. In a shady bend of the road came a merry motor zooming along and Doggerel's friend, Jarden Guenther, at the wheel. Mr. Guenther was doubtless amazed to see Doggerel in this remote spot, but he was going the other way, and passed with a cheerful halloo. Then, by the old Defense Signal tree on the Paoli road, came a flivver, which rescued the two plodders and took them two miles or so on their way. By the Tredyffrin golf course they were set down before a winding byway, which they followed with tingling shanks and hearts full of achievement.

A shady lane by the now stripling Darby brought them to a quiet pool under leaning willows, and a silver gush of water over a small dam beneath which a bronze Venus bathes herself thoughtfully. Madrigal wore the face of one entering into joy rarely vouchsafed to battered poets. Doggerel, in his paltry way, was likewise of blithe cheer. Through a gap in the hedge they scaled a knoll and reached their haven. And here they found what virtuous walkers have ever found at the end of an innocent journey—a bath, a beer, and a blessing.

# THE PARADISE
# SPECIAL

THE BIG BUS known to thousands of Philadelphia children as the Paradise Special was standing ready at 1621 Cherry street. Inside, in one of the large classrooms of the Friends' Select School, twenty small boys, each carefully tagged and carrying his bundle, were waiting impatiently. It was half-past eight in the morning, and the bus was about to leave for Paradise Farm with the Tuesday morning consignment of urchins for the summer camp run by the Children's Country Week Association. The doctor was looking over them and one poor youngster was trying to conceal his tears from the rest. The doctor had found a spot in his throat and he had a high temperature. He was not to be allowed to go this week; his turn would have to come later. They were all a bit impatient by this time. Most of them had been up since half-past five, counting every minute.

If you enjoy a shrill treble uproar, and find it amusing to watch a busload of small boys enjoying themselves at the top of their versatile powers, I recommend a trip on the Paradise Special. Throughout the week the bus is busy taking children and mothers to the various farms and camps run by the Association, but Tuesday morning is boys' day. Not the least amusing feature of the trip is to watch the expressions of those the bus passes on the road. It creates a broad grin wherever it goes. That shouting caravan of juvenile glee is indeed an entertaining sight.

There were nineteen boys on board when we left Cherry street—an unusually small load for the Paradise Special. Others were going out by train. But nineteen boys, aged from seven to thirteen, comprise a considerable amount of energy. Three or four of them had been to Paradise Farm before, and immediately took the lead in commenting on all that befell. Mickey Coyle was one of these, lamenting that as he would be thirteen in September this would probably be his last visit. "But I'm lucky I ain't dead," he said philosophically. "I've a brother twenty years old who's dead. He died on my birthday. He had bronnical pneumonia and typhoid and flu."

We passed along the Parkway. "This is a Bollyvard, ain't it?" said one. Entering the Park, another cried, "Is this the country?" "Sure, them's the Rocky Mountains," said Mickey in scorn.

The first question in the minds of all the passengers was to know exactly how soon, and at what precise point, they would be "in the country." The Park, though splendid enough, was not "the country." As we sped along City Line road there was intense argument as to whether those on one side of the bus were in the country while those of us on the other side were still in the city. Another game that seemed to underlie all their thoughts was that this expedition was in some way connected with misfortune for Germany. Every time we overhauled another car or truck—which happened not infrequently, for the Paradise Special travels at a good clip—that car was set down as German. Every time a swift vehicle passed us we were said to be in danger of being torpedoed. For some period of time we were conceived to be a load of German prisoners who had been captured by the Yanks. Then again one small enthusiast shouted out that we were "bullsheviks" who had been arrested.

Once satisfied that we were really in the country—and they were not quite at ease on this point until the last of the suburban movies had been left behind—their attention focused itself on the question of apple trees. Even so experienced a Country Weeker as Mickey (this was his fifth visit to the Farm) was vague on this point. To a city youngster almost every tree seems to be an apple tree. And everything that looks in the least reddish is a strawberry. Unripe blackberries along the hedges were hailed with tumult and shouting as strawberries. Every cow with horns was regarded a little fearfully as a bull. And a cow in the unfamiliar posture of lying down on top of a hill was pointed out (from a distance) as a "statue."

After we passed Daylesford and Green Tree and the blue hills along the Schuylkill came into view, the cry, "Look at that scenery!" became incessant. Any view containing hills is known as "scenery" to the Country Weekers. When the scenery began eleven-year-old Charley Franklin could contain himself no longer. He began to tear off the clean shirt and new shoes in which his mother had sent him from home, and, digging in his bundle, hauled out a blouse and tattered pair of sneakers that satisfied his idea of fitness for the great adventure. He proudly showed me his small bathing suit, carefully wrapped up in a Sunday comic supplement. His paper bag of cookies had long since been devoured, and the question of how soon another meal would come his way was beginning to worry him. Then we turned off the high road, past a signpost saying Paradise Farm, and they were all on their toes. The long, echoing tunnel under the high railway embankment was greeted with resounding cheers. More cheers for the swimming hole just beyond. We drew up at the foot of a steep flight of wooden steps leading up the hill. All piled out with yells. At the top of the stairs stood a rather glum group of forty similar urchins. These responded without much acclaim to the applause of the newcomers. They were the batch going home on the bus. Their week at Paradise was over.

When we left, a few minutes later, the arrivals were already being assigned to their bunks in the various camp bungalows, and were looking around exultantly at the plentiful "scenery" and evidences of plentiful food to come. But the temper of the returning load was not quite so mirthful. They also had been up since an early hour, but play had languished as they had put on their clean clothes and had carefully bundled up their other stores in small newspaper wrappings. One small cynic told me that he had learned the necessary connection between green apples and castor oil. Another, with flaming red hair, seemed to have tears in his eyes. Whether these were due to green apples or to grief I could not determine. But the way they all shouted good-by to Mr. and Mrs. Steel (who have charge of the camp) showed how they appreciated their week's adventure. "Good-by swimming hole!" they shouted, and then "Good-by snakes!" explaining that they had killed four small garter snakes in the meadow. They cheered up greatly when they saw a freight train puffing along the railway, and it was evident that we would have a fair race with that train all the way in to Overbrook. Immediately the train was set down as a German menace, and the cheerful chauffeur was implored to do his best for his country. It should be said that we beat the German train to Overbrook by about one hundred yards.

The latter part of the ride was marked by a sudden panic on the part of the passengers concerning sundry nickels and dimes which seemed to have disappeared. Nathan Schumpler, aged eight, turned his blouse pocket inside out a dozen times without finding the dime he was sure he had had. This was a terrible blow, because he told me he had lost a quarter through a crack in the porch the day before. This started all the others exploring. Knotted and far from clean handkerchiefs were hastily untied to make sure of the precious coinage for homeward carfare. At last Nathan found his dime, in the very pocket he had been turning upside down for fifteen minutes. When they got back to Cherry street they were overjoyed to find a number of toy trains and tracks waiting on the floor. My last sight of the Country Weekers was when they were playing with these while their guardians checked off their lists and made sure that each had carfare to take him home and knew how to get there. "Yes," said the chauffeur, as he lit a cigarette and watched them disperse, "they're a great bunch. But if you want to hear noise, you should listen to the girls when they go out."

# HAVERFORD

To be deeply rooted in a place that has meaning is perhaps the best gift a child can have. If that place has beauty and a feeling of permanence it may suggest to him unawares that sense of identity with this physical earth which is the humblest and happiest of life's intuitions.

Over the lawns of Haverford in the late '90s there shone the cheery simplicity of an older mode. A college of only a hundred students, which had outgrown some of the anxious problems of its youth, still combined the traditional plainness of its Quaker inheritance with an undergraduate life of busy hilarity and horseplay. "How like an English nobleman's park!" was once the naïve exclamation of a British visitor on seeing the college's beautiful domain; and indeed there was a certain agreeable paradox in finding these young Pennsylvania puritans revelling at their ease in a landscaped arcadia worthy of the Duke of Marlborough. Philadelphia Friends have never allowed their ethical "plainness" to interfere with carnal comfort, and a Haverford boyhood's earliest impression was quite likely to be of the rich feastings in front of Founders Hall at Commencement time. Under the bronze glimmer of copper beech trees the long tables were set out. When were there ever such great bowls of strawberries and chicken salad; such largesse of ice cream? On the cricket field were flannels and scarlet blazers; tally-ho parties came driving up the noble avenue of elms; through the long sweetness of a June day would continue the annual match with the University of Pennsylvania, with interval for al fresco lunch. Cricket is not a "game," it is always a "match"; and it is by no means devoid of occasion for hardihood. Perhaps it is not a sport apt for the American temper, but if the day comes when leisurely tourneys no longer pattern Cope Field with white

266

figures, and no connoisseurs sit contentedly smoking on the long weatherstained benches in the shade, something of great charm will have passed away. In the general herd stampede of American life Haverford was always just a little different—not in the least by ostentation or intent; she happened to grow that way.

So it is that the young Mistletoe of whom I write can never be grateful enough for the early glimpse of an arcadian quietness. It is an instructive experience to have grown up astraddle of two epochs. It is interesting to remember the days when there were no taxis at the Haverford station, but old McGurk with his queer-smelling hack; when small boys ran yelling across the campus to see the first horseless carriage; when the Main Line trains were still drawn by those dainty P.R.R. locomotives with the rakish cowcatcher and a slender funnel with a fluted rim; when elderly Friends had their coat collars cut away at the back of the neck, collars and lapels being considered Babylonish. (John Woolman sailed in the steerage of the ship *Mary and Elizabeth*, instead of in the cabin, because he found in the vessel's cabin quarters "sundry sorts of carved work and imagery," which put his mind "under a deep exercise.") It is always the inconsistencies of any doctrine that are most lovable. It gives one pleasure to remember that in the era of Haverford's greatest rigor, when music and fiction were stringently excluded from official countenance, the college built Barclay Hall (1877). For purposes of worldly flourish they abandoned the fine old simplicity of Founders Hall and went in for a vast barrack of clumsy pseudo-Gothic bravado. It even had a spire, the thing which more than anything else caused George Fox epilepsies. This edifice, named for a worthy old Scottish apologist, was so greatly admired that the same architect was later engaged to start the career of Bryn Mawr College with an even more sinister nondescript, Taylor Hall. In course of time Barclay Hall has grown well-loved for its jocund associations, but it exists as

267

a large reminder that even men of immaculate piety are not always delicate in taste.

So much of living is irrelevant, and the phases of it that we learn to have deep dear meaning seem to arrive perilously haphazard. It can hardly be amiss to look inward upon our only sure treasure and try to discern what were the flashes of quintessence. It implies a very profound humility, and an incurable passion for living; but more than that it lays itself upon one by unexplained necessity. In old days of Friends' meeting one sitting in the silence who felt himself moved by some "concern" was supposed to stand and deliver. Just so Mistletoe feels, and has long felt, a concern to explore the memories of thirty years or so and say, This was beautiful; this had a meaning. As he approaches forty (wondering why Thackeray in his ballad represents that age as one of such settled sobriety?) he is acutely aware of the fantastic antinomy between life as it is actually experienced and life as reported to us by the accredited expounders. At that period one should be ready to begin to try to educate himself in the things that matter. No wonder, then, that for his own composure he hankers to set down some hard-won inflexions from his own grammar of surprise. The paradigms that are most beautiful can scarce be discussed in prose. (It is not that poets are granted greater license; it is that they have fewer—and more understanding—readers.) But the time will come when none will be able to put down for you these flairs and furies of your own. Once in the humble little Friends' meetinghouse in Oxford a shy homely girl in a plain tweed suit suddenly got up in the silent sitting. It was a clear spring forenoon, with that moist English savor in the air. Her voice trembled with terror, but she managed to say "I'm thinking of the sky and the trees and the shadows of the trees, and the wind, and the smell of everything." She sat down, subsiding into a shaken privacy of tears; but we understood. Of all the outgivings he heard in his years of Friends' meeting, Mistletoe remembers that one best.

It would be hard to imagine a happier childhood. He did not often in later years allow himself to think back about it, so far from those placid scenes had subsequent preoccupations led him. Save only that there was no salt water near, Haverford was a perfect place for such purposes as his. It is a lively suburb now, but in the 'nineties it was still country. West of the college tall regiments of corn stretched in rustling files toward sunset; all was wood and farmland to the immortal water of Darby Creek. Oh Darby, unspoiled even now, is there none to celebrate you but he?

Haverford was provincial then in the best sense, a social and sectarian integer, drawing its students mostly from a solid (and probably rather unimaginative) swath of Quaker families. One would not, and did not, expect any rare passion for intellectual frenzy in so placid a commune. But in subtle ways one felt influences at work. It was good to come into life in that little world while Isaac Sharpless was its presiding officer. He was a man in somewhat the antique mould, with almost an Abraham Lincoln flavor in his gravity and his humor. It takes one back to excellent simplicities to remember that his first call to the vocation of teaching came to him when he was ploughing in a field near Westtown, where he was waited upon by a committee of Westtown School. Nor does one forget his telling how in the difficult days of his early service at Haverford, for relief from anxieties he would retire at night to the college observatory to study the stars. That little domed retreat, camped in a cluster of confidential pine trees and suggesting a mystic Oriental shrine, was a place of romantic riddle to Mistletoe from earliest days. And somehow he connects Isaac Sharpless's evenings there with a bequest long afterward noted in the college catalogue, "to encourage the ennobling study of the heavens."

Remembered impressions of childhood are under suspicion; it is difficult not to interpolate into them significances we became aware of later. But it is important to reintegrate what one may of the pure artistic permeability of that prime. I believe all the little group of urchins who grew together on the college lawns (the Haverford faculty was always comfortably proliferous) early relished a notion of their sylvestered world as a place apart. In the Little School (as it was always known), a yellow cottage by the meeting house, or in overheard conversation of their elders, these small fry gathered a vague idea of the modest but honorable traditions of their birthplace. James Russell Lowell had visited there, yes, and even (I think) Matthew Arnold; and the body of Lincoln had passed by our own grounds on the way to burial in Illinois. These legends certainly meant less than the Swarthmore Game; but they were in the background of one's pride. More important still was the realization, felt in the passive acceptance of nonage, that there was beauty on that lawn. Few places can show such comely sweeps of turf and shrubbery. To begin life there was to learn later that almost every bush and tree had unconsciously become a personal friend. The old mulberry by the ruined arch, the prostrate mock-orange tree below the cricket-shed, the tall pines by Chase Hall, the feathery clumps of pampas grass, the copper beeches, the fallen flukes of mapleseeds, all such became part of one's innocence. In spring there was the constant drowsy whirr of the big lawnmower, drawn by a horse who wore huge leather slippers on his feet to spare the sod. Nor he, nor the rhododendrons, not anything else in that perfect picture, were in vain. One had an idea of peace. It would not be until many years later one might divine an almost ominous loveliness in some lights and shades. Under the copper beeches, in Pennsylvania's reckless sun, there is a lustred shimmer that knows no argument, "such tawny shining as gilds the gipsy's knees." The library, brave outwork of austerity, stands on its green terrace; its long lancet windows, fringed with creeper, have the right monastic shape, to admit the maximum of light with the least of worldly view; but the whiff of grassy air comes through to mingle with the savor of old leathers. Rambling in those groves you will sometimes be aware that the woodlands of Penn have never been wholly won back from wilderness. Whatever that visitor may have said, those are not the tame trees of "an English nobleman's park," they are still forest timber, and sometimes the voice they whisper is not of Penn but of Pan.

# MAKING MARATHON
# SAFE FOR THE URCHIN

THE URCHIN and I have been strolling about Marathon on Sunday mornings for more than a year, but not until the gasolineless Sabbaths supervened were we really able to examine the village and see what it is like. Previously we had been kept busy either dodging motors or admiring them as they sped by. Their rich dazzle of burnished enamel, the purring hum of their great tires, evokes applause from the Urchin. He is learning, as he watches those flashing chariots, that life truly is almost as vivid as the advertisements in the *Ladies' Home Journal*, where the shimmer of earthly pageant first was presented to him.

Marathon is a village so genteel and comely that the Urchin and I would like to have some pictures of it for future generations, particularly as we see it on an autumn morning when, as I say, the motors are kenneled and the landscape has ceased to vibrate. In the douce benignance of equinoctial sunshine we gaze about us with eyes of inventory. Where my observation errs by too much sentiment the Urchin checks me by his cooler power of ratiocination.

Marathon is a suburban Xanadu gently caressed by the train service of the Cinder and Bloodshot. It may be recognized as an aristocratic and patrician stronghold by the fact that while luxuries are readily obtainable (for instance, banana splits, or the latest novel by Enoch A. Bennett), necessaries are had only by prayer and advowson. The drug store will deliver ice cream to your very refrigerator, but it is impossible to get your garbage collected. The cook goes off for her Thursday evening in a taxi, but you will have to mend the roof, stanch the plumbing and curry the furnace with your own hands. There are ten trains to take you to town of an evening, but only two to bring you home. Yet going to town is a luxury, coming home is a necessity. The supply of grape juice seems almost unlimited, yet coal is to be had catch-as-catch-can.

Another proof that Marathon is patrician at heart is that nothing is known by its right name! The drug store is a "pharmacy," Sunday is "the Sabbath," a house is a "residence," a debt is a "balance due on bill rendered." A girls' school is a "young ladies' seminary." A Marathon man is not drafted, he is "inducted into selective service." And the railway station has a porte cochère (with the correct accent) instead of a carriage entrance. A furnace is (how erroneously!) called a "heater." Marathon people do not die—they "pass away." Even the cobbler, good fellow, has caught the trick; he calls his shop the "Italo-American Shoe Hospital."

This is an innocent masquerade! If Marathon prefers not to call a flivver a flivver, I shall not expostulate. And yet this quaint subterfuge should not be carried quite so far. Stone walls are made for sunny lounging; yet stone walls in Marathon are built with uneven vertical projections to discourage the sedentary. Nothing is more delightful than a dog; but there are no dogs in Marathon. They are all airedales or spaniels or mastiffs. If an ordinary dog should wag his tail up our street the airedales would cut him dead. Bless me, Nature herself has taken to the same insincerity. The landscape round Marathon is lovely, but it has itself well in hand. The hills all pretend to be gentle declivities. There is a beautiful little sheet of water, reflecting the trailery of willows, a green salute to the eye. In a robuster community it would be a swimming hole—but with us, an ornamental lake! Only in one spot has Nature forgotten herself and been so brusque and rough as to jut up a very sizable cliff. This is the loveliest thing in Marathon: sunlight and shadow break and angle in cubist magnificence among the oddly veined knobs and prisms of brown stone.

Yet this cliff or quarry is by common consent taboo among us. It is our indelicacy, our indecency. Such "residences" as are near modestly turn their kitchens toward it. Only the blacksmith and the gas tanks are hardy enough to face this nakedness of Mother Earth—they, and excellent Pat Lemon, Marathon's humblest and blackest citizen, who contemplates that rugged and honest beauty as he tills his garden on the land abandoned by squeamish burghers. That is our Aceldama, our Potter's Field, only approached by the athletic, who keep their eyes from Nature's indiscretion by vigorous sets of tennis in the purple shadow of the cliff.

Life is queerly inverted in Marathon. Nature has been so bullied and repressed that she fawns about us timidly. No well-conducted suburban shrubbery would think of assuming autumn tints before the ladies have got into their fall fashions. Indeed none of our chaste trees will even shed their leaves while any one is watching; and they crouch modestly in the shade of our massive garages. They have been taught their place. In Marathon it is a worse sin to have your lawn uncut than to have your books or your hair uncut. I have been aware of indignant eyes because I let my back garden run wild. And yet I flatter myself it was not mere sloth. No! I want the Urchin to see what this savage, tempestuous world is like. What preparation for life is a village where Nature comes to heel like a spaniel? When a thunderstorm disorganizes our electric lights for an hour or so we feel it a personal affront. Let my rearward plot be a deep-tangled wildwood where the happy Urchin may imagine something more ferocious lurking than a posse of radishes. Indeed, I hardly know whether Marathon is a safe place to bring up a child. How can he learn the horrors of drink in a village where there is no saloon? Or the sadness of the seven deadly sins where there is no movie? Or deference to his betters where the chauffeurs, in their withered leather legs, drive limousines to the drug store to buy expensive cigars, while their employers walk to the station puffing briar pipes?

I had been hoping that the war would knock some of this topsy-turvy nonsense out of us. Maybe it has. Sometimes I see on the faces of our commuters the unaccustomed agitation of thought. At least we still have the grace to call ourselves a suburb, and not (what we fancy ourselves) a superurb. But I don't like the pretense that runs like a jarring note through the music of our life. Why is it that those who are doing the work must pretend they are not doing it; and those not doing the work pretend that they are? I see that the motor messenger girls who drive high-powered cars wear Sam Browne belts and heavy-soled boots, whereas the stalwart colored wenches who labor along the tracks of the Cinder and Bloodshot console themselves with flimsy waists and light slippers. (A fact!) By and by the Urchin will notice these things. And I don't want him to grow up the kind of chap who, instead of running to catch a train, loiters gracefully to the station and waits to be caught.

# FOOTNOTE ON
# PHILADELPHIA
# CRICKET

Roslyn Heights
Long Island, N.Y.
March 15, 1951

**D**EAR JOHN:
The best I can do—and a bit feverishly, I fear:
your letter reached me in the final figuring of an income
tax, and the prostration of a sweep of flu—is write you a
footnote why I can't possibly do a preface for your *Century
of Philadelphia Cricket*. It would sharply annoy the old experts and veterans on whose good will the book must count
for support. They would inevitably think I had pushed
myself in where I don't belong, and I wouldn't blame
them. And Philadelphians can think of quite enough reasons for not buying a book without our putting fresh ones
in their minds. I would be l.b.w. on the very first ball. For
your sake, and for my own humble decency, I beg off.

You see (since you force me to think back) cricket is to
me a feeling, an idea, an emotion, a childhood memory; a
noumenon if you wish; shadow-patterns on the wall of
Plato's cave; and ideality never, for me, put to the touch of
crude participation. I never played except in the childhood
games after supper in front of Founders Hall. I know
nothing about Philadelphia cricket; all I knew was what I
saw as a child at Haverford, of which *pars magna fuisti*. It
was an ideality which never came to the carborundum of
the mill. Yes, I have watched cricket in later years; in village
games in England and in Canada; I have known such
screwball players as you mention—Sir James Barrie and
E. V. Lucas—and have seen good old Sir Jack Squire, after

too heavy a lunch of shepherd's pie and village Treble-X, fall on his face while making his absurdly long run to deliver his first ball. I think it was Jack Squire's country eleven that succeeded Barrie's in literary renown. I doubt if he ever bowled a maiden over! (I wish my income tax could say the same.) As I heard a Surrey spectator say, watching Sir Jack trudging over the shaggy meadow (fingers so hopefully curved and palpated on the red ball) "Oi blieve e'd do better if 'e wouldn't go so far down 'ill."

I remember too the notice that used to flutter on the bulletin board on Founders Porch: *The following freshmen turn out tomorrow to Roll the Crease.*—

If I had the knowledge, or the impudence (dear John) I'd hurry to help roll your crease. But my cricket lore, however dear to me, is entirely private. It includes the permanent vision of old Henry Cope (class of '69, wasn't he?) for whom our immortal field is named, and who used to stand end-lessly under the great elm trees watching every stroke. In those days there were still the old benches discarded from the Meeting House, whitewashed for fifty years and at last fell to pieces. When I was watching a cricket match at Haverford a year ago I suddenly realized that I, even I myself, out of college forty years and whiskered, was of the same superannuation as the old Henry I remembered.

There is certainly some psychic reason why cricket in America was born in Philadelphia, flourished, passed away, and now—in our instinctive hunger for some last remaining uncommercialized sport—shows tender signs of revival. But I can't write about such things. Cricket to me is our adored old teacher Frank Gummere, sitting on the front steps of 1 College Circle in those spring afternoons of the first decade, and knowing—as he would know the prosody of the Roman de la Rose—the snick, the click, the whack, the crack, the slock, the knock, of every batsman's stroke, how it sounded on the cunningly molded willow, and how much it was likely good for. And of all games ever invented, it is the game for Philadelphians; if you don't think you can score, you don't have to run. What a cricketer John Wanamaker might have been; but don't let me get frisky.

Your distinguished memoirists know, better than I, the things that endear the game to me: the smell of grass, the creak of straps on pads, the thud of running feet chasing a near-boundary. I have not forgotten that I was a mascot (in a very tiny scarlet-and-black blazer) in your own team of 1896 that played Cambridge University; and I still remember the lissom and darkling Prince Ranjitsinhji, delicate and devilish at the bat as any of Kipling's panthers. But, I repeat, I know cricket only as dream and poetry. For a hundred years cricket has been the only kind of poetry Philadelphia has really approved. And all your participants—Frankford, Germantown, Merion, and U. of P., and the others—were poets without knowing it. Isn't that the most delicious of all our dear old Home Town's achievements? Its greatest triumphs by accident.

Think of the different tunes and tones of the laminated willow (so severely wound with thread, so deeply and cunningly sprung with an autographed XXXX sheave, mostly from Birmingham?) and twirl the bat for chance; was it, they used to say, flat or round? I don't remember. But cricket was always to me just a notion, a love afloat. Those who actually played it, beautiful as they were (even bulging a bit in the midriff like some Scattergoods at the wicket, and how slick they were with their How's That's?) were the hardworking actors. I was, and I remain, and fade away into my pitiful silence, the unspoiled spectator.

Speaking of Barrie, I always wondered how it was possible for him to handle a ball. I'm sure that cricket was just one of his island fancies. Did you ever see his hands? Tiny little dimpled clumps, like the puds of a little girl of ten. Whereas E. V. Lucas had great corned-beef lunch-hooks. But for both of them, as for Philadelphia in her reminiscence, cricket was a fairy tale. An excuse to get out into the afternoon air, the smell of maple-pollens, the gentle choreography of white pants in pattern on the turf, the batsman thumping down some pimple of sod, the bowler waving his field into some fanciful expertise (like income tax inspectors), the umpires in their long white surplices— these are what spectators, like professors of literature, can relish and sizzle in their membranes. These are part of cricket, and part of Philadelphia.

And so, to have been born, by chance, into cricket's Golden Age at Haverford, in the 90's, was like having been born among the dramatists of Elizabeth the Queen (in the 1590's) or among the Wordsworth-Coleridge-Yarnalls (of the 1790's). It was being born into something beautiful and unique. In my childhood (which seems to have lasted too long) a Lester, or a Scattergood, or a Hal Furness (to mention one of my own era whose mild and wary art was perfect) made drives, or cuts, or slices, or even unforgivable slogs, that were like Elizabethan sonneteers hoisting an Amoretto clear across Maple Avenue.

I love to think of the story of Henry Pleasants, who, thrilled beyond belief to play against Sir Arthur Conan Doyle at Lord's (1904, was it?) had two chances for a catch—and dropped them both. Henry was too gentlemanly to admit the truth; he allowed Sir Arthur to think that reverence for Sherlock and Watson had unnerved him. Actually, he had a painful blood-poison in his hand. If it had been basketball of 1951, what might we have thought?

I have one tangible souvenir of what Quiller-Couch, or maybe Andrew Lang, called "sweet hours, and the fleetest of time." When the old batting-shed was gently collapsing—it stood deserted for years, abaft the Library, in a sort of tropic jungle of overgrown sumacs; like one of the Malayan bungalows where Mr. Somerset Maugham puts his poor pukka-sahibs through such psychosomatic despairs, his District Officers with outwashed shorts and their memsahibs with such preshrunken tempers—I picked up an

279

ancient forgotten cricket-ball; a bit sideswiped in shape, as though once smitten by a Baily or a Biddlebanks, or a Gummere or a Comfort, of ancient kindlier time. I keep it in a mug, an empty mug, on top of a bookcase. More intellectual sensualists would have plaster busts of Homer or Halitosis, the classical warnings; but that head of an Amazon victim, almost indeed like the parched walnut of poor glorious little Sir James Barrie's suffering skull, is what I sometimes look at. I keep it in the same mug with an old dusty and equally defeated battle flag of the Confederacy. My only honesty is that I was always the first to admit defeat. So here is the ball that was never hit, in the game that was never played, in the story that will never be written.

So you see now (dear John) because the collector is at the door, why I can't write. If you want to use this as a footnote to your own personal chapter, pray do so; but not as a Preface. I love Philadelphia, and cricket, more than they love themselves. But I love them, as (God help him) the artist only can, a pattern of incidental, and exquisite, and simply perfect beauty. Only Philadelphia, which has these rhythms in its heart unawares, can guess what we are talking about. So Night now.

CHRISTOPHER

# THE SHORE IN
# SEPTEMBER

THE SANDS ARE lonely in the fall. On those broad New Jersey beaches, where the rollers sprawl inward in ridges of crumbling snow, the ocean looks almost wistfully for its former playmates. The children are gone, the small brown legs, the toy shovels and the red tin pails. The familiar figures of the summer season have vanished: the stout ladies who sat in awninged chairs and wrestled desperately to unfurl their newspapers in the wind; the handsome mahogany-tanned lifesavers, the vamperinoes incessantly drying their tawny hair, the corpulent males of dark complexion wearing ladies' bathing caps, the young men playing a degenerate baseball with a rubber sphere and a bit of shingle. All that life and excitement, fed upon hot dogs and vanilla cones, anointed with cold cream and citronella, has vanished for another year.

But how pleasant it is to see the town (it is Fierceforest we have in mind) taking its own vacation, after laboring to amuse its visitors all summer long. Here and there in the surf you will see a familiar figure. That plump lady, lathered by sluicing combers as she welters and wambles upon Neptune's bosom, is good Frau Weintraub of the delicatessen, who has been frying fish and chowdering clams over a hot stove most of July and August, and now takes her earned repose. Yonder is the imposing bulge of the real estate agent, who has been too busy selling lots and dreaming hotel sites to visit the surf hitherto. Farther up the shore is the garage man, doing a little quiet fishing from the taffrail of a deserted pier. The engineer of the "roller coaster" smokes a cigar along the deserted boardwalk and discusses the league of nations with the gondolier-in-chief of the canals of Ye Olde Mill. The hot-dog expert, whose

281

merry shout, "Here they are, all red hot and fried in butter!" was wont to echo along the crowded arcade, has boarded up his stand and departed none knows where.

There is a tincture of grief in the survey of all this liveliness coffined and nailed down. Even the gambols of Fierceforest's citizens, taking their ease at last in the warm September surf, cannot wholly dispel the mournfulness of the observer. There is something dreadfully glum in the merry-go-round seen through its locked glass doors. All those gayly caparisoned horses, with their bright Arabian housings, their flowing manes and tossing heads and scarlet-painted nostrils, stand stilled in the very gesture of glorious rotation. One remembers what a jolly sight that carrousel was on a warm evening, the groaning pipes of the steam-organ chanting an adorable ditty (we don't know what it is, but it's the tune they always play at the movies when our favorite Dorothy Gish comes on the screen), children laughing and holding tight to the wooden manes of the horses, and flappers with their pink dresses swirling, clutching for the brass ring that means a free ride. All this is frozen into silence and sleep, like a scene in a fairy tale. It is very sad, and we dare not contemplate the poor little silent horses too long.

Bitterly does one lament the closing of the Boardwalk auction rooms, which were a perpetual free show to those who could not find a seat in the movies. There was one auctioneer who looked so like Mr. Wilson that when we saw his earnest gestures we always expected that the league of nations would be the subject of his harangue. But on entering and taking a seat (endeavoring to avoid his eye when he became too persuasive, for fear some involuntary gesture or the contortion of an approaching sneeze would be construed as a bid for a Chinese umbrella stand) we always found that it was a little black box full of teacups that was under discussion. He would hold one up against an electric bulb to show its transparency. When he found his audience unresponsive he would always say, "You know I don't have to do this for a living. If you people don't appreciate goods that have quality, I'm going to pack up and go to Ocean City." But he never went. Almost every evening, chagrined by some one's failure to bid properly for a cut-glass lady-finger container or a porcelain tooth-brush-rack, he would ask the attendant to set it aside. "I'll buy it myself," he would cry, and as he kept on buying these curious tidbits for himself throughout the summer, we used to wonder what his wife would say when they all arrived.

Along the quiet Boardwalk we saunter, as the crisp breeze comes off the wide ocean spaces. Bang! bang! bang! sound the hammers, as the shutters go up on the beauty parlor, the toy shop, the shop where sweet-grass baskets were woven, and the stall where the little smiling doll known as Helene, the Endearing Beach Vamp, was to be won by knocking down two tenpins with a swinging pendulum. How easy it was to cozen the public with that! A bright red star was painted at the back of the pendulum's swing, and the natural assumption of the simple competitor was that by aiming at the star he would win the smiling Helene. Of course, as long as one aimed at the star success was impossible. The Japanese dealers, with the pertinacity of their race, are almost the last to linger. Their innocent little gaming boards, their fishponds where one angles for counterfeit fish and draws an eggcup or a china cat, according to the number inscribed on the catch, their roulette wheels ("Ten Cents a Chance—No Blanks")—all are still in operation, but one of the shrewd orientals is packing up some china at the back of the shop. He knows that trade is pretty well done for this season. We wondered whether he would go down to the beach for a swim before he left. He has stuck so close to business all summer that perhaps he does not know the ocean is there. There is another thrifty merchant, too, whose strategy comes to our attention. This is the rolling-chair baron, who has closed his little kiosque, but has taken care to paint out the prices per hour of his vehicles, and has not marked any new rates. Cautious man, he is waiting until next summer to see what the trend of prices will be then.

Across the fields toward the inlet, where the grasses have turned rusty bronze and pink, where goldenrod is minting its butter-yellow sprays and riotous magenta portulacas seed themselves over the sandy patches, the rowboats are being dragged out of the canal and laid up for the winter. The sunburned sailorman who rents them says he has had a good season—and he "can't complain." He comes chugging in with his tiny motorboat, towing a string of tenderfeet who have been out tossing on the crabbing grounds for a couple of hours, patiently lowering the fishheads tied on a cord and weighted with rusty bolts. His patient and energetic wife who runs the little candy and sarsaparilla counter on the dock has ended her labors. She is glad to get back to her kitchen: during the long, busy summer days she did her family cooking on an oil stove behind the counter. The captain, as he likes to be called, is about to make his annual change from mariner to roofer, the latter being his winter trade. "It's blowing up for rain," he says, looking over his shoulder at the eastern sky. "I guess the season's pretty near over. I'll get up the rest of them boats next week."

In September the bathing is at its best. Particularly at sunset, when every one is at supper. To cross those wide fields of wiry grass that stretch down to the sand, is an amazement to the eye. Ahead of you the sea gleams purple as an Easter violet. The fields are a kind of rich palette on which every tint of pink, russet and bronze are laid in glowing variation. The softly wavering breeze, moving among the coarse stalks, gives the view a ripple and shimmer of color like shot silk. A naturalist could find hundreds of species of flowers and grasses on those sandy meadows.

There are great clumps of some bushy herb that has already turned a vivid copper color, and catches the declining sunlight like burnished metal. There are flecks of yellow, pink and lavender. A cool, strong odor rises from the harsh, knife-edged grasses—a curiously dry, brittle scent, familiar to all who have poked about sand dunes.

The beach itself, colored in the last flush of the level sun, is still faintly warm to the naked foot, after the long shining of the day; but it cools rapidly. The tide is coming in, with long, seething ridges of foam, each flake and clot of crumbled water tinged with a rose-petal pink by the red sunset. All this glory of color, of movement, of unspeakable exhilaration and serenity, is utterly lonely. The long curve of the beach stretches away northward, where a solitary orange-colored dory is lying on the sand. The air is full of a plaintive piping of sea-birds. A gull flashes along the beach, with a pink glow in its snowy underplumage.

At that hour the water is likely to be warmer than the air. It may be only the curiously magical effect of the horizontal light, but it seems more foamy, more full of suds, than earlier in the day. Over the green top of the waves, laced and marbled with froth, slides a layer of iridescent bubble-wash that seems quite a different substance from the water itself—like the meringue on top of a lemon pie. One can scoop it up and see it winking in points of sparkling light.

The waves come marching in. It is a calm sea, one would have said looking down from the dunes, but to the swimmer, elbowing his way under their leaning hollows, their stature seems tremendous. The sunlight strikes into the hills of moving water, filling them with a bluish spangle and tremor of brightness. It is worth while to duck underneath and look up at the sun from under the surface, to see how the light seems to spread and clot and split in the water like sour cream poured into a cup of tea. The sun, which is so ruddy in the evening air, is a pale milky white when seen from under water.

A kind of madness of pleasure fills the heart of the solitary sunset swimmer. To splash and riot in that miraculous color and tumult of breaking water seems an effective answer to all the grievances of earth. To float, feeling the poise and encircling support of those lapsing pillows of liquid, is mirth beyond words. To swim just beyond the line of the big breakers, dropping a foot now and then to feel that bottom is not too far away—to sprawl inward with a swashing comber while the froth boils about his shoulders—to watch the light and color prismed in the curl and slant of every wave, and the quick vanishing of brightness and glory once the sun is off the sea—all this is the matter of poems that no one can write.

The sun drops over the flat glitter of the inland lagoons; the violet and silver and rose-flushed foam are gone from the ocean; the sand is gray and damp and chilly. Down the line of the shore comes an airplane roaring through the upper regions of dazzling sunlight, with brightness on its varnished wings. The lighthouse at the Inlet has begun to twinkle its golden flash, and supper will soon be on the table. The solitary swimmer takes one last regretful plunge through a sluicing hill of green, and hunts out his pipe. He had left it, as the true smoker does, carefully filled, with a match-box beside it, in a dry hollow on the sand. Trailing a thread of blue reek, he plods cheerfully across the fields, taking care not to tread upon the small hoptoads that have come out to hail the evening. Behind him the swelling moon floats like a dim white lantern, penciling the darkening water with faint scribbles of light.

But there are still a few oldtimers in Fierceforest, cottagers who cling on until the first of October, and whose fraternal password (one may hear them saying it every time they meet) is "Sure! Best time of the year!" Through the pink flush of sunrise you may see the husbands moving soberly toward the early commuters' train, the 6:55, which is no longer crowded. (A month ago one had to reach it half an hour early in order to get a seat in the smoker.) Each one transports his satchel, and also curious bundles, for at this time of year it is the custom to make the husband carry home each week an instalment of the family baggage, to save excess when moving day comes. One totes an oilstove; another, a scales for weighing the baby. They trudge somewhat grimly through the thin morning twilight, going back for another week at office and empty house or apartment. Leaving behind them the warm bed, the little cottage full of life and affection, they taste for a moment the nostalgic pang that sailors know so well when the ship's bow cuts the vacant horizon. Over the purple rim of sea the sun juts its scarlet disk. You may see these solitary husbands halt a moment to scan the beauty of the scene. They stand there thoughtful in the immortal loneliness of dawn. Then they climb the smoker and pinochle has its sway.

# TOWARD MICKLE STREET

# THE WHITMAN
# CENTENNIAL

Y ESTERDAY—Memorial Day—was a true Walt Whitman day. The ferries thronged with cheerful people,
the laughing, eager throng at the Camden terminal, piling
aboard trolley cars for a holiday outing—the clang and thud
of marching bands, the flags and flowers and genial human
bustle, pervaded now and then by that note of tribute to
the final mystery—surely all this was just such a scene as
Walt loved to watch and wonder. And going on pilgrimage
with two English editors to Mickle street and Harleigh
Cemetery, it was not strange that our thoughts were largely
with the man whose hundredth birthday we bear in mind
today.

By just so far (it seems to me) as we find it painful to read
Walt Whitman, by just so far we may reckon our divergence
from the right path of human happiness. If it perturbs us to
read his jottings of "specimen days" along Timber creek,
wrestling with his twelve-foot oak sapling to gain strength,
sluicing in clear water and scouring his naked limbs with
his favorite flesh-brush, ruminating in blest solitude among
the tints of sunset, the odor of mint-leaves and the moving
airs of the summer meadow—if this gives us a twinge, then
it is probably because we have divorced ourselves from the
primitive joyfulness of the open air. If we find his trumpet-
ings of physical candor shameful or unsavory, perhaps it is
because we have not schooled our thoughts to honest
cleanliness. (Though Anne Gilchrist's gentle comment
must not be forgotten: "Perhaps Walt Whitman has forgotten the truth that our instincts are beautiful facts of nature,
as well as our bodies; and that we have a strong instinct of
silence about some things.") If we find him lacking in
humor or think some of his catalogues tedious—there are

catalogues and shortage of humor even in some books considered sacred. And Whitman, if not a humorist himself, has been (as Mr. Chesterton would say) the cause of humor in others. How adorably he has lent himself to parody! But this by the way. The point is, Whitman is a true teacher: first the thrashing, then the tenderness. No one ever found him exhilarating on the first reading. But he is a hound of heaven. He will hunt you down and find you out. Expurgate him for yourself, if you wish. He cannot be inclosed in a formula. He asks you to draw up your own formula as you read him. Rest assured, William Blake would not have found him obscure. "If you want me again, look for me under your bootsoles." Is not that the very accent of Blake?

There is marvelous drama in Camden for the seeing eye. The first scene is Mickle street, that dingy, smoke-swept lane of mean houses. The visitors from oversea stood almost aghast when they saw the pathetic vista. For years they had dwelt on Whitman's magnificent messages of pride and confidence:

> See, projected through time,
> For me an audience interminable.

Perhaps they had conjured to mind a clean little cottage such as an English suburb might offer: a dainty patch of wallflowers under the front door, a shining brass knocker, a sideboard of mahogany with an etching of Walt on the wall. No wonder, then, that the deathplace of the poet with "audience interminable" came as a shock.

And yet, one wonders, is not that faded box, with its flag hanging from the second story and little Louis Skymer's boyish sign in the window—*Rabbits for sale cheap*—and the backyard littered with hutches and the old nose-broken carved bust of Walt chucked away in a corner—is it not in a way strangely appropriate? Would not Walt almost have preferred it to be so, with its humble homeliness, so instinct with humanity, rather than a neatly tidied mauso-leum? If Walt had believed that a man must live in a colonial cot in a fashionable suburb in order to write great poetry he would not have been Walt.

> The great matter is to reveal and outpour the Godlike suggestions pressing for birth in the soul.

And then it must be remembered that Walt didn't live much on Mickle street until he became a confirmed invalid, and his pack of listeners kept him talking so hard he didn't know where he was. He lived on the ferries, up and down Chestnut street, or (for that matter) in the constellation Orion.

The second scene of the Camden drama is at Harleigh Cemetery. Here, among that sweet city of the dead, in a little dell where the rhododendrons yield their fragrance to the sun-heavy air, the massive stone door stands ajar. A great mass of flowers, laid there by the English-Speaking Union, was heaped at the sill. More instinctively than in many a church, the passer lifts his hat.

> Has any one supposed it lucky to be born?
> I hasten to inform him or her it is just as lucky to die,
> and I know it.

I thought of what a little girl who was standing on the pavement of Mickle street had said to me as we halted in front of the Whitman house. "My father was sick, and he died."

Yesterday—Memorial Day—was a day of poignant thoughts. Walt wrote once in "Specimen Days":

> Somehow I got thinking today of young men's deaths—not at all sadly or sentimentally, but gravely, realistically, *perhaps a little artistically*.

293

What a curious note of apology there is in the last admission! He who was so rarely "artistic"! He who began his career as a writer of incredibly mawkish short stories and doggerels, and rigidly trained himself to omit the "stock" touches! Let us not try to speak of Walt, or of death, in any "artistic" vein.

"Stop this day and night with me" (Walt said) "and you shall possess the origin of all poems." By which he meant, of course, you shall possess your own soul. You shall grasp with sureness and ecstasy the only fact you can cling to in this baffling merry-go-round—the dignity and worth of your own life. In reading Whitman one seems to burst through the crust of perversity, artificial complexity and needless timidity that afflicts us all, to meet a strong river of sanity and courage that sweeps away the petty rubbish. Because it is so far from the course of our meaningless gestures, we know instinctively it is right and true. There is no heart so bruised, there is no life so needlessly perplexed, but it can find its message in this man. "I have the best of time and space," he said. So have we all, for our little moment. Read his defiant words, great and scornful as any ever penned:

What place is besieged, and vainly tries to raise the siege?
Lo, I send to that place a commander, swift, brave,
   immortal,
And with him horse and foot, and parks of artillery,
And artillerymen, the deadliest that ever fired gun.

He sends you your own soul.

As we rode back to Camden on the trolley one of my companions spied the Washington statue in front of the courthouse (which I had been hoping he would miss). He smiled at the General grotesquely kneeling in stone. "Only giving one knee to his Maker," was his droll comment.

It was so with Walt. He wanted to be quite sure what he was kneeling to before he gave both knees.

Perhaps the most curious (and gruesome) story in connection with Whitman comes to me from James Shields. He has showed me a monograph by the late Dr. E.A. Spitzka, professor of anatomy at the Jefferson Medical College, which gives a brief review of scientific post-mortem measurements made of the brains of 130 notable men and four women. In this monograph, reprinted by the American Philosophical Society in 1907, occurs the following paragraph:

87. WHITMAN, WALT, American poet. The weight of Walt Whitman's brain is variously given as 45.2 ounces (1282 grams) and 43.3 ounces (1228 grams). His stature was six feet and in health he weighed about 200 pounds. The brain had been preserved, but some careless attendant in the laboratory let the jar fall to the ground; it is not stated whether the brain was totally destroyed by the fall, but it is a great pity that not even the fragments of the brain were rescued.

# ANNE GILCHRIST'S HOUSE

THE KENSINGTON car that goes northward on Seventh street carries one straightway into a land of adventure. Hardly have you settled in your seat when you see a sign, The Pickwick Cafe, 53 North Seventh street. Admirable name for a chophouse! Glancing about, across the aisle is a lady with one of those curious hats which permit the wearer to scrutinize through the transparent brim while her head is apparently bent demurely downward. The surprising effect of impaling oneself upon so unexpected a gaze is startling. Bashfully one turns elsewhere. On a hoarding stares a theatrical sign: "Did You Tell Your Wife ALL Before Marriage?"

I got off at Master street and walked stolidly west. It is a humble causeway in that region, rich in junk shops and a bit shaky in its spelling. At the corner of Warnock is an impromptu negro church, announcing "Servers every Sunday, 3 p. m." The lithograph which is such a favorite on South street, crops up again: the famous golden-haired lassie with a blue dress, asleep under a red blanket, guarded by a white dog with a noble, steadfast expression. Fawn and Camac streets reappear and afford quiet vistas of red brick with marble trimmings. I believe this is Fawn's first venture north of Bainbridge. As its name implies, a shy, furtive street. One could spend a lively day afoot tracing the skip-stops of these two vagabonds. Camac street has tried to concentrate attention on itself between Walnut and Spruce, calling itself arrogantly the Greatest Little Street in the World. But it leads a multiple life. I have found it popping up around Race street, at Wallace, and even north of that most poetically named of all Philadelphia's thoroughfares, Rising Sun avenue.

The greenery of Ontario Park is likely to lure the way-farer from Master street for a detour. There is a large public school there, and an exceedingly pretty young teacher in a pink dress and shell spectacles was gravely leading a procession of thirty small urchins for their morning recess in the open air. Two by two, with decent gravity, they crossed the street, and demobilized in the park for hair ribbons, shoelaces and blouse strings to be retied.

As it approaches Broad street, Master goes steadily up grade, both physically and in the spirit. At the corner of Broad it reaches its grand historic climax in the vast ornate brown pile where Edwin Forrest died in 1872. A tablet says, "This house was the residence of Edwin Forrest, the greatest tragedian of his time." It is interesting to remember (with the aid of an encyclopedia) that one of Forrest's favorite rôles was Spartacus. Until the arrival of Liebknecht he was supreme in that accomplishment.

At the top of the hill, at Fifteenth street, Master street becomes almost suburban and frisky. It abounds in gracious garden vistas, rubber plants and an apartment house of a Spanish tinge of architecture. A patriotic Presbyterian church has turned its front lawn into a potato patch. At 1534 one of the smallest and most delightful black puppies ever seen was tumbling about on a white marble stoop. He was so young that his eyes were still blue and cloudy, but his appeal for a caress was unmistakable. I stopped to pay my respects, but a large Airedale appeared and stood over him with an air of "You haven't been introduced."

A few blocks further on one abuts upon Ridge avenue, the Sam Browne belt of Philadelphia. In its long diagonal course from Ninth and Vine up to Strawberry Mansion, Ridge avenue is full of unceasing life and interest. It and South street are perhaps the two most entertaining of the city's humbler highways. Master street crosses it at a dramatic spot. There is a great cool lumber yard, where the piled-up wood exhales a fragrant breath under the hot sun, and lilac-breasted pigeons flap about among the stained rafters. A few yards away one catches a glimpse of the vast inclosure of Girard College, where the big, silvery-gray parthenon rises austerely above a cloud of foliage.

One aspect of Ridge avenue is plain at a glance. It is the city's stronghold of the horse. You will see more horses there than anywhere else I know (except perhaps down by the docks). From horseshoeing forges comes the mellow clang of beaten iron. As the noon whistles blow, scores of horses stand at their wagons along the curb, cheerfully chewing oats, while their drivers are dispatching heavy mugs of "coffee with plenty" in the nearby delicatessens. Ridge avenue conducts a heavy trade in furniture on the pavements. Its favorite tobaccos are of a thundering potency: Blue Hen, Sensation, Polar Bear, Buckingham cut plug. There is a primitive robust quality about its merchandising. "Eat Cornell's Sauer Kraut and Grow Fat," says a legend painted across the flank of a pickle factory. "Packey McFarland Recommends Make-Man Tablets," is the message of a lively cardboard "cutout" in a druggist's window. Odd little streets run off the avenue at oblique angles: Sharswood, for instance, where two horses stood under the shade of a big tree as in a barnyard picture. On a brick wall on Beechwood street I found the following chalked up:

CLAN OF THE EAGLE'S EYE
*Lone Wolf*
*Red Hawk*
*Arrowfire*
*Red Thunder*
*Deerfoot*

This seemed a pathetic testimony that not even the city streets can quench the Fenimore Cooper tradition among American youth. And, oddly enough, below this roster of braves some learned infant had written in Greek letters,

"Harry a dam fool." Evidently some challenge to a rival tribe.

Twenty-second street north of Ridge avenue is a quiet stretch of red brick, with occasional outcroppings of pale yellow-green stone. At the noon hour it is a cascade of children, tumbling out of the Joseph Singerly Public School. Happily for those juveniles, there is one of the best tuck shops in Philadelphia at the corner of Columbia avenue. It is worth a long journey to taste their cinnamon buns. And in the block just behind the school, at 1929 North Twenty-second, there is a little three-story yellow-green house with a large bay window, which gives Whitman lovers a thrill. That little house is associated with one of the most poignant and curious romances in the story of American letters. For it was here that Mrs. Anne Gilchrist and her children came in September, 1876, and lived until the spring of 1878. Mrs. Gilchrist, a noble and talented English woman, whose husband had died in 1861, fell passionately in love with Walt after reading *Leaves of Grass*. Her letters to Walt, which were published recently by Thomas Harned, are among the most searchingly beautiful expressions of human attachment. After Whitman's paralytic stroke Anne Gilchrist insisted on coming from London to Philadelphia to be near the poet and help him in any way she could; and to this little house on Twenty-second street Walt used to go day after day to take tea with her and her children. Walt had tried earnestly to dissuade her from coming to America, and his few letters to her seem a curiously enigmatic reply to her devotion. Perhaps, as Mr. Harned implies, his heart was engaged elsewhere. At any rate, his conduct in this delicate affair seems sufficient proof of what has sometimes been doubted, that he was at heart a gentleman—a banal word, but we have no other.

The present occupant of the house is Mrs. Alexander Wellner, who was kind enough to grant me a few minutes' talk. She has lived in the house only a year, and did not know of its Whitman association. The street can hardly have changed much—save for the new public school building—since Centennial days. The gardens behind the houses are a mass of green shrubbery, and in a neighboring yard stands an immense tree in full leaf. Perhaps Walt and his good friends may have sat out there for tea on warm afternoons forty-two years ago. But it seems a long way from Camden!

As I came away, thinking of that romantic and sad episode in the lives of two who were greatly worthy of each other, the corner of my eye was caught by a large poster. In a random flash of vision I misread it in accordance with my thoughts. THE GOOD GRAY POET, it seemed to say. For an instant I accepted this as natural. Then, returning to my senses, I retraced my steps to look at it again. THAT GOOD GULF GASOLINE!

# WALT WHITMAN
# MINIATURES

## I

A DECENT respect to the opinions of mankind requires that one should have some excuse for being away from the office on a working afternoon. September sunshine and trembling blue air are not sufficient reasons, it seems. Therefore, if any one should brutally ask what I was doing the other day dangling down Chestnut Street toward the river, I should have to reply, "Looking for the *Wenonah.*" The *Wenonah,* you will immediately conclude, is a moving picture theater. But be patient a moment.

Lower Chestnut Street is a delightful place for one who does not get down there very often. The face of wholesale trade, dingier than the glitter of uptown shops, is far more exciting and romantic. Pavements are cumbered with vast packing cases; whiffs of tea and spice well up from cool cellars. Below Second Street I found a row of enormous sacks across the curb, with bright red and green wool pushing through holes in the burlap. Such signs as WOOL, NOILS AND WASTE are frequent. I wonder what noils are? A big sign on Front Street proclaims TEA CADDIES, which has a pleasant grandmotherly flavor. A little brass plate, gleamingly polished, says HONORARY CONSULATE OF JAPAN. Beside immense motor trucks stood a shabby little horse and buggy, restored to service, perhaps, by the war-time shortage of gasoline. It was a typical one-horse shay of thirty years ago.

I crossed over to Camden on the ferryboat *Wildwood,* observing in the course of the voyage her sisters, *Bridgeton, Camden, Salem* and *Hammonton.* It is curious that no matter where one goes, one will always meet people who are traveling there for the first time. A small boy next to me was gazing in awe at the stalwart tower of the Victor Company, and snuffing with pleasure the fragrance of cooking tomatoes that makes Camden savory at this time of year. Wagonloads of ripe Jersey tomatoes making their way to the soup factory are a jocund sight across the river just now.

Every ferry passenger is familiar with the rapid tinkling of the ratchet wheel that warps the landing stage up to the level of the boat's deck. I asked the man who was running the wheel where I would find the *Wenonah*. "She lays over in the old Market Street slip," he replied, and cheerfully showed me just where to find her. "Is she still used?" I asked. "Mostly on Saturday nights and holidays," he said, "when there's a big crowd going across."

The *Wenonah*, as all Camden seafarers know, is a ferryboat, one of the old-timers, and I was interested in her because she and her sister, the *Beverly*, were Walt Whitman's favorite ferries. He crossed back and forth on them hundreds of times and has celebrated them in several paragraphs in *Specimen Days*. Perhaps this is the place to quote his memorandum dated January 12, 1882, which ought to interest all lovers of the Camden ferry:

"Such a show as the Delaware presented an hour before sundown yesterday evening, all along between Philadelphia and Camden, is worth weaving into an item. It was full tide, a fair breeze from the southwest, the water of a pale tawny color, and just enough motion to make things frolicsome and lively. Add to these an approaching sunset of unusual splendor, a broad tumble of clouds, with much golden haze and profusion of beaming shaft and dazzle. In the midst of all, in the clear drab of the afternoon light, there steamed up the river the large new boat, the *Wenonah*, as pretty an object as you could wish to see, lightly and swiftly skimming along, all trim and white, covered with flags, transparent red and blue streaming out in the breeze.

302

Only a new ferryboat, and yet in its fitness comparable with the prettiest product of Nature's cunning, and rivaling it. High up in the transparent ether gracefully balanced and circled four or five great sea hawks, while here below, mid the pomp and picturesqueness of sky and river, swam this creature of artificial beauty and motion and power, in its way no less perfect."

You will notice that Walt Whitman describes the *Wenonah* as being white. The Pennsylvania ferryboats, as we know them, are all the brick-red color that is familiar to the present generation. Perhaps older navigators of the Camden crossing can tell us whether the boats were all painted white in a less smoky era?

The *Wenonah* and the *Beverly* were lying in the now unused ferry slip at the foot of Market Street, alongside the great Victor Talking Machine works. Picking my way through an empty yard where some carpentering was going on, I found a deserted pier that overlooked the two old vessels and gave a fair prospect on to the river and the profile of Philadelphia. Sitting there on a pile of pebbles, I lit a pipe and watched the busy panorama of the river. I made no effort to disturb the normal and congenial lassitude that is the highest function of the human being: no Hindoo philosopher could have been more pleasantly at ease. (O. Henry, one remembers, used to insist that what some of his friends called laziness was really "dignified repose.") Two elderly colored men were loading gravel onto a cart not far away. I was a little worried as to what I could say if they asked what I was doing. In these days casual loungers along docksides may be suspected of depth bombs and high treason. The only truthful reply to any question would have been that I was thinking about Walt Whitman. Such a remark, if uttered in Philadelphia, would undoubtedly have been answered by a direction to the chocolate factory on Race Street. But in Camden every one knows about Walt. Still, the colored men said nothing beyond

303

returning my greeting. Their race, wise in simplicity, knows that loafing needs no explanation and is its own excuse.

If Walt could revisit the ferries he loved so well, in New York and Philadelphia, he would find the former strangely altered in aspect. The New York skyline wears a very different silhouette against the sky, with its marvelous peaks and summits drawing the eye aloft. But Philadelphia's profile is (I imagine) not much changed. I do not know just when the City Hall tower was finished: Walt speaks of it as "three-fifths built" in 1879. That, of course, is the dominant unit in the view from Camden. Otherwise there are few outstanding elements. The gradual rise in height of the buildings, from Front Street gently ascending up to Broad, gives no startling contrast of elevation to catch the gaze. The spires of the older churches stand up like soft blue pencils, and the massive cornices of the Curtis and Drexel buildings catch the sunlight. Otherwise the outline is even and well-massed in a smooth ascending curve.

It is curious how a man can stamp his personality upon earthly things. There will always be pilgrims to whom Camden and the Delaware ferries are full of excitement and meaning because of Walt Whitman. Just as Stratford is Shakespeare, so is Camden Whitman. Some supercilious observers, flashing through on the way to Atlantic City, may only see a town in which there is no delirious and seizing beauty. Let us remind them of Walt's own words:

> A great city is that which has the greatest men and women,
> If it be a few ragged huts it is still the greatest city in the
>   whole world.

And as I came back across the river, and an airplane hovered over us at a great height, I thought how much we need a Whitman to-day, a poet who can catch the heart and meaning of these grievous bitter years, who can make plain the surging hopes that throb in the breasts of men. The world has not flung itself into agony without some unexpressed vision that lights the sacrifice. If Walt Whitman were here he would look on this new world of moving pictures and gasoline engines and U-boats and tell us what it means. His great heart, which with all its garrulous fumbling had caught the deep music of human service and fellowship, would have had true and fine words for us. And yet he would have found it a hard world for one of his strolling meditative observancy. A speeding motor truck would have run him down long ago!

As I left the ferry at Market Street I saw that the Norwegian steamer *Taunton* was unloading bananas at the Ericsson pier. Less than a month ago she picked up the survivors of the schooner *Madrugada,* torpedoed by a U-boat off Winter Bottom Shoal. On the *Madrugada* was a young friend of mine, a Dutch sailor, who told me of the disaster after he was landed in New York. To come unexpectedly on the ship that had rescued him seemed a great adventure. What a poem Walt Whitman could have made of it!

## II

It is a weakness of mine—not a sinful one, I hope—that whenever I see any one reading a book in public I am agog to find out what it is. Crossing over to Camden this morning a young woman on the ferry was absorbed in a volume, and I couldn't resist peeping over her shoulder. It was "Hans Brinker." On the same boat were several schoolboys carrying copies of Myers' *History of Greece.* Quaint, isn't it, how our schools keep up the same old bunk! What earthly use will a smattering of Greek history be to those boys? Surely to our citizens of the coming generation the battles of the Marne will be more important than the scuffle at Salamis.

My errand in Camden was to visit the house on Mickle Street where Walt Whitman lived his last years. It is now occupied by Mrs. Thomas Skymer, a friendly Italian woman, and her family. Mrs. Skymer graciously allowed me to go through the downstairs rooms.

I don't suppose any literary shrine on earth is of more humble and disregarded aspect than Mickle Street. It is a little cobbled byway, grimed with drifting smoke from the railway yards, littered with wind-blown papers and lined with small wooden and brick houses sooted almost to blackness. It is curious to think, as one walks along that bumpy brick pavement, that many pilgrims from afar have looked forward to visiting Mickle Street as one of the world's most significant altars. As Chesterton wrote once, "We have not yet begun to get to the beginning of Whitman." But the wayfarer of to-day will find Mickle Street far from impressive.

The little house, a two-story frame cottage, painted dark brown, is numbered 330. (In Whitman's day it was 328.) On the pavement in front stands a white marble stepping-block with the carved initials W. W.—given to the poet, I dare say, by the same friends who bought him a horse and carriage. A small sign, in English and Italian, says: *Thomas A. Skymer, Automobiles to Hire on Occasions*. It was with something of a thrill that I entered the little front parlor where Walt used to sit, surrounded by his litter of papers and holding forth to faithful listeners. One may safely say that his was a happy old age, for there were those who never jibbed at protracted audience.

A description of that room as it was in the last days of Whitman's life may not be uninteresting. I quote from the article published by the Philadelphia *Press* of March 27, 1892, the day after the poet's death:

Below the windowsill a four-inch pine shelf is swung, on which rests a bottle of ink, two or three pens and a much-rubbed spectacle case.

(The shelf, I am sorry to say, is no longer there.)

The table—between which and the wall is the poet's rocker covered with a worsted afghan, presented to him one Christmas by a bevy of college girls who admired his work—is so thickly piled with books and magazines, letters and the raffle of a literary desk that there is scarcely an inch of room upon which he may rest his paper as he writes. A volume of Shakespeare lies on top of a heaping full waste basket that was once used to bring peaches to market, and an ancient copy of Worcester's Dictionary shares places in an adjacent chair with the poet's old and familiar soft gray hat, a newly darned blue woolen sock and a shoe-blacking brush. There is a paste bottle and brush on the table and a pair of scissors, much used by the poet, who writes, for the most part, on small bits of paper and parts of old envelopes and pastes them together in patchwork fashion.

In spite of a careful examination, I could find nothing in the parlor at all reminiscent of Whitman's tenancy, except the hole for the stovepipe under the mantel. One of Mrs. Skymer's small boys told me that "He" died in that room. Evidently small Louis Skymer didn't in the least know who "He" was, but realized that his home was in some vague way connected with a mysterious person whose memory occasionally attracts inquirers to the house.

Behind the parlor is a dark little bedroom, and then the kitchen. In a corner of the back yard is a curious thing: a large stone or terra cotta bust of a bearded man, very much like Whitman himself, but the face is battered and the nose broken so it would be hard to assert this definitely. One of the boys told me that it was in the yard when they moved in a year or so ago. The house is a little dark, standing

between two taller brick neighbors. At the head of the stairs
I noticed a window with colored panes, which lets in spots
of red, blue and yellow light. I imagine that this patch of
vivid color was a keen satisfaction to Walt's acute senses.
Such is the simple cottage that one associates with America's literary declaration of independence.

The other Whitman shrine in Camden is the tomb in
Harleigh Cemetery, reached by the Haddonfield trolley.
Doctor Oberholtzer, in his *Literary History of Philadelphia*,
calls it "tawdry," to which I fear I must demur. Built into a
quiet hillside in that beautiful cemetery, of enormous slabs
of rough-hewn granite with a vast stone door standing
symbolically ajar, it seemed to me grotesque, but greatly
impressive. It is a weird pagan cromlech, with a huge
triangular boulder above the door bearing only the words
WALT WHITMAN. Palms and rubber plants grow in pots
on the little curved path leading up to the tomb; above it is
an uncombed hillside and trees flickering in the air. At this
tomb, designed (it is said) by Whitman himself, was held
that remarkable funeral ceremony on March 30, 1892, when
a circus tent was not large enough to roof the crowd, and
peanut venders did business on the outskirts of the gathering. Perhaps it is not amiss to recall what Bob Ingersoll said
on that occasion:

"He walked among verbal varnishers and veneerers,
among literary milliners and tailors, with the unconscious
dignity of an antique god. He was the poet of that divine
democracy that gives equal rights to all the sons and daughters of men. He uttered the great American voice."

And though one finds in the words of the naïve Ingersoll
the squeaking timber of the soapbox, yet even a soapbox
does lift a man a few inches above the level of the clay.

Well, the Whitman battle is not over yet, nor ever will
be. Though neither Philadelphia nor Camden has recognized 330 Mickle Street as one of the authentic shrines of
our history (Lord, how trimly dight it would be if it were in

New England!), Camden has made a certain amend in putting Walt into the gay mosaic that adorns the portico of the new public library in Cooper Park. There, absurdly represented in an austere black cassock, he stands in the following frieze of great figures: Dante, Whitman, Molière, Gutenberg, Tyndale, Washington, Penn, Columbus, Moses, Raphael, Michael Angelo, Shakespeare, Longfellow and Palestrina. I believe that there was some rumpus as to whether Walt should be included; but, anyway, there he is.

You will make a great mistake if you don't ramble over to Camden some day and fleet the golden hours in an observant stroll. Himself the prince of loafers, Walt taught the town to loaf. When they built the new postoffice over there they put round it a ledge for philosophic lounging, one of the most delightful architectural features I have ever seen. And on Third Street, just around the corner from 330 Mickle Street, is the oddest plumber's shop in the world. Mr. George F. Hammond, a Civil War veteran, who knew Whitman and also Lincoln, came to Camden in '69. In 1888 he determined to build a shop that would be different from anything on earth, and well he succeeded. Perhaps it is symbolic of the shy and harassed soul of the plumber, fleeing from the unreasonable demands of his customers, for it is a kind of Gothic fortress. Leaded windows, gargoyles, masculine medusa heads, a sallyport, loopholes and a little spire. I stopped in to talk to Mr. Hammond, and he greeted me graciously. He says that people have come all the way from California to see his shop, and I can believe it. It is the work of a delightful and original spirit who does not care to live in a demure hutch like all the rest of us, and has really had some fun out of his whimsical little castle. He says he would rather live in Camden than in Philadelphia, and I daresay he's right.

# EPILOGUE

# A CITY NOTEBOOK

IT WOULD be hard to find a more lovely spot in the flush of a summer sunset than Wister Woods. Old residents of the neighbourhood say that the trees are not what they were fifteen and twenty years ago; the chestnuts have died off; even some of the tall tulip-poplars are a little bald at the top, and one was recently felled by a gale. But still that quiet plateau stands in a serene hush, flooded with rich orange glow on a warm evening. The hollyhocks in the back gardens of Rubicam Street are scarlet and Swiss-cheese-coloured and black; and looking across the railroad ravine one sees crypts and aisles of green as though in the heart of some cathedral of the great woods.

Belfield Avenue, which bends through the valley in a curve of warm thick yellow dust, will some day be boule-varded into a spick-and-span highway for motors. But now it lies little trafficked, and one might prefer to have it so, for in the stillness of the evening the birds are eloquent. The thrushes of Wister Woods, which have been immortal-ized by T. A. Daly in perhaps the loveliest poem ever written in Philadelphia, flute and whistle their tantalizing note, while the song sparrow echoes them with his confi-dent, challenging call. Down behind the dusty sumac shrubbery lies the little blue-green cottage said to have been used by Benjamin West as a studio. In a meadow beside the road two cows were grazing in the blue shadow of overhanging woodland.

Over the road leans a flat outcrop of stone, known locally as "The Bum's Rock." An antique philosopher of those parts assured the wayfarer that it is named for a romantic vagabond who perished there by the explosion of a can of Bohemian goulash which he was heating over a small fire of sticks; but one doubts the tale. Our own conjecture is that

it is named for Jacob Boehm, the old time brewer of Germantown, who predicted in his chronicles that the world would come to an end in July, 1919. From his point of view he was not so far wrong.

Above Boehm's Rock, in a grassy level among the trees, a merry little circle of young ladies was sitting round a picnic supper. The twilight grew darker and fireflies began to twinkle. In the steep curve of the Cinder and Bloodshot (between Fisher's and Wister stations) a cheerful train rumbled, with its engine running backward just like a country local. Its bright shaft of light wavered among the tall tree trunks. One would not imagine that it was less than six miles to the City Hall.

A quarter to one A.M., and a hot, silent night. As one walks up Chestnut Street a distant roaring is heard, which rapidly grows louder. The sound has a note of terrifying menace. Then, careering down the almost deserted highway, comes a huge watertank, throbbing like an airplane. A creamy sheet of water, shot out at high pressure, floods the street on each side, dashing up on the pavements. A knot of belated revellers in front of the Adelphia Hotel, standing in mid-street, to discuss ways and means of getting home, skip numbly to one side, the ladies lifting up their dresses with shrill squeaks of alarm as the water splashes round them. Pedestrians plodding quietly up the street cower fearfully against the buildings, while a fine mist envelops them.

After the tank comes, more leisurely, a squad of brooms. The street is dripping, every sewer opening clucks and gurgles with the falling water. There is something unbelievably humorous in the way that roaring Niagara of water dashes madly down the silent street. There is a note of irony in it, too, for the depressed enthusiasts who have been sitting all evening in a restaurant over lemonade and ginger ale. Perhaps the chauffeur is a prohibitionist gone mad.

While eating half a dozen doughnuts in a Broad Street lunchroom at one o'clock in the morning, we mused happily about our friends all tucked away in bed, sound asleep. There is one in particular on whom we thought with serene pleasure. It was charming to think of that delightful, argumentative, contradictory, volatile person, his active mind stilled in the admirable reticence of slumber. He, so endlessly speculatory, so full of imaginative enthusiasms and riotous intuitions and troubled zeals concerning humanity, lost in a beneficent swoon of unconsciousness! We could not just say why, but we broke into chuckles to think of him lying there, not denying any of our statements, absolutely and positively saying nothing. To have one's friends asleep now and then is very refreshing.

Off Walnut Street, below Fifth, and just east of the window where that perfectly lovely damsel sits operating an adding machine—why is it, by the way, that the girls who run adding machines are always so marvellously fair? Is there some secret virtue in the process of adding that makes one lovely? We feel sure that a subtracting engine would not have that subtle beautifying effect—just below

Fifth Street, we started to say, there runs a little alley called (we believe) De Silver Court. It is a sombre little channel between high walls and barred windows, but it is a retreat we recommend highly to hay fever sufferers. For in one of the buildings adjoining there seems to be a warehouse of some company that makes an "aromatic disinfector." Wandering in there by chance, we stood delighted at the sweet medicinal savour that was wafted on the air. It had a most cheering effect upon our emunctory woes, and we lingered so long, in a meditative and healing ecstasy, that young women immured in the basement of the aromatic warehouse began to peer upward from the barred windows of their basement and squeak with astonished and nervous mirth. We blew a loud salute and moved away.

We entered a lunchroom on Broad Street for our favourite breakfast of coffee and a pair of crullers. It was strangely early and only a few of the flat-arm chairs were occupied. After dispatching the rations we carefully filled our pipe. With us we had a copy of an agreeable book, *The Calamities and Quarrels of Authors*. It occurred to us that here, in the brisk serenity of the morning, would be a charming opportunity for a five-minute smoke and five pages of reading before attacking the ardours and endurances of the day. Lovingly we applied the match to the fuel. We began to read:

> Of all the sorrows in which the female character may participate, there are few more affecting than those of an authoress——

A stern, white-coated official came over to us and tapped us on the shoulder.

"There's a sign behind you," he said.

We looked, guiltily, and saw:

## POSITIVELY
## NO SMOKING

The cocoateria on Eighth Street closes at one A.M. Between twelve-thirty and closing time it is full of busy eaters, mostly the night shift from the Chestnut Street newspaper offices and printing and engraving firms in the neighbourhood. Ham and eggs blossom merrily. The white-coated waiters move in swift, stern circuit. Griddle cakes bake with amazing swiftness toward the stroke of one. Little dishes of baked beans stand hot and ready in the steam-chest. The waiter punches your check as he brings your frankfurters and coffee. He adds another perforation when you get your ice cream. Then he comes back and punches it again.

"Here," you cry, "let it alone and stop bullying it!"

"Sorry, brother," he says. "I forgot that peach cream was fifteen cents."

317

One o'clock. They lock the door and turn out the little gas jet where smokers light up. As the tables empty the chairs are stacked up on top. And if it is a clear warm evening the customers smoke a final weed along the Chestnut Street doorsteps, talking together in a cheery undertone.

No man has ever started upon a new cheque-book without a few sourly solemn thoughts.

In the humble waters of finance wherein we paddle we find that a book of fifty cheques lasts us about four months, allowing for two or three duds when we start to make out a foil payable to bearer (self) and decide to renounce that worthy ambition and make it out to the gas company instead.

It occurs to us that if Bunyan had been writing *Pilgrim's Progress* nowadays instead of making Christian encounter lions in the path he would have substituted gas meters, particularly the quarter-in-the-slot kind that one finds in a seaside cottage. However——

Four months is quite a long time. It may be weak of us, but we can never resist wondering as we survey that flock of empty cheques just what adventures our bank account is going to undergo during that period, and whether our customary technique of being aloof with the receiving teller and genial and commentary with the paying ditto is the right one. We always believe in keeping a paying teller in a cheerful frame of mind. We would never admit to him that we think it is going to rain. We say, rather, "Well, it may blow over," and try not to surmise how many hundreds there are in the pile at his elbow. Probably we think the explanation for the really bizarre architecture of our bank is to keep depositors' attention from the money. Unquestionably Walt Whitman's tomb over in Harleigh—Walt's vault— was copied from our bank.

The cheques in our book are blue. We have always

regretted this. If we had known it beforehand perhaps we would have inflicted our problems upon another bank. Because there are so many more interesting colours for cheques, tints upon which the ink shows up in a more imposing manner. A pale pink or cream-coloured cheque for $2.74 looks much more exciting than a blue cheque for $25. We have known gray, pink, white, brown, green and salmon-coloured cheques. A friend of ours once showed us one that was a bright orange, but refused to let us handle it. But yellow is the colour that appeals to us most strongly. When we were very young and away from home our monthly allowance, the amount of which we shall not state, but it cost us less effort than any money we ever received since, came to us by way of pale primrose-coloured cheques. For, after all, there are no cheques like those one used to get from one's father. We hope the Urchin will think so some day.

We like to pay homage to the true artist in all lines. At the corner of Market and Marshall streets—between Sixth and Seventh—the collarclasp orator has his rostrum, and it seems to us that his method of harangue has the quality of genuine art. He does not bawl or try to terrify or bully his audience into purchase as do the auctioneers of the "pawn-brokers' outlets." How gently, how winningly, how sweetly he pleads the merits of his little collar clasp! And there is shrewd imagination in his attention-catching device, which is a small boy dressed in black, wearing a white hood of cheesecloth that hides his face. This peculiar silent figure, with a touch of mystery about it, serves to keep the crowd wondering until the oration begins.

With a smile, with infinite ingratiation and gentle persuasion, our friend exhibits the merits of his device which does away with the traditional collar-button. His art is to make the collar-button seem a piteous, almost a tragic thing. His eyes swim with unshed tears as he describes the discomfort

319

of the man whose collar, fastened by the customary button, cannot be given greater freedom on a hot, muggy day. He shows, by exhibition on his own person, the exquisite relief afforded by the adjustable collar clasp. "When the day grows cool," he says, "when you begin to enjoy yourself and want your collar tighter, you just loosen the clasp, slide the tabs closer together, and there you are. And no picking at your tie to get the knot undone. Now, how many of you men have spoiled an expensive tie by picking at it? Your fingers come in contact with the fibres of the silk and the first thing you know the tie is soiled. This little clasp"— and he casts a beam of affection upon it—"saves your tie, it saves your collar, and it saves your patience." A note of yearning pathos comes into his agreeable voice, and he holds out a handful of the old-fashioned collar-buttons. "You men are wearing the same buttons your great-grandfathers wore. Don't you want to get out of collar slavery? *Don't* you want to quit working your face all out of shape struggling with a collar-button? Now as this is a manufacturing demonstration——"

On a warm evening nothing is more pleasant than a ride on the front platform of the Market Street L, with the front door open. As the train leaves Sixty-ninth Street it dips down the Millbourne bend and the cool, damp smell of the Cobb's Creek meadows gushes through the car. Then the track straightens out for a long run toward the City Hall. Roaring over the tree tops, with the lights of movies and shops glowing up from below, a warm typhoon makes one lean against it to keep one's footing. The airy stations are lined by girls in light summer dresses, attended by their swains. The groan of the wheels underfoot causes a curious tickling in the soles of the feet as one stands on the steel platform.

This groan rises to a shrill scream as the train gathers speed between stations, gradually diminishing to a reluctant grumble as the cars come to a stop. In the distance, in a peacock-blue sky, the double gleam of the City Hall tower shines against the night. Down on the left is the hiss and clang of West Philadelphia station, with the long, dim, amber glow of the platform and belated commuters pacing about. Then the smoky dive across the Schuylkill and the bellow of the subway.

From time to time humanity is forced to revise its customary notions in the interests of truth. This is always painful.

It is an old fetich that the week-end in summer is a time for riotous enjoyment, of goodly cheer and mirthful solace. A careful examination of human beings during this hebdomadal period of carnival leads us to question the doctrine.

When we watch the horrors of discomfort and vexation endured by simple-hearted citizens in pursuit of a light-hearted Saturday and Sunday, we often wonder how it is that humanity will so gleefully inflict upon itself sufferings which, if they were imposed by some taskmaster, would be called atrocious.

We observe, for instance, women and children standing sweltering in the aisles of trains during a two-hour run to the seashore. We observe the number of drownings, motor accidents, murders, and suicides that take place during the Saturday to Monday period. We observe families loaded down with small children, who might have been happy and reasonably cool at home, struggling desperately to get away

for a day in the country, rising at 5 A.M., standing in line at the station, fanning themselves with blasphemy, and weary before they start. We observe them chased home by thunderstorms or colic, dazed and blistered with sunburn, or groaning with a surfeit of ice cream cones.

It is a lamentable fact (and the truth is almost always lamentable, and hotly denied) that for the hard-working majority the week-end is a curse rather than a blessing. The saddest fact in human annals is that most people are never so happy as when they are hard at work. The time may come when criminals will be condemned, not to the chair, but to twenty successive week-ends spent standing in the aisles of crowded excursion trains.

Strolling downtown to a well-known home of fish dinners, it is appetizing to pass along the curve of Dock Street in the coolness of the evening. The clean, lively odours of vegetables and fruit are strong on the air. Under the broad awnings of the commission merchants and produce dealers the stock is piled up in neat and engaging piles ready to be carted away at dawn. Under the glow of pale arcs and gas lamps the colours of the scene are vivid. Great baskets of

eggplant shine like huge grapes, a polished port wine colour; green and scarlet peppers catch points of light; a flat pinkish colour gleams on carrots. Each species seems to have an ordered pattern of its own. Potatoes are ranged in a pyramid; watermelons in long rows; white and yellow onions are heaped in sacks. The sweet musk of cantaloupes is the scent that overbreathes all others. Then, down nearer to the waterfront, comes the strong, damp fishy whiff of oysters. To stroll among these gleaming piles of victuals, to watch the various colours where the lamps pour a pale silver and yellow on cairns and pyramids of vegetables, is to gather a lusty appetite and attack the first oyster stew of the season with a stout heart.

It being a very humid day, we stopped to compliment the curly-headed sandwich man at Ninth and Market on his décolleté corsage, which he wears in the Walt Whitman manner. "Wish we could get away with it the way you do," we said, admiringly. He looked at us with the patience of one inured to bourgeois comment. "It's got to be tried," said he, "like everything else."

We stopped by the Weather Man's little illuminated booth at Ninth and Chestnut about 10 o'clock in the evening. We were scrutinizing his pretty coloured pictures, wondering how soon the rain would determine, when a slender young man appeared out of the gloom, said "I'm sorry to have to do this," switched off the light, and pulled down the rolling front of the booth. It was the Weather Man himself.

We were greatly elated to meet this mythical sage and walked down the street a little way with him. In order to cheer him up, we complimented him on the artistic charm of his little booth, with its glow of golden light shining on the coloured map and the bright loops and curves of crayon. We told him how almost at any time in the evening groups of people can be seen admiring his stall, but his sensitive heart was gloomy.

"Most of them don't understand it," he said, morosely. "The women are the worst. I've gone there in the evening and found them studying the map eagerly. Hopefully, I would creep up behind to hear their comments. One will say, 'Yes, that's where my husband came from,' or 'I spent last summer over there,' pointing to some place on the map. They seem to think it's put there for them to study geography."

We tried to sympathize with the broken-hearted scientist, but his spirit had been crushed by a long series of woes.

"The other evening," said he, "I saw a couple of girls gazing at the map, and they looked so intelligent I really was charmed. Apparently they were discussing an area of low pressure that was moving down from the Great Lakes, and I lent an ear. Imagine my chagrin when one of them said: 'You see the colour of that chalk line? I'm going to make my next knitted vestee just like that.' And the other one said: 'I think the whole colour scheme is adorable. I'm going to use it as a pattern for my new camouflage bathing suit.'

"Thank goodness," cried the miserable Weather Man,

"I have another map like that down at the Bourse, and the brokers really give it some intelligent attention."

We went on our way sadly, thinking how many sorrows there are in the world. It is grievous to think of the poor Weather Man, lurking with beating pulses in the neighbourhood of Ninth and Chestnut in the hope of finding someone who understands his painstaking display. The next time you are standing in front of his booth do say something about the Oceanic High in the South Atlantic or the dangerous Aleutian Low or the anticyclonic condition prevailing in the Alleghanies. He might overhear you, and it would do his mournful heart good.

It was eight o'clock, a cool drizzling night. Chestnut Street was gray with a dull, pearly, opaque twilight. In the little portico east of Independence Hall the gas lamp under the ceiling cast a soft pink glow on the brick columns.

Independence Square was a sea of tremulous, dripping boughs. The quaint heptahedral lamps threw splashed shimmers of topaz colour across the laky pavement. "Golden lamps in a green night," as Marvell says, twinkled through the stir and moisture of the evening.

# PUTTING THE CITY
# TO BED

I T WAS A delicious cool evening when I strolled abroad to observe the town composing itself for slumber. The caustic Mrs. Trollope, who visited Philadephia in 1830, complained bitterly that there was no carousal or cheer of any kind proceeding in the highways after sunset: "The streets are entirely dark, scarcely a step is heard, and for a note of music, or the sound of mirth, I listened in vain." But the lady would find us much more volatile now.

The Weather Man tries to set us a good example by pulling down the front of his little booth at Ninth and Chestnut soon after 10 o'clock, but there are few who take the hint. It was a night almost chilly—67 degrees—a black velvety sky to the northward, diluted to a deep purple and blue where the moon was shining in the south. At 10:45 letter writing was in full scratch along the counters of the main postoffice. Every desk was busy; the little stamp windows were lively caves of light. Hotel signs—the old signs that used to say ROOMS $1 UP, and now just say ROOMS—were beaconing along the street. Crowds were piling out of movies. The colored man who letters cards with delicate twirls of penmanship was setting up his little table on Market street. In spite of the cool air every soda fountain was lined with the customary gobs. The first morning papers were beginning to be screamed about the streets, with that hoarse urgency of yelling that always makes the simple-minded think that something fearful has happened.

A crowd gathered hastily in front of a big office building on Chestnut street. Policemen sprang from nowhere. A Jefferson ambulance clanged up. Great agitation, and prolonged ringing of the bell at the huge iron-grilled front door. What's up? Finally appeared a man with blood spattered over his shirt and was escorted to the ambulance. The engineer had walked too near an electric fan and got his head cut. Lucky he didn't lose it altogether, said one watcher.

Eleven o'clock. In a cigar store served by a smiling damsel, two attractive ladies were asking her if it would be safe for them to visit a Chinese restaurant a little farther up the street. "We're from out of town," they explained, "and all alone. We want some chop suey. Is that the kind of place ladies can go to?" The cigar saleslady appealed to me, and I assured the visitors they would be perfectly serene. Perhaps if I had been more gallant I should have escorted them thither. Off they went, a little timorous.

Eleven fifteen. The first of the typical nighthawk motors begin to appear: huge runabouts, with very long bonnets and an air of great power. One of them, a vivid scarlet with white wheels, spins briskly round the City Hall. Trills and tinklings of jazz clatter from second-story restaurants. But Chestnut street is beginning to calm down. Lights in shop windows are going off. The old veteran takes his seat on a camp-stool near Juniper street and begins to tingle his little bell merrily. If you drop something in his box, he will tell you the sign of the zodiac under which you were born, prognosticate your lucky days and planetary hours and advise you when to take a journey. He explained to me that this happened to be the night of Venus. I had been sure of it already after some scrutiny of the pavements. As the lights are dimmed along the street, the large goldfish in a Chestnut street cafe window grow more placid and begin to think of a little watery repose.

Half-past eleven. The airy spaces round the City Hall are full of a mellow tissue of light and shadow. The tall lamp standards are like trees of great pale oranges. The white wagons of the birchbeer fleet are on their rounds. The seats where the band concerts are held are deserted save for one ·

meditative vagrant, drooping with unknown woes. Swiftly flowing cars flit mysteriously round the curve and bend into the long expanse of North Broad street where their little red sternlights twinkle beneath the row of silver arcs stretching away into the distance. Broad Street Station is comparatively quiet, though there is the usual person gazing up at the window lettered SCRIP CLERGY STOPOVERS COMMUTATION. He wonders what it means. I do not know, any more than he. Standing at the corner of the station the lights of the sky are splendid and serene. Over the Finance Building a light wispy plume of steam hovers and detaches itself, gleaming in the moonshine like a floating swan's feather. The light catches the curves of the trolley rails like ribbons of silver.

Midnight. The population seems to have sorted itself into couples. Almost all the ladies in sight wear silk sports skirts, and walk with their escorts in a curiously slow swishing swing. Some of them may have been dancing all evening, and still pace with some of the rhythm of the waxed floor. In darkened banks are little gleams of orange light behind trellises of bars, where watchmen sit and grind away the long hours. Down the dark narrow channel of Sansom street it is very silent. The rear of a ten-cent store shows a gush of brightness, where some overhauling of stock is going on. The back door is open, and looking in I can see a riotous mouse darting about under the counters, warily watching the men who are rearranging some display. The Jefferson Hospital is silent, with occasional oblongs of light in windows. I seem to detect a whiff of disinfectants, and wonder how the engineer is getting on.

Market street is still lively. A "dance orchard" emits its patrons down a long stair to the street. Down they come, gaily laughing. The male partners are all either gobs, who love dancing even more than ice cream soda; or youths with tilted straw hats of coarse weave, with legs that bend backward most oddly below the knee, very tightly and briefly trousered. Two doughboys with ace of spades shoulder insignia greet the emerging throng, showing little booklets for sale. They urge the girls to buy, with various arts of cajolery and bright-eyed persuasion. "Who'll buy a book?" they say, "forty short stories, put out by a wounded soldier." The girls all wear very extensive hats, and are notably pretty. "Which way do we go?" is the first question on reaching the street. It is usually the way to the nearest soda fountain.

Twelve forty. The watering tank roars down Chestnut street, shedding a hissing tide from curb to curb. The fleet of To Hire night taxis wheel off one by one as fares leap in to escape from the deluge, which can be heard approaching far up the silent street. It is getting quiet, save in the all-night lunch rooms, where the fresh baking of doughnuts and cinnamon buns is being set out, and the workers of the night shift are streaming in for their varied and substantial meals. They eat leisurely, with loud talk, or reading the morning papers.

One fifteen. The population consists mostly of small groups on corners waiting patiently for cars, which are rare after one o'clock. Chauffeurs sit in twos, gossiping over the fares of the evening. Along the curb of the Federal Building on Ninth street linger a few resolute loungers, enjoying the calm of the night. A fruit stall man is wondering whether to trundle home. The pile of fresh doughnuts in the lunch room is rapidly diminishing. Street cleaning trucks are on their nightly round. It's time to go to bed.